D0994825

# The Degunking 12-Step Program

Here is the basic 12-step degunking process that you should follow to fully degunk your PC:

1. Physically clean your PC and all of the peripherals and devices that you use (Chapter 3).

2. Do an overhaul of your work area and clean out all of the configurations of the hardware that you use (Chapter 4).

3. Properly configure and set up your PC or laptop (if you use one) and all of its key components—monitor, printers, and so on (Chapter 5).

4. Properly configure and set up all of your PC support peripherals, including digital cameras, scanners, PDAs, and smart displays (Chapter 6).

5. Set up USB and FireWire connections for your equipment to get better performance when transferring data (Chapter 7).

6. Set up a basic system so that you can optimize and share a dial-up Internet connection around your home (Chapter 8).

7. Get rid of your dial-up Internet connection and move to a faster cable or DSL connection if you have access to these services (Chapter 9).

8. Link up all of the computers around your home or small office with a low-cost but efficient network (Chapter 10).

9. Set up a wireless networking system to allow you to use your PC wherever you want in your home or small office (Chapter 11).

10. Back up your system on a regular basis (Chapter 12).

11. Perform some cost-effective tasks to really speed up the performance of your PC (Chapter 13).

12. Degunk a new PC, and learn how to get rid of (or recycle) older equipment (Appendix A).

# Degunking with Time Limitations

To get the full benefits of degunking, we highly recommend that you complete all of the main degunking tasks in the order that they are presented. Performing all of these tasks will require quite a bit of time, though. If your time is limited, here are some suggestions for valuable degunking tasks that you can perform in the time you *do* have—whether it's 10 minutes, 3 hours, or half a day.

# Ten-Minute Degunking

If you have a very short amount of time—less than half an hour, say—you should focus on taking small steps to physically clean and degunk your PC and your work area:

1. Clean the dust and fingerprints from your monitor (page 26).
2. Clean your mouse (page 45).
3. Clean scanner glass, Web cam lenses, and digital camera lenses (page 55).
4. Choose a peripheral to get rid of, such as an unused Web cam or PDA (page 75).
5. Designate a drawer for peripherals you want to keep and begin moving peripherals, chargers, and cables into it (page 75).
6. Configure your monitor with a screen resolution that works for you (page 95).
7. Verify that you're getting the required updates and service packs (page 105).

# Thirty-Minute Degunking

If you only have 30 minutes or so, we recommend you perform the 10-minute degunking tasks and then the following tasks to further degunk your PC, peripherals, and work area:

1. Perform ink-jet printer maintenance tasks such as cleaning the heads and nozzles (page 48).
2. Hide hardware you don't access often like hubs, switches and routers, and cable modems and their cables (page 82).
3. Improve the performance of your PDA or other handheld device using our file synchronization techniques and tips for saving media by learning what to keep and what not to keep (page 126).
4. Disable programs that run in the background and aren't necessary (page 334).
5. Set parental controls in Windows Media Player so your kids can't view what you don't want them to view (page 340).
6. Give away hardware and peripherals you no longer need to friends, family, or charities (Appendix A).
7. Back up your Outlook Express address book, mail account settings, and messages (page 283).
8. Create a schedule for Microsoft Backup so that it runs automatically (page 293).
9. Find, download, and use free Windows Media Player PowerToys and plug-ins (page 335).

# One-Hour Degunking

If you have an hour to degunk your PC, you have some time to perform some deep-cleaning and deep-degunking tasks:

1. Learn how to degunk the photos you take, as well as your printer, by reading about how to take a good picture, choose the best inks, and configure the printer appropriately (page 109).
2. Degunk your scanner by setting the correct scanning resolution and dpi and making sure the scanner has the resources it needs to function properly (page 124).

3. Download and install a free anti-adware or anti-spyware application and use it to scan your PC (page 170).

4. Create a backup of valuable data using the method of your choice (page 279).

5. Create a hardware profile on your laptop or desktop PC (page 319).

6. Degunk a multiple-user PC by turning on Fast User Switching, making applications available to all users, and using shared folders to avoid duplicate data on the PC (page 329).

## Three-Hour Degunking

If you have three hours to work on your PC, there are some truly important activities you really must perform:

1. Clean the outside and the inside of your PC's tower (page 29).

2. Disconnect everything from the PC's tower, including all cables and cords, and label them (page 36).

3. Share a dial-up Internet connection with users on a network (page 163).

4. Install a TV tuner card, or upgrade an existing video or sound card (page 316).

## Half-Day Degunking

As you move forward through the book, you'll run across some tasks that will take at least half a day:

1. Set up a basic network with a hub, switch or router, and Ethernet cables (page 158).

2. Upgrade from dial-up to DSL (page 177). This may take two half-day sessions.

3. Set up a wireless network (Chapter 12 ).

4. Add more RAM (page 313). This is a half-day task because it involves finding and purchasing the right RAM, opening the case, and installing it.

5. Degunk your new PC by removing unnecessary programs, trial software, and desktop icons (Appendix A).

## Spare Moment Degunking

There may be times when you are doing something with your computer and you discover that you have a few minutes to spare. These tasks do not need to be performed in any specific order. Simply select a task and perform it to help clean your PC. (Of course, any of the 10-minute degunking tasks can also be performed!)

1. Delete icons off of your desktop, especially if you have a newer PC, including those for a free trial of AOL service, free trial software or limited use software, and for applications you don't need or use (page 351).

2. Use compressed air to clean the vents in the PC's tower (page 32). You can also use the compressed air to blow dirt out of the keyboard and dust off of your desk.

3. Take any steps that time allows to degunk under the desk (see the before and after

photos on pages 37 and 38).

4. Disable system-hogging themes (page 104).

5. Download and install a Registry checking application and use it regularly (page 108).

6. Organize a junk drawer that contains peripherals, cables, and cords (page 119).

7. Delete unwanted images from your digital camera before they ever make it onto your hard drive (page 120).

8. Obtain and install antivirus software and keep it up-to-date (page 168).

9. Always practice safe Web-surfing practices (page 173).

10. Make use of Windows tools, specifically scannow, Disk Cleanup, and Disk Defragmenter, especially if you've noticed problems (page 201).

11. Drag and drop today's work to an external hard disk or burn the data to a CD or DVD (page 289).

Joli Ballew

Jeff Duntemann

**President**
*Keith Weiskamp*

**Editor-at-Large**
*Jeff Duntemann*

**Vice President, Sales, Marketing, and Distribution**
*Steve Sayre*

**Vice President, International Sales and Marketing**
*Cynthia Caldwell*

**Production Manager**
*Kim Eoff*

**Cover Designers**
*Kris Sotelo*

**Paraglyph Press, Inc.**
4015 N. 78th Street, #115
Scottsdale, Arizona 85251
Phone: 602-749-8787
**www.paraglyphpress.com**

Paraglyph Press ISBN: 1-933097-03-5.

Printed in the United States of America
10  9  8  7  6  5  4  3  2  1

**P PARAGLYPH**
P R E S S

# What Readers Are Saying About
# The Degunking™ Series!

"[*Degunking Windows* is] a great new book that explains why computers lose their vigor over time. It offers easy-to-follow instructions for cleaning out your hard drive, tweaking programs, eliminating spyware, sorting e-mail and updating your system."
—From *Parade Magazine*, Robert Mortiz in the "Gadget Guide" section

"Do you own a PC or Mac computer and use it regularly? Then, it has gunk. Gunk is all the unnecessary junk on your computer that can slow down performance and ultimately cause system malfunction. It's those fuzzy photos that never got tossed, e-mail you've filed and forgotten, old programs you never use, hidden programs you don't want and too many programs that launch at startup. I found very useful advice from two books: "*Degunking Windows* by Joli Ballew and Jeff Duntemann, and *Degunking Your Mac* by Joli Ballew."
— *Seattle Times*

"The cheapest infusion of power to a Windows XP computer can now be had for a mere $24.99. It's not a faster processor or more memory but a well-done book titled "*Degunking Windows*."
—*Miami Herald*

"I am impressed. [*Degunking Windows*] makes a very useful companion for step-by-step computer maintenance....My copy is filled of highlighter marks and 3M page markers."
—Memphix PC User's Group

"Duntemann is a PC guru who can clean your system out with one hand tied behind his back."
—Dingbat Magazine

"Only one word is needed to summarize "[*Degunking Windows*]: terrific! The authors display an awesome knowledge of Windows XP and its workings, and tell us how to use them to good advantage. The information provided in the book is comprehensive and detailed, yet highly readable."
—Sierra Vista (AZ) IBM PC User Group

"Read this book [*Degunking Windows*] and you can degunk your computer in just a few hours using a set of tried-and-true techniques."
—Fallbrook PC Users Group

"Joli Ballew and Jeff Duntemann do an excellent job of helping you to find the things that are slowing down and cluttering up your system. Keep the book handy because you will need to go through this cleanup periodically—maybe a couple times a year."
—Tony Bradley (**netsecurity.about.com**)

*Recently Published by Paraglyph Press:*

**Degunking eBay**
*By Greg Holden*

**Degunking Your Email, Spam, and Viruses**
*By Jeff Duntemann*

**Degunking Windows**
*By Joli Ballew*
*and Jeff Duntemann*

**Degunking Your Mac**
*By Joli Ballew*

**Game Coding Complete, Second Edition**
*By Mike McShaffry*

**Small Websites, Great Results**
*By Doug Addison*

**A Theory of Fun**
***For Game Design***
*By Raph Koster*

**Perl Core Language Little Black Book**
*By Steven Holzner*

**3D Game-Based Filmmaking: The Art of Machinima**
*By Paul Marino*

**Windows XP Professional: The Ultimate User's Guide,
Second Edition**
*By Joli Ballew*

**Jeff Duntemann's Wi-Fi Guide**
*By Jeff Duntemann*

**Visual Basic .NET Core Language Little Black Book**
*By Steven Holzner*

**The SQL Server 2000 Book**
*By Anthony Sequeira*
*And Brian Alderman*

*For my family, Mom, Dad, Jennifer, and Cosmo.*
*—Joli Ballew*


*For Bishop Elijah of the Old Catholic Church*
*Dominus Vobiscum!*
*—Jeff Duntemann*

❧

# About the Authors

**Joli Ballew** is a full time writer and digital enthusiast who also teaches, creates Web sites, and consults from her home in Dallas, Texas. Joli has written over a dozen books, including co-authoring the wildly popular book *Degunking Windows* with Jeff Duntemann. Joli continues to serve as a regular *Microsoft Expert Zone* columnist and blogger, and is an avid golfer.

**Jeff Duntemann** is an author, editor, programmer, lecturer, and technology columnist, with over a dozen books under his belt, including *Jeff Duntemann's Wi-Fi Guide, Degunking Your Email, Spam, and Viruses*, and *Assembly Language Step-by-Step*. Jeff has written for many major magazines and industry journals including *Byte, Dr. Dobb's Journal*, and *PC Week*. He is the founding editor of *PC Techniques* and *Visual Developer Magazine*. Jeff has published his ContraPositive Web diary since 1998 (see **www.duntemann.com/Diary.htm**). He lives with his wife Carol in Colorado Springs.

# Acknowledgments

Thanks once again to the Paraglyph Press team, including Steve, Keith, Cynthia, Kim, and Jeff, for bringing me back into the fold for another go-round with the Degunking series. I've been creating Degunking books since the beginning, and am always honored when approached to do another one—especially another one with Jeff—who is indeed a joy to work with.

I'd like to add another note of thanks here to my agent, Neil Salkind, as well as all of the other folks at Studio B, including Elsa and David. They've kept me in books and projects up to my ears, and I'm certainly thankful to remain a busy and employed author, technical editor, columnist, and <paid!> blogger.

Finally, my family continues to be supportive, even though most of the time they don't have a clue what I'm writing about, or even what I'm talking about, or why I need five PCs, or what this gadget or that gadget is, or why I sometimes get so involved I don't leave the house for days. Thanks for listening anyway, even if I sometimes bore you to tears.

—Joli Ballew


Behind each Jeff Duntemann book is a small army of advisors and reality checkers, and it would be difficult to mention them all by name, but they include Bill Roper, Jim Mischel, Frank Thornton, David Beers, Bill Dillon, and (like they used to say on the *Bullwinkle Show*) a host of others. Many thanks to everybody, along with Keith, Steve, Cynthia and the gang back at Paraglyph HQ, to Joli for hammering out some of the best material I've seen on the subject, and of course to Carol for being patient while I was noisily "doing hardware" downstairs.

—Jeff Duntemann

## The Paraglyph Mission

This book you've purchased is a collaborative creation involving the work of many hands, from authors to editors to designers to technical reviewers. At Paraglyph Press, we like to think that everything we create, develop, and publish is the result of one form creating another. And as this cycle continues on, we believe that your suggestions, ideas, feedback, and comments on how you've used our books is an important part of the process for us and our authors.

We've created Paraglyph Press with the sole mission of producing and publishing books that make a difference. The last thing we all need is yet another tech book on the same tired, old topic. So we ask our authors and all of the many creative hands who touch our publications to do a little extra, dig a little deeper, think a little harder, and create a better book. The founders of Paraglyph are dedicated to finding the best authors, developing the best books, and helping you find the solutions you need.

As you use this book, please take a moment to drop us a line at **feedback@paraglyphpress.com** and let us know how we are doing—and how we can keep producing and publishing the kinds of books that you can't live without.

Sincerely,

Keith Weiskamp & Jeff Duntemann
Paraglyph Press Founders
4015 N. 78th Street, #115
Scottsdale, Arizona 85251
email: **feedback@paraglyphpress.com**
Web: **www.paraglyphpress.com**

# Contents at a Glance

# Contents

## Chapter 3
## Physically Cleaning Your PC and Peripherals ............................ 25

## Chapter 4
## Degunking and Configuring Your PC Work Area ...................... 59

## Chapter 5
## Degunking Your Main PC Components ....................................... 93

## Chapter 6
## Degunking Your Peripherals ..................................... 115

## Chapter 7
## Untangling Your USB and FireWire Connections ..................... 133

## Chapter 11
## Going Wireless While Staying Gunk-Less ............................. 237

# Introduction

If you have a PC, you have gunk. That's a given. Whether or not you have gunk isn't the question here. The question is, *Just how much gunk do you have?* If you're like most computer and digital enthusiasts, you probably have a lot. However, it may have accumulated so slowly and quietly over the past few months or years that you really didn't take notice—well, at least not until you became aware that you were buried up to your eyeballs in peripherals, cables, power cords, chargers, dirt, and dust. And *that's* why you're reading this book. We understand.

Now, one PC does not necessarily make a gunked-up mess. But that's not all you have, is it? If you have more than one PC, you've got a double whammy of gunk. If they're not networked, a triple whammy. If you have other hardware—for instance, a laptop, a digital camera, a DV camera, a Web cam, or a handful of printers—you have even more. And if you add into the mix a cable modem, a hub, a switch or router, a PDA, a smart display, a backup device, or a scanner, you probably no longer have any control whatsoever over your PC and peripherals. If you have broken peripherals or ones that don't work at all, you need our help more than ever. If you have a media center that you use to watch and record TV, connect to a network, and burn CDs and DVDs—and it's in the family room—forget about it!

So, what's a body to do? We have the answers you need. We know what the problems are and we have figured out the solutions. We know you want to keep most of your stuff but you have no idea where to keep it. You can't vacuum under your desk, and it's getting mighty dusty under there. You can't find the cables you need when you want to charge up the DV camera and make a movie. And you don't know how to organize your peripherals so they can be easily used and accessed but not in the way. You have questions too: How on earth does one go about cleaning the *inside* of a PC? And with all of the networking choices, backup choices, and Internet choices, how can you ever even choose how to degunk? That's what we're here to show you.

You can degunk your PC in just a few days using a set of tried-and-true techniques. With this step-by-step guide, *Degunking Your PC,* you can quickly clean, speed up, secure, and organize your PC, and in the process, organize your office and your life.

Of course, you'll want to network multiple PCs, speed up your Internet service, and configure your peripherals so they work well too, and that's all just for starters.

As you've probably surmised, this book isn't about how to *use* your PC and peripherals. We figure you have all of those printers, scanners, cameras, and routers pretty much figured out. This book is an easy-to-read and concise guide showing you how to *improve* the performance of your PC and peripherals, how to get organized, and how to remove clutter.

# Why You Need This Book

We've talked with scores of PC owners, and the common problem they *all* had was what we've termed *gunk:* they all have too much stuff and not enough places to store it. What they do have doesn't work as it should, or it's just plain grimy.

Gunk can come from anywhere. Think *outside* the box for a minute. Each peripheral you acquire has at least two cables, often more. There may be chargers or sync cables too, all of which add to the piles of gunk you keep. Not only do these items cause physical gunk, the way you have them connected can cause performance gunk. If you have a cat that sleeps on the tower, that's another form of external gunk.

Now, think *inside* the box. Open your PC's tower and we guarantee you'll find lots of dust. This dust can actually cause your PC to perform poorly or even fail. On the hard drive, you'll find software that belongs with each peripheral, duplicate and unnecessary software and applications, and free trials of this or that. Gunk, gunk, gunk.

What you *don't* have can cause gunk too. If you don't get regular software updates and regular operating system updates, or if you don't own and keep up-to-date antivirus software and anti-adware and anti-spyware applications, you're in trouble. You also have to keep regular backups and configure hardware to work the way it was meant to work. You have to use reliable surge protectors. If you don't do these things, you'll create your own dangerous gunk!

## *Degunking Your PC* to the Rescue

This book is a unique guide that can save you hundreds of hours of valuable time, hundreds of dollars of unnecessary repairs, and a bundle of desktop space. Without regular maintenance and applied organizational skills, all PCs and all peripherals will get gunked up. The goal of this book is to show you how to degunk all of this yourself. Here are some of the unique ways this book can help you:

√ Shows you where gunk accumulates on a PC and how it can slow your PC down—even though you might not realize you have gunk!

√ Provides an easy-to-follow 12-step degunking process that you can put to work immediately.

√ Includes explanations, in everyday terms, of how to easily fix common problems that create gunk on and around your PC.

√ Provides information on how to save money with free degunking tools that are easily found on the Internet.

√ Includes a unique "GunkBuster's Notebook" feature in every chapter to help you reduce the clutter on and around your PC.

√ Features degunking maintenance tasks that you can perform on a regular basis to keep your PC in top form.

√ Provides instructions on how to degunk every one of your peripherals. This feature can really save you a lot of time and headaches!

√ Features advice on how to keep your PC and peripherals gunk-free so you won't create the same gunk again.

√ Tells you how to get rid of old hardware and how and why you need to degunk a new PC.

√ Tells you how to organize your office, your PC, your peripherals, and yes, even a bit of your life!

# How to Use This Book

*Degunking Your PC* is structured around the order of the degunking process that you should follow. The book starts off by explaining the importance of degunking and why PCs require it. Each subsequent chapter describes important degunking tasks, explained in plain English with step-by-step instructions.

---

**TIP: This book is designed around a 12-step program (outlined in Chapter 2) that we recommend you follow, starting with Chapter 3 and continuing through the end of the book. We highly recommend you follow the process in the order that it is presented here. This will result in the most benefit from the time you spend degunking your PC.**

---

Once you've completely degunked your PC, you can perform different degunking operations at different times, depending on your needs. We hope you follow the schedules we've created for you, though. That's certainly the best way to stay on top of things. We expect that this book will become one of your most-used computer books, and we'll bet that it will end up on the bookshelf that's right next to your PC.

# A Note on Windows Versions

The degunking tasks presented in this book were written to work with the current version of Windows XP Home Edition and Windows XP Professional Edition. Some of the operations presented, such as backing up Windows using Microsoft Backup, are specific to Windows XP as they are detailed in this book. However, most of the degunking PC tasks are not operating-system specific. Most are generic operations that do not require a specific OS, including but not limited to the following:

√ Cleaning monitors, lenses, scanners, and Web cams

√ Cleaning the inside of the PC

√ Cleaning laptops

√ Cleaning keyboards and mice

√ Hiding cables, cords, and power supplies

√ Labeling and organizing cables and cords

√ Cleaning and maintaining ink-jet and laser printers

√ Choosing and installing a new monitor, printer, or all-in-one unit

√ Hiding the tower

√ Purchasing and installing wireless equipment

√ Getting rid of peripherals and their related software

√ Configuring monitor resolution, dpi, and icon size

√ Overriding Internet Explorer and Outlook Express defaults

√ Getting good prints

√ Configuring peripherals such as cameras, scanners, and Web cams for best performance

√ Getting the best performance from USB devices

√ Setting up a basic network

√ Installing security software

√ Upgrading from dial-up to DSL

√ Creating and degunking a wireless network

√ Creating a backup strategy

√ Upgrading RAM, the CPU, and video and sound cards

A few things in this book do require XP though, including using Internet Connection Sharing for sharing a dial-up connection, using specific software such as TweakUI and TweakMP, working with XP's themes, setting up a network with XP's Network Setup Wizard, and tweaking system properties. However, you can perform most of these tasks with other OSes; you'll just have to look past the directions for XP here and stretch the explanation a little.

# A Note on PC Makes and Models

PCs come in all flavors: some are compact, some are large, some are laptops, and some, like media centers, may not come with a tower. Some PCs are proprietary, meaning *if* you can get inside, you might not find anything replaceable in there, unless you order it from the manufacturer. Be careful, because sometimes opening a case may void the warranty too. This is especially true of printers and scanners.

When you're ready to open the case and look inside, blow out the dust, add cards or other components, or replace internal parts, you'll need to take into account that your PC may be different from the generic PC we talk about here. PCs are PCs though; they all have a motherboard, RAM, cards, fans, and air vents. They also have USB ports, printer ports, and a place to plug in a monitor, keyboard, and mouse. So even if you're following the directions to a T, remember, your PC may be different from ours.

# The Degunking Mindset

The more you learn about degunking your PC, the more you'll realize that degunking is a mindset, not just a set of technical skills. We view degunking as mostly psychology, not just technology. Rather than simply thinking about it as a series of steps and tasks, you should think of degunking as a disciplined approach to making your PC last longer and perform better. If you follow the degunking process outlined in this book, you'll give yourself an insurance policy and save yourself from aggravation down the road. There's nothing worse than being charged $75 by a technician who tells you your motherboard was fried because of all the dust that accumulated in there! *Degunking Your PC* will make your time on your PC more efficient, more productive, and probably even more enjoyable.

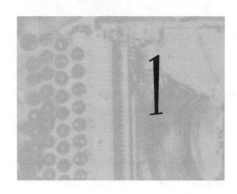

# Why Is My PC All Gunked Up?

## Degunking Checklist:

√ Understand how and why your PC is gunked up and the differences between internal and external gunk.

√ Learn the basic steps to degunking your PC, work area, and hardware.

√ Know that having too many peripherals can get in your way.

√ Learn how software that comes with hardware gunks up the inside of your PC.

√ Convince yourself that you need to get rid of unnecessary, broken, or duplicate hardware.

√ Understand that cables and cords must be treated with care and improper use can cause problems that can be difficult to diagnose.

√ Learn that dial-up connections are gunk and why moving to broadband is a better option.

√ Understand that degunking tasks are tasks that must be done regularly, and follow the scheduling tips for best results.

R elax. It's nobody's fault. You have a problem—your PC is gunked up. No matter who you are or how you use your PC, you likely have excess gunk and clutter that is getting in your way. And you likely have your equipment set up in such a way that you can't get the best use out of it. Maybe you have a printer that doesn't work or prints really slowly because of the way it was first installed. Or perhaps you have so much software installed on your PC that you can't find anything you are looking for. You might even have a Pocket PC that you never use or an old digital camera you've replaced with a newer one. Perhaps the sea of cords and cables underneath your desk or an unsafe number of power supplies and connected peripherals are driving you crazy. (When was the last time you had the nerve to look under your desk, anyway?) Clutter like this is a fact of modern life. You acquire things, buy things, install things, configure things, break things (or things break), and, well, the stuff just piles up.

# Types of Gunk

There are two types of gunk: internal and external. *Internal gunk* is "virtual" gunk, like installed software for hardware you no longer own. Internal gunk can make your PC run more slowly than it should and cause various other problems. *External gunk* is "physical" gunk. External gunk can make it difficult to work at your desk and impossible to vacuum underneath it. Let's take a closer look at both.

## Hazards of Internal Gunk

Internal gunk, the virtual gunk you acquire after months or years of using your PC, can cause a myriad of problems. Adware, spyware, and viruses can disable a system that's not properly protected. It can also cause your network to become unreliable or to crash. Unsigned drivers or poorly installed or configured hardware can make it impossible to use a device as it's meant to be used and can cause the blue screens of death (a complete failure of the system) that are difficult to diagnose.

Internal gunk also comes from the failure to configure devices like monitors, printers, scanners, Web cams, and other hardware properly. If you can't read what's on a Web site because the print is too small, that's gunk! Here are some other signs that you have internal gunk, each of which we'll address in this book:

√  Your PC runs slowly and you don't know why.

√  When you look at the All Programs list, you see lots of software you never use or you don't know what it is used for.

√  You have software installed for hardware you no longer own.

√  You don't get good prints from your ink-jet printer.

√ Every time you use your Web cam, your PC reboots or hangs.

√ You are not getting the same performance from your USB devices as you used to.

√ You have to disconnect from the Internet on your PC when someone else in the family wants to connect from theirs.

√ You still transfer data from one PC to another via floppy disk, CD, or DVD.

√ Your wireless network doesn't work well and is not reliable.

√ You have some backups, but you hope you never have to use them because they are so unorganized.

√ You have voice recognition software but you can't get it to work as well as you'd like.

## And Then There's External Gunk

External gunk can cause plenty of problems too. The dirt and grime that accumulates inside the mouse will make it skip and jump. The smudge on the scanner can make your pictures look weird. You might have a USB port that's not the right type or is limiting or causing problems with the available bandwidth to devices. You might still be using a dial-up connection to the Internet and want to move to something else but don't know how. Here are some other signs that you have external gunk, each of which we'll address in this book:

√ There are fingerprints and grime on your flat-screen monitor, and you don't know how to clean it without harming it.

√ You can see dust on the intakes of your PC.

√ Your ink-jet printer always prints vertical lines on your prints, or the ink isn't applied properly.

√ You purchase printer after printer because every time you replace a cartridge, you can never get it to print right again.

√ You receive memory errors with lots of weird numbers listed.

√ You can't pay a bill at your desk because of all the hardware on it.

√ You use power strips but you don't know if they also protect against power surges or sags.

√ You have hardware that you don't use or is broken and you don't know what to do with it.

√ You can't vacuum under your desk.

√ You can't reach the back of the PC to switch out your USB printer for your USB camera.

Gunk happens!

## So, Now What?

So what's a body to do? Well, that's what we're here to show you. In this book you'll learn first just how much gunk you have and then what steps to take to reduce or eliminate it. Depending on how long you've had your PC and how many hobbies you've acquired (scanning, digital photography, chatting with microphones and Web cams, and so on), you may have quite a bit of work to do. If you've only been computing a year or so, maybe all you need is some physical cleaning and to perform a few organizational tasks.

The first order of business is to take the "Vacuum" and the "Bill Paying at Your Desk" tests. If you can't vacuum under your desk, or if you have to move *anything* to pay a bill, you're gunked!

---

**TIP: As with all books in the Degunking series, you should work through this book in order for best results.**

---

# Can Degunking Your PC Really Help?

Anyone who has used their PC for a while and taken the time to do a little degunking quickly realizes that getting rid of clutter and fixing and optimizing what you have left can really save you a lot of time. It's easy to fall into the trap of wasting a lot of time trying to use equipment that doesn't work properly or that gets in your way. Often we think that because our equipment is not working properly, we need to run out and purchase a new PC and other peripherals. Fortunately, degunking can really help in situations like this and might even save you money by eliminating the need to buy replacement equipment you don't actually need.

Once you really get your PC running the way that you want it to and make a good work area for yourself, you'll be a lot more productive and have much more fun using your PC. You won't have to constantly hunt for things and you won't get frustrated by things that don't work. PCs are much like cars: they need a little upkeep now and then. With a little bit of care you'll get much more performance out of your PC and peripherals and you'll be able to prolong the life of your equipment.

Unfortunately, most books don't provide much information to really help you clean up your PC and your peripherals and get everything set up so that you can be more productive. Most books focus on either basic user techniques or power user tips and tricks and leave you to your own devices when it comes to figuring out how to get organized and clutter free. What we are about to show you in this book really isn't difficult. You just need to set aside some time and try to discipline yourself a little. It's important to realize that you'll get the best benefit if you perform certain degunking maintenance tasks on a regular basis. And by following the sequential steps that we present, you can improve your experiences with your PC considerably.

Our process is divided into four key areas:

1.  *Cleaning out the physical gunk.* As we use our PCs, we always seem to be adding new peripherals and other gadgets. This can really make the gunk build up. Here we'll focus on how you can physically clean your PC and all of your peripherals that are sitting there dying for attention. Believe it our not, we'll actually get out the cleaning supplies and show you how to clean everything that you have. We'll even show you how to clean up your work area so that all of your equipment fits together very nicely and you can see your desk. When you finish with this process, you'll feel really good. You might even feel that you've given new life to your PC and your peripherals.

2.  *Getting everything connected and configured for optimum performance.* PC communications and networking technologies have come a long way over the past few years. You no longer need to connect to the Internet using a slow dial-up connection, and you no longer need to pass disks around to copy files from one PC in your home to another. You also don't need to use all of the cumbersome wires you have cluttering up your home or office. You can go wireless and really increase your productivity. Once you've physically cleaned your equipment, we'll show you how to apply the degunking mindset to getting all of your equipment connected. You'll be able to make your PCs more secure and you'll be able to do more with the PCs you have.

3.  *Backing up.* The more you use your PC and the more you communicate with others and share files, the more you'll need a backup system that really works. Here we'll help you get organized and take control over everything that you store on your PC or home network. If you are like most PC users, you are probably currently taking on more risk than you realize by not backing up regularly and not storing your backups in a safe place. We'll show you how to set up a simple but reliable system that is easy to follow on a regular basis.

4.  *Opting for performance.* Once you've completed the important process of degunking your PC and peripherals, it's time to focus on performance issues so that you can carry out tasks such as upgrading video cards, upgrading your CPU if you need to, adding RAM, and much more. You can make improvements that will help you prolong the life of your PC and make it perform much faster. PCs are prone to becoming obsolete quickly because of new technology coming out all the time. Fortunately, there are measures you can take to get more out of what you currently have, and we'll show you what they are.

# Understanding How Gunked Up You Really Are

As you work through the chapters in this book, you'll find you've accumulated *a lot* of gunk. Once you've accepted that idea, you'll learn what to throw away, what to hide and where, what to put away in a drawer or closet, and what duplicate hardware is in use that you can get rid of. For instance, you may have purchased a new flat-screen monitor (one that has its own speakers built in) but still use those two large and clumsy speakers that came with your PC. Those speakers are now unnecessary and taking up valuable workspace. In addition, although you use your digital camera occasionally, you really don't need it sitting on the desk, connected to the USB port, plugged in, and connected to the FireWire port. This is gunk and complicates your life and your desk, and removing it or storing it somewhere else quickly solves this problem.

## Let's Talk About *Serious* Gunk

Go ahead and poke your head under your desk. If you see a myriad of power cords, power strips, USB cables, FireWire cables, mouse and keyboard cables, and network cables, you're not alone. Figure 1-1 shows an example. You can't vacuum under here.

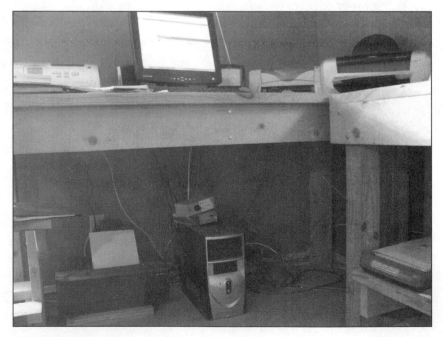

**Figure 1-1**
This is a gunked-up workspace.

The image shows lots of gunk. Look closely; there are four printers, a scanner, and what looks to be a single power outlet for all of it. There's a printer switch box (unnecessary in this day and age of USB hubs and USB printers (someone hasn't been keeping up), an external hard disk used for backups precariously placed on top of the PC's tower, and a mini TV, with an antennae for goodness sake! This setup is a real mess. If any part of this photo looks familiar to you, you've got a lot of work to do.

To start degunking this mess (as well as whatever else you've got going on), you'll have to start at the beginning of this book and work through every page. Table 1-1 outlines how the gunk in this photo affects both the user and the PC.

**Table 1-1    Problems Related to Internal and External Gunk**

| Problem | The Gunk It Creates |
| --- | --- |
| Dust | Dust can get into the PC tower and cause RAM and other internal components to fail. Not physically cleaning the inside and the outside of the computer a few times a year can render it inoperable. |
| Multiple printers | Multiple printers take up space on your desk, underneath your desk, and beside your desk. Each also adds two more cables to the mix: a power cord and a USB or parallel printer cable. |
| Printer software | Software for printers that aren't being used takes up hard drive space and can use system resources looking for software updates or monitoring ink levels. |
| Printer switch box | An old printer switch box not only encourages a user to collect printers, it also runs on parallel port technology. That's slower than USB and needs to be removed. |
| External hardware device (precariously perched) | If the tower is knocked over and damaged, the backup device will be too. If a toddler or small animal gets near it, it could be knocked off. |
| Television | No one uses antennae anymore. Reception is too poor. |
| Wires and cables | Too many wires and cables make it impossible to vacuum and locate cords when you need them. When cords are gunked up like this, there's generally lots of unnecessary stuff there too. |
| Power outlets, surge protectors, and overload. | Too many power cords can create a fire hazard by overloading the outlet or the home electrical system. Power strips do not provide protection for surges or sags either, and one good jolt could leave your PC inoperable. |
| Scanner | We're guessing the scanner in this image hasn't had its scanner glass cleaned in a while. |
| Keyboard and mouse cords | If keyboard and mouse cords aren't long enough, the user will be uncomfortable working. |
| Tower | If a tower is placed on the floor, it could be knocked over. It could also be destroyed by a busted water heater. Beyond that, it's difficult to insert CDs or connect equipment when you have to get on your knees to do it. |

## Too Many Peripherals and Connections

As noted in Figure 1-1, some gunk is due to peripherals. Cameras, scanners, printers, Pocket PCs, speakers, hubs, switches, routers, keyboards, mice, microphones, Web cams, and backup drives all contribute. Count the peripherals you can see. If you can see, on or underneath your desk, more than six or seven, you're likely having a hard time keeping the cords, cables, and work area organized.

Think about it logically: one DV camera has 3 connections. One is the charger or power supply, one is the connection to the computer's USB port, and one is to the computer's FireWire port. The scanner and printer have 2 connections each: one connection is the power supply, the other is the one that connects it to the PC. A pocket PC can have 2 or 3 as well. If you multiply 10 peripherals by 2.5 (a fair average) you'll have between 20 and 30 cords to deal with. Too many peripherals equals too much gunk.

### GunkBuster's Notebook: Software Adds Up Too

When you install new hardware, software is sure to follow. Almost all hardware comes with some sort of software. This may be in the form of a driver, an application, or a group of applications. Most users tend to install whatever comes with the hardware, and much of it is unnecessary. Figure 1-2 shows software packaged with a new Hewlett-Packard printer. Most of this is unnecessary (in most instances). Users usually have other printing software programs.

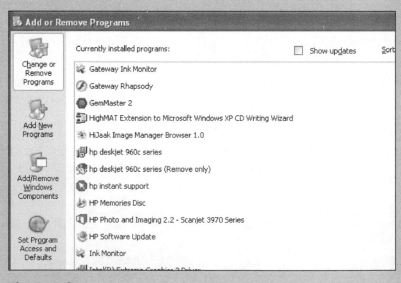

**Figure 1-2**
Most hardware comes with unnecessary (or unused) software.

This extra software takes up space on your PC's hard drive, often runs in the background, and can slow down the performance of the machine. The software is doubly unnecessary if you no longer own the hardware. You probably have a bit of this software running on your PC now. In this book, you'll learn that removing software is just as important as any other degunking task.

## Be Wary of Nonfunctional, Outdated, Unnecessary, or Duplicate Hardware

What did you do with your last digital camera, the one you replaced with the new DV camera you recently purchased? What about the older scanner or printer that connected through a printer cable, or the Web cam that always made your computer freeze up? If they are still on or underneath your desk, or if their cords and cables are, that's gunk. If you put them in a closet or drawer, just in case you might need them some day, you should rethink that decision. If you haven't used the hardware in over a year, you probably never will. What about the software? Did you remove it from your PC when you put that old camera in the closet?

It's okay. Almost everyone has broken, outdated, or duplicate hardware somewhere, so you're not alone. If you're a pack rat, it may be difficult to say goodbye. However, as you'll learn in Appendix A, you can give functional, even though outdated, hardware to your favorite charity, an elderly parent who doesn't know the difference between a printer cable and a USB cable, or a child who can't be trusted with a thousand dollar digital camera. We'll teach you how to get rid of gunk. We promise you'll be happier and more productive, even if it's a little painful at first.

### GunkBuster's Notebook: How Many Extra Printers Do You Have?

Printers, printers, printers, everywhere. *I (Joli) have, like, eight of them around the house.* Some work, some don't. One of them used to work before I tried refilling the cartridges with the do-it-yourself-ink-refilling-cartridge kit, and no one makes cartridges for two of them anymore. What a gunked-up mess. Printers are my weakness.

You may have a weakness for things too; it may be a weakness for old Web cams or digital cameras. It's okay; we'll help you say goodbye. Take inventory, admit you are powerless over your printer collection, and then hop on board the Degunking Your PC wagon and start letting go.

# Other Common Gunk Signs

There are lots of other signs of gunk. Some are obvious, such as having equipment sitting around that doesn't work any longer, and some aren't so obvious, such as having overloaded surge protectors, crimped network cables, or unorganized or nonexistent backups for your PC. There are chapters dedicated to these topics throughout the book to show you how to deal with them using the degunking techniques that we provide.

## Your Hardware Is So Dusty and Dirty That You Are Afraid to Have Visitors

If you are avoiding having friends or family members come to visit you because your PC and other peripherals are so dusty and dirty, then you are really in trouble. (You might even want to jump to Chapter 3 immediately if you are in this situation and learn how to start cleaning up your gunk!) You probably aren't this bad off, but all of us could use some advice and encouragement to clean and dust a little more often.

When it comes to your PC and other peripherals, dust and dirt is not your friend. Dust that accumulates around your PC also accumulates inside of it. As mentioned earlier, dust inside the PC will collect on the memory, the motherboard, and other internal components and can cause them to stop working. Internal parts are very delicate.

In addition to the technical side of dusting and cleaning your equipment, dusting and cleaning gives you the opportunity to take inventory of what you have too. There's no better way to count printers than by cleaning their print nozzles and heads. Cleaning will also take you inside the mouse and keyboard, under the scanner glass, and inside the tower. If you've never had the pleasure of blowing compressed air into a computer tower after years of use, well, you've missed a pretty spectacular and dusty experience!

Cleaning the outside will lead to cleaning up the work area and getting a handle on cords, cables, hubs, and power supplies. Once the work area is sparkling clean, you can move on to other degunking tasks.

## Your PC Is Working against You and Not for You

There are many things that can happen with your PC and peripherals that start to make them work against you:

√ Your monitor is configured improperly and is thus putting a lot of strain on your eyes.

√ Your mouse has so much gunk build-up in it that you can't even slide it across the desk.

√ Your PC has so much old software installed on it that it takes forever to start up.

√ The new keyboard is configured properly and you don't even know how to use many of the features it provides.

√ You get system errors that you simply ignore when you boot up and use your PC.

√ Your printer isn't configured with the proper drivers and it doesn't always print correctly and occasionally causes your PC to lock up.

√ You don't know how to use your CD-ROM burner because you never installed the proper software.

√ Your hard drive makes grinding noises when you perform resource-intensive tasks.

√ When your PC boots up, it often runs through an additional disk scan.

√ You have programs you don't recognize.

√ You don't know anything about Disk Cleanup, Disk Defragmenter, cache files, temporary Internet files, or history files.

√ You have not tweaked any Internet Explorer settings or you notice problems with it. For instance, your home page has been changed or you get too many pop-ups.

√ Someone has e-mailed you stating that you sent them a virus.

√ You can't find files you know you've saved.

These kinds of problems can build up over time and nag you to death. Some of them are easy to ignore, but the end result is that they can slow you down and make you feel cluttered as you work. Some of these problems might even make your PC crash more often than it should, which in the end could really cost you. The worst thing you could possibly do is ignore critical PC problems, not back up your files, and then have something bad happen and not be able to recover them.

This type of gunk is something that you must attack as soon as you can. Fortunately, help is right around the corner. Soon we'll be showing you ways to degunk your monitor, keyboard, and mouse, as well as other necessary computer components. For instance, the monitor has lots of resolution settings, and one is right for you. It might not be the one that's configured, though, so we'll work through the various choices. You can also use Windows Display Properties to configure how large icons and fonts are, configure screen savers, and set the computer's colors so they work for you instead of you working for them.

If you've purchased a newer keyboard or mouse, you may not be aware that those items come with software than can be used to configure everything from how fast the mouse scrolls to what happens when you press the specialty keys on the keyboard. On many keyboards now, you can even configure what the function keys do!

Of course, you'll want to degunk your CD burning software packages by choosing one you like and getting rid of the other five, and you'll want to choose the right kind of connections for your peripherals, get your USB ports and hubs working properly, and perhaps even add additional cards for additional components. All of that is part of degunking.

## You're Still on Dial-Up

Another common form of gunk is the old dial-up connection. Sure, that may be a budget matter for many people, but for others, failing to move to DSL or cable is the result of a fear of the unknown. Using a dial-up connection can really waste a lot of your time. Think about all of the time you have to sit there and wait for your PC to connect and all of those times when you are doing something important (like shopping for shoes online) and you lose your connection. Wouldn't it be much cheaper and smarter in the long run to switch over to a more reliable and faster connection? Fear no more. Because in Chapter 9, you'll learn all you need to know to make the move, add the hardware, set up the connection, and get the best deal.

## You Have Multiple Computers That Aren't Networked

If you have multiple computers in the house, they should ideally be networked. There are many reasons for this: you can share a single Internet connection, share pictures and music, and move data from one computer to another without having to carry it on a floppy disk, CD, or flash drive. You can set up a network through a single null modem cable, a hub, a router, a switch, or even through a wireless access point.

Going wireless is the best option if you can afford it, and it's the optimal way to degunk. You can get rid of lots of cables. If you don't want to go wireless though, purchase a $30 hub and a few Category 5 cables and you're good to go. You'll learn about setting up both (and degunking what you have already) in later chapters.

## Backups Are Randomly Created and Not Organized

Degunking doesn't just have to do with getting rid of stuff, cleaning up what you have, and configuring optimal settings for monitors and other hardware. It can mean adding things too. For instance, there's one often overlooked degunking technique: adding a backup system. This might be an external backup drive, or it may just be a strategy to back up once a week using a CD or DVD burner.

Backing up brings more gunk into play, though. CDs, DVDs, unorganized backup hard drives, unreliable backups—all of these things can cause you to acquire more gunk than you will get rid of. So, when creating backups and a backup strategy, you have to figure out how you'll organize what you create. That's all covered in Chapter 12.

## Living with Slow Performance

If you got up this morning and drove to work and realized that your car could only go half as fast as it did a year ago or that your brakes were hardly working, you'd probably be on the phone as quickly as possible trying to make an appointment to get your car fixed. But when it comes to our PCs, we often put up with poor and declining performance. We often think that our PCs are supposed to age quickly and that there is nothing we can do about it. There is.

Slow performance might be caused by a number of things. You might not have enough RAM, your CPU may no longer have enough horsepower to run the newer software you are using, you might be using incorrect drivers for some of your peripherals, and so on. The good news is that there really is something that you can do.

If your computer is bogged down with software or you don't have enough RAM to use effectively the software you have, the computer is gunked. Make the computer perform better and you'll be a happier camper.

Improving performance can also mean completing these tasks:

√   Adding more RAM

√   Upgrading the CPU or purchasing a new tower

√   Installing better video or sound cards

√   Configuring hardware profiles

√   Tweaking system properties

√   Learning to work more efficiently

As was mentioned earlier, sometimes, adding hardware can do just as much for improving your computer as removing things can. If it all seems overwhelming now, don't worry, each chapter takes you though the process step-by-step, and we promise to be gentle.

## Summing Up

The most difficult part of getting your PC back in tip-top shape involves dedicating time to the tasks. As we move on and look at the different degunking techniques, we'll arrange the tasks in the order that will likely get you the best results in the shortest amount of time. Our approach will be to show you not only how to fix things, but how to get yourself in the habit of keeping them that way once finished. If you're new to the world of degunking, don't worry. It's much easier than putting together a swing set for your kids or an entertainment center for your parents.

# Degunking Your PC

## Degunking Checklist:

√ Understand that the best degunking results are obtained by working, in order, through our proven degunking 12-step program.

√ Know what questions to ask to get the best degunking results.

√ Learn that physically cleaning your computer is just as important as managing your work area and taking control of cords and cables.

√ Understand that you *can* get rid of hardware you don't use, like old Web cams, digital cameras, and printers that don't print.

√ Learn that you can network computers in both wired and wireless configurations and share a single Internet connection with multiple networked computers.

√ Understand why you should be on a regular backup schedule and why you should organize archived data.

√ See how to enhance computer performance by adding hardware and removing unnecessary peripherals.

As you learned in the first chapter, there are lots of ways to acquire gunk. You may have broken, unnecessary, or duplicate hardware, non-networked computers, a slow Internet connection, or a myriad of cables and cords under your desk. You may not be able to find the USB cables required to plug in your digital camera or have so much dust on your monitor it's hard to make out what's displayed on it. A thousand things could have caused you to get gunked up. In this chapter, you'll learn how to start applying the degunking mindset.

Our degunking mindset isn't about just technical issues. We call it a mindset because it involves how you think about the technology you use, how you get organized, and how you maintain your equipment. The mindset isn't something that you adopt for a little while and then forget all about. It requires a little discipline, but as you'll soon see, the results you'll get are well worth the effort. In this chapter, we'll quickly introduce you to the degunking strategy that we'll be using, and then in Chapter 3 we'll hit the ground running and give you some tasks to perform so that you can start degunking your PC. Taking a moment to understand the degunking mindset is important because what we have to say will really help you understand why it is important to perform some degunking tasks in a specific order, what degunking tasks you should focus on when you have specific problems, and what degunking tasks you should schedule and make part of the routine of using your PC. The best part is that you won't need a lot of time to get some quick results.

# The Proven Method for Degunking Your PC

The first thing to keep in mind as you read this book is that when we talk about "degunking your PC," we'll be referring to any desktop or laptop PC you might have, as well as all of the other peripherals that you use with your system, such as your printers, scanners, digital cameras, networks, and so on. As we all know, PCs don't operate in a vacuum, and it's important to look at everything that you connect to your PC. Often, performance problems and clutter annoyances are caused by all of the stuff that you might be using with your PC. We like to think of this as the "holistic" approach to making your PC operate at its peak. We hate to say it, but if Dr. Phil wrote a computer book, he'd probably give you the same lecture (sorry, we won't go there anymore).

When we wrote the first degunking book (*Degunking Windows*) we developed a 12-step program that has proven to be a big hit with Windows users. In fact, we've received numerous comments and reviews from readers around the world, all indicating that having a 12-step program really helped keep them focused and on track as they went about their work of degunking. So the good news is that we'll be introducing another 12-step program in this chapter, but this time it will be designed specifically to help you degunk your PC and your peripherals. By starting with the most basic tasks and moving to the more advanced ones, you can clean up your PC by building on what you've done previously. For instance, you wouldn't want to defragment your hard drive first and then delete gigabytes of unwanted data and applications; you'd only have to defragment the drive again when you finished! And, you wouldn't want to hide or mount your external speakers just before you discover that your new flat-screen monitor has speakers already built in!

That's the point of the degunking program: to do things in the right order and minimize the work you do while maximizing the results you get. By the time you get to the end of this chapter, you'll understand our 12-step program for degunking your PC. We want you to get very familiar with it because we'll be using it throughout the book. It's okay to even make a copy of it and tape it to your wall if you need some encouragement.

## Important Questions to Ask Yourself

As you use your PC and peripherals and work at your desk, you need to ask yourself the following questions. Your answers will help you decide where to focus your energy and time while degunking:

√ Have I ever opened the computer case and used compressed air to clean the inside of the system?

√ Do I clean the scanner glass, the Web cam eye, or the print nozzle heads?

√ Does the sheer size of my monitor overpower my desktop?

√ Do I have more than 7 peripherals on or under my desk?

√ Can I see more than 15 cords and cables under my desk?

√ Do I have multiple hubs when one larger one would suffice? Or worse, do I need a switch or a router?

√ How many peripherals do I have that I haven't used in a year or more?

√ Is the software installed for my hardware configured properly—or needed at all?

√ Do I have to switch out USB devices because I don't have enough ports, or do I get error messages when using them?

√ Is my Internet connection as fast and effective as I want it to be?

√ Are my computers networked and is the network functional?

√ Do I have reliable and up-to-date backups?

√ Can I add more RAM, a faster CPU, or other internal hardware to enhance performance?

√ Is my PC secured with the latest updates, virus definitions, and device drivers?

√ Is my PC crashing more than it should?

√ Am I having trouble finding the programs and files that are stored on my computer?

√ Is my hard drive running so slowly that it takes forever to get any work done?

√ Should I go wireless?

Answering these questions helps you understand what needs to be done and how gunk accumulates, and this will lead you to understand how the degunking program works and how it is useful. You'll find that our 12-step strategy is a good way to get organized, and in this book you'll work though it chapter by chapter. Before you know it, you'll be free of all that clutter and unnecessary hardware and you'll be zipping along at breakneck speed!

## Physically Cleaning Your PC

Physically cleaning your PC is important. Sticky mice, problematic keys on a keyboard, gunk on the monitor, clogged print nozzles, and the dust and grime that accumulates inside the computer tower can all cause headaches, if not complete failure of the device. Cat hair, smoke particles, and dust inside the monitor, for instance, can cause internal components like RAM to stop working completely or produce errors that are difficult to diagnose. Additionally, bent prongs on a monitor connection, loose hardware connections, or bent cables can also cause problems. The first step in degunking is to clean, clean, clean. Just think of how good you feel when you clean the inside of your home or your garage. Cleaning your PC and all of the peripherals you use can leave you with the same feeling of bliss.

## Managing Your Work Area

There are a million reasons why your work area could be gunked up. Your monitor takes up your entire desk, speakers are not hidden and cables are everywhere, the tower is either taking up space on the desk or unattainable under it, or you have multiple hubs (a patchwork network) when one larger one would do. You might also have mice and keyboard cords on the desk or peripherals and their cords everywhere.

There are lots of ways to overcome a gunked-up work area. Going with a flat-screen monitor will free up a lot of space if you can afford it, and wireless hardware is always a plus. Wireless mice and keyboards are inexpensive, and wireless printers are coming around in price too.

Of course, purchasing a small storage bin for all of your electronic equipment like digital cameras, PDAs, Pocket PCs, iPods, and smart displays is also a smart idea. There's no reason for these things to be under or on your desk if you rarely use them. Storage bins also make a good place to keep extra cables, power supplies, and cords used to connect devices. Figure 2-1 shows an example.

**Figure 2-1**
Degunking is bliss!

## Managing Cords and Cables

Managing your cords and cables isn't just cosmetic; it's a necessary and required part of degunking. Overloaded power strips can cause a fire, while overloaded computers can perform sluggishly. Being unable to vacuum or clean under the desk and around the cables can cause dust and dirt to build up in the computer case, as well in the keyboard and mouse. And last but not least, if you want to plug in a device but don't know which cord goes to it, you're just not going to be able to use it.

Getting a handle on the countless number of cables under your desk is a multi-step process. First, you'll need to choose the right power strips, ones that will actually protect you if lightning strikes or there's a power surge. Chances are good that the one you purchased for $9.99 isn't going to do the trick. You also need to take inventory of just how many power strips you have in a single room. There is such a thing as overload!

Next, you'll need to label all of the cables and cords you have, even the ones that are stored. There's nothing worse than looking for the power charger when the battery goes dead on the PDA or when you need to charge up your DV camera.

Finally, you'll need to learn the right ways to handle and hide network cables and run wires around or under doors. You'll also want to optimize how you use cable ties and split conduit for managing what you have. It's all a part of the degunking process, and one you must do before you begin other degunking tasks.

## Managing and Degunking Peripherals (and Computer Components)

Managing and degunking peripherals (and computer components) are two different things. Managing peripherals and components can mean labeling cords and hiding or storing unused items, while degunking them can mean setting the correct resolution for your monitor or using the software with your wireless keyboard to create shortcuts to documents or Internet Web sites. Degunking tasks can also include getting rid of unnecessary software; many people have four or five CD burning software programs or four or five printer applications. You'll have to take inventory to see just what you need to manage.

Additionally, managing tasks can mean optimizing USB ports, hubs and routers, or perhaps even switches. To get the most out of your USB devices, you have to understand how connecting them to USB hubs affects performance. To get the most out of hubs, routers, and switches, you have to understand the difference between them all first. These are more advanced degunking tasks and are thus further down in the degunking 12-step program than others are.

## Degunking Internet Connections

When multiple PCs are connected, they can all share a single Internet connection. Sharing a dial-up Internet connection between two or more PCs is the most basic networking strategy. To share an Internet connection, you'll need to understand the hardware and software requirements and set up Internet Connection Sharing in Windows. You'll also need to be aware of security issues and get each computer its own antivirus software.

Dial-up is also the most basic Internet strategy. In order to fully degunk your Internet connections, you'll want to consider moving to DSL, cable, or some other form of broadband. When making the move, it's important to understand how to choose a provider; select between modems, routers, or switches; set up the hardware you decide to use, and learn how to get the most out of the connection once it's set up. Degunking your Internet connections is also an advanced degunking strategy and will take more time than previously mentioned degunking tasks.

## Wired Networking

If you've set up Internet Connection Sharing, you have a basic network. This network may have been created using a null modem cable, a hub and Ethernet cables, or a switch or router. However, keeping the network operational and optimized requires more thought.

To degunk the network or create a new one of course requires the best hardware, but you'll also need to make sure everything is connected properly, and study the best and worst configurations for wired networks. Understanding what works well and what doesn't will help you create a better network or optimize the one you already have.

## Wireless Networking

Going wireless is an excellent way to degunk. Wireless networking says it all: no wires, no gunk. When you're ready to go wireless, you can learn how in Chapter 11. From installing wireless access points and adapters to installing antennas, cables, and connectors, you can get the ultimate degunked network.

Degunking an already created wireless network can be tricky, though. There are specific ways to test the network and troubleshoot problematic connections and interference. Knowing how to optimize placement of access points and how to increase throughput for media and music is important. Once you get a wireless network set up and degunked properly, you'll be amazed at how much more productive you can become. Many people think that using a wireless network is dangerous because they are not as secure as wired networks, but the reality is that wireless networking is actually safe if you set things up properly.

## Managing Backups and Archived Data

Everyone should have a backup strategy, as well as a way to organize archived data. The backup strategy can be as simple as dragging files to an external hard drive or as primitive as saving to a floppy disk. Whatever the choice though, it's essential to back up regularly, either once a day or once a week.

In Chapter 13, you'll learn what kinds of backup devices are available and how to organize what you've backed up. You can opt for the Windows backup utility, or you can use third-party programs. Either way, the object of Chapter 12 is to get you on a regular program for backing up your data. Once you learn to make your backups a regular activity, you'll create a level of protection for yourself that you'll wish you always had.

## Enhancing Performance

We all can't afford a screaming machine, but we can increase the performance of the one we have. In general, it's fairly inexpensive to add RAM, and adding as little as 128 MB can really speed up performance. Nowadays, anything less than 256 is simply not enough. Programs like Photoshop CS suggest you have a minimum of 256, and that's just to get minimal functionality from the program.

It's also possible to upgrade your CPU, upgrade sound and video cards, and add items like TV tuners or FireWire ports. Adding or upgrading hardware, assuming your computer meets the requirements for such, can really spice up the performance of a computer.

It's also a good idea to create hardware profiles if you use your PC for multiple tasks. For instance, if you have a laptop you take to work, you can create a profile that includes work printers and scanners, network connections, and e-mail. If you come home and use the same machine for gaming online, you can create a separate profile for gaming. The gaming profile won't have unnecessary programs or other components loaded, offering you more resources for playing games.

Finally, you can tweak your system's properties so your computer opts for either best performance or best appearance or uses processor scheduling for either programs or background services, and you can enhance memory usage and virtual memory settings. All of these things can help improve performance.

# Getting a New PC and Getting Rid of Old Equipment

In Appendix A, we'll talk about what to do with unnecessary and unwanted peripherals, and older PCs you no longer need or have replaced. There are lots of ways to recycle older equipment, including selling it, donating it, or passing it on to a family member or friend. Since the need for getting rid of older hardware almost always follows obtaining newer stuff, we'll also talk about degunking any new PC you've purchased. New PCs come with all kinds of gunk, including trial versions of software, ads for Internet service, and unnecessary programs.

## Degunking Finesse

In Appendix B, we'll finish up by going over a little degunking finesse. You'll learn about voice recognition programs and how to use them to surf the Web. You'll learn about new messaging programs that let you play games and visit online and that also let you set up a video phone to talk while visiting through a Web cam. You'll also learn how to replace the battery when your system and system clock starts to fail and how to deal with multiple users on a single PC.

# The Degunking 12-Step Program

We introduced the concept of the 12-step program earlier in the chapter. It's now time to present it to you so that you have your degunking road map. The more you work with it, the more you'll discover how easy it is to follow and how it can save you a lot of valuable time in the long run.

1.  Physically clean your PC and all of the peripherals and devices that you use (Chapter 3).
2.  Do an overhaul of your work area and clean out all of the configurations of the hardware that you use (Chapter 4).
3.  Properly configure and set up your PC or laptop (if you use one) and all of its key components—monitor, printers, and so on (Chapter 5).
4.  Properly configure and set up all of your PC support peripherals, including digital cameras, scanners, PDAs, and smart displays (Chapter 6).
5.  Set up USB and FireWire connections for your equipment to get better performance transferring data (Chapter 7).
6.  Set up a basic system so that you can optimize and share a dial-up Internet connection around your home (Chapter 8).
7.  Get rid of you dial-up Internet connection and move to a faster cable or DSL connection if you have access to these services (Chapter 9).

8. Link up all of the computers around your home or small office with a low-cost but efficient network (Chapter 10).

9. Set up a wireless networking system to allow you to use your PC wherever you want in your home or small office (Chapter 11).

10. Back up your system on a regular basis (Chapter 12).

11. Perform some cost-effective tasks to really speed up the performance of your PC (Chapter 13).

12. Safely sell, donate, or dispose of the PC equipment that you no longer need (Appendix A).

# Summing Up

It's time to start degunking in earnest. By now, you should understand that your PC is gunked up and have an idea of what things contributed to it. You should know all about the 12-step degunking strategy and how and why we'll start where we will. So, get out that duster, dry cloth, and can of compressed air and turn the page. It's time to degunk!

# 3

# Physically Cleaning Your PC and Peripherals

**Degunking Tasks:**

√ Safely clean any type of monitor that you might have, including CRTs and flat panel LCDs.

√ Clean the inside and outside of your desktop case (tower).

√ Take precautions to protect your PC from electrostatic discharge.

√ Clean both the inside and outside of your laptop, if you use one.

√ Properly clean any printers that you use, including both ink-jets and lasers.

√ Learn how to clean a scanner, a Web cam, and a camera lens.

√ Know what environmental issues cause computer prob-lems—including pollen, pet dander, smoke, and tempera-ture extremes—and how to minimize damage.

√ Setup a regular maintenance schedule for cleaning your PC and your key peripherals.

What would happen if you never cleaned your reading glasses? We guarantee you'd notice a problem after only a few days. What about wiping down the bathroom mirror or the kitchen sink? If you didn't do that occasionally, you'd end up with a nasty mess on your hands rather quickly. Now, think about how often you clean your PC, computer monitor, scanner, or printer. You don't, you say? It's the same thing!

Believe it or not, your PC gets physically gunked up every time you use it, just like your glasses or any appliance in your home. Your fingers have oil on them, the monitor attracts dust and dirt, you drop food crumbs in the keyboard (or more gross, skin cells), the mouse gets grimy with who knows what, the cat sheds all over the tower…, in short, well, it's yucky.

Just as you have to clean your house, you have to clean your PC. We're not talking about cleaning up files or updating drivers here; we're not taking out the trash. We're talking about good, old-fashioned scrubbing with a rag and cleansers. With computers, though, you'll also need a screwdriver, some compressed air, an electrostatic wrist strap, and other non-conventional cleaning supplies. In this chapter, you'll learn all you need to know about physical cleaning and more. Break out the supplies, get under the desk, and let's have a go at it!

## Clean Any Type of Monitor You Use

Few people ever think about cleaning their computer, much less the monitor. You'd think people would remember to do that as the screen colors fade when fingerprints collect on it, and when your kid writes "Wash Me" in the dust perched there. Unfortunately, that's not the case, and our bet is that you have collected quite a bit of grime over the years.

Cleaning the monitor is easy, but it's equally simple to do it incorrectly. There are rules. You don't want to scratch the monitor with something abrasive, spray window cleaner directly on the screen, or use a damp cloth on a flat-screen monitor. Different monitors require different care. Let's look first at CRTs.

---

**TIP:** *To get the best view of dirt and grime possible, and to prevent damage or electrical shock, turn off your monitor before cleaning it.*

---

### CRTs

CRTs (cathode-ray tubes) are those big, clunky monitors with glass screens. A CRT monitor is shown in Figure 3-1. They're the ones that take up half your desktop. If you have the instruction booklet for your monitor, you should read

**Figure 3-1**
CRT monitors are quite large.

it before doing anything else. If you know the brand and model, you can also look up the information on the Internet. This is an important first step because some screens have a special coating to reduce reflections and static electricity and cleaning the surface with a mild glass cleaner (or detergent) can damage it.

If you can't find any specific instructions for your monitor, you're probably safest cleaning the screen with non-abrasive, lint-free, cotton (or equivalent) cloth and a non-alcohol, non-abrasive cleanser. If you're not sure, just use a damp cloth.

Here are some things to remember when cleaning a CRT screen:

√   Never spray any solution directly on the screen itself. It could drip and damage the screen. Instead, spray the solution onto the rag first.

√   Don't use a paper towel, although some folks will encourage you to do so. Paper towels are made from wood pulp and can scratch. A cotton rag is best.

√   Never touch the inside of the monitor or take it apart. The voltage could kill you.

√   Consider a cleaner like Endust for Electronics or specialty screen cleaning wipes, pads, spray, and cloths. Visit **www.keysan.com** for a listing of products.

√   When cleaning the screen, wipe from top to bottom and then from left to right. Repeat until your monitor is clean.

# Flat Panel LCDs

If you have an LCD (liquid crystal display) monitor, you'll need to take a different approach. LCD monitors are often called flat screens because the screens are thin and flat. Laptops have LCD screens.

LCD screens are a little more delicate than CRTs. Before cleaning these screens, you should read the instruction booklet that came with your monitor. If you know the brand and model, you can also look up the information on the Internet. This is an important first step because these monitors are generally quite fragile and cleaning the surface with the wrong tools can damage it.

Here are some tips you should follow when cleaning an LCD flat monitor:

√ Always use a soft, dry, non-abrasive cloth.

√ If necessary, add a touch of vinegar or isopropyl alcohol to the cleaning cloth.

√ Never spray anything directly onto the screen.

√ Don't use a paper towel.

√ Don't use ammonia or strong cleaners. Instead, consider special LCD cleaning cloths.

√ When cleaning, wipe from top to bottom and then from left to right. Repeat until your monitor is clean.

## GunkBuster's Notebook: Watch Out for Loose D-Connector Hardware

There's a special hazard connected with the D-connectors used in most VGA-style video adapters and old-style serial ports. D-connectors (named for the shape of the flange surrounding the pins or holes) used in PC cases are mounted to the case with a pair of short hexagonal posts. These posts have a threaded hole in the outside end, into which a mating thumbscrew threads to secure the connector plug to the chassis jack. See Figure 3-2.

The hexagonal posts are fastened to the PC case with a short threaded stud, a lock washer, and a hex nut. These are tightened at the factory when the PC is assembled, but many cycles of connecting and disconnecting a video or old-style serial port cable can loosen the interior hex nut that holds the hexagonal post to the case.

The hazard is simple: If the interior hex nut or lock washer gets so loose it falls off the hexagonal post's threaded stud, it can fall into the interior of the PC. If it lands on a circuit board (either the motherboard or an expansion board), it can short out printed

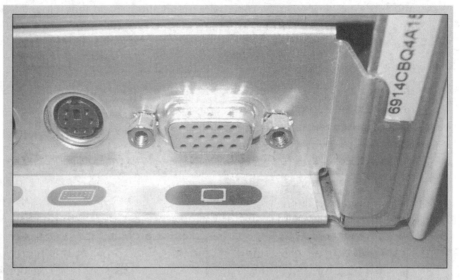

**Figure 3-2**
D-connectors and their hexagonal posts.

circuit traces and damage or destroy the board. This can render your PC inoperable and cost you hundreds of dollars in parts and service fees for a replacement motherboard.

During your periodic PC degunkings, check the hexagonal posts on all your D-connectors. They should be tight and should neither wiggle nor rotate. If you find any loose ones, tighten them carefully using a 3/16-inch nut driver. In some cases, this may require that you remove the covers from the PC and place a finger or a pair of pliers on the interior hex nut to keep it from rotating while you tighten the post from the outside of the case.

The best way to keep the hexagonal posts from loosening over time is to *not* overtighten the thumbscrews of your video or old-style serial cables. The thumbscrews are there to ensure that the plugs do not wiggle free of the chassis connectors. You don't even have to turn the thumbscrews tight. Just turn them until the plug is securely seated in the socket and does not wiggle nor back out when tugged.

# Clean Your Desktop Tower

Cleaning the outside of the tower is similar to cleaning the outside of your home. If you don't clean the stucco, siding, or gutters occasionally, your house starts to look bad. And, just as clogged gutters cause problems with drainage and birds' nests can cause problems with air intakes and fans, clogged air vents in a computer tower cause problems with airflow, which causes overheating and other damage.

The inside of the case can't be ignored either. Dust and other gunk accumulate there just as cat hair, spider webs, and similar items invade the deepest corners of your home. Although you don't have to clean your tower that often, you still have to put it on your spring-cleaning "to do" list.

## Gunkbuster's Notebook: Keep Your System Box!

When you bring home a new PC, you'll also bring home a fat handful of manuals (most of which you'll never read) and possibly a front-panel plate displaced by a ZIP or second CD-ROM drive installed by the retailer, plus several CD-ROMs containing OS recovery files and bundled software. Most of this material isn't useful while things go well, and so this stuff tends to come home with you and be dispersed in your office, among file cabinets, hardware drawers, and CD racks. That's a mistake: It's much better to keep it all together. Lose those CDs, and you will lose the ability to fully recover the software that you paid for, in the event of a catastrophic hard disk failure or the need to reinstall Windows after a bad spyware or virus attack.

Some PC manufacturers actually ship a nicely printed cardboard box with the PC, in which all this will (probably) fit. Unfortunately, in this age of cost saving, most manufacturers do not. We recommend finding a shoebox-sized cardboard box in which all this system-specific stuff can live. Label it with the make and model of the PC to which it belongs, and store it someplace where you can get at it without risking your neck in the attic or the rafters above the garage. In the event that you need to restore the system, or (heavens!) actually read those fabulous manuals, you won't have to go hunting—and the manuals and CDs will not be contributing to the clutter gunk invariably gathering in your home office.

# Cables, Connectors, and the Outside of the Tower

If you look at the back (and often the front) of your computer tower, you'll see lots of connections. There's USB and FireWire ports, a place to plug in the monitor and printer, speaker connections, a network interface card, and more. We are sure you've never cleaned those! It's never too late to take charge though, so in this section we'll do a full cleaning of all connectors and cables. Before we get started, pull your tower out so that you can see the back of it (assuming that is where your connections are located) and try to familiarize yourself with the various connections. If your connections are in the front, you won't have to move your tower.

The first step to taking control of your computer may seem a bit overwhelming. Are you sitting down? You need to disconnect everything from your tower, place it on a desk, and clean all of the parts on the outside. Ouch! (And we haven't even addressed cleaning the *inside*!) It's not as hard as it seems, though, and if you take a few precautions while doing it, you won't have any problems putting it back together. Just make sure that the first thing you disconnect is your power cord. We can't think of any degunking task that is so important that it is worth getting a serious shock over.

Ready? Gather up a pen and some masking tape (or stickers you can write on) first. We prefer the smallest Avery labels. Then, follow these steps:

1.  Make sure you computer is shut down and unplugged. (We know we already mentioned this, but telling you twice emphasizes the importance of this step!)

2.  Gently move the tower (with all connections intact) to an area where you can see the connections, both front and back.

3.  Remove the USB and FireWire hardware and cables. Set them aside, together. Use the pen and masking tape (or stickers) to make a note about what was connected, and to what port. For instance, you might unplug your digital camera, noting that the digital camera's USB connection plugs into the USB connection in the front of the case. Then, create another note that says "Digital Camera Connection" and attach it to the USB cable, the FireWire cable, and the electrical plug. Place the hardware aside, with the cables. (Don't forget printers, Web cams, and scanners here.)

4.  Unplug the keyboard and mouse. These are located on the back of the tower. Label these items with masking tape and a pen, and then move the cords out of the way.

5.  Remove the tower's power cord. Label it appropriately.

6.  Unplug speakers and the microphone, if they exist, and label the cords and connections. Unplug the speakers from the outlet. Set aside.

7.  Unplug the monitor and disconnect it from the back of the computer. Label the monitor's power cord.

8.  Disconnect network cables, router or modem connections, and phone line connections. Label appropriately.

9.  Place the tower on a clean area of the desktop.

10. If any additional cords are connected but you can't figure out what they go to, set them aside. You'll probably figure it out later. (In degunking one of our computers, we ended up with several additional cords. We're still not sure what some of them are for.)

With the tower disconnected, get out the trusty vacuum and its peripherals. Vacuum the dust out of the air intakes and vents using the brush attachment, use compressed air to blow out remaining dust and dirt, clean all crevices with a dry cotton swab, and finally, clean the outside of the tower with a rag sprayed with a mild nonabrasive cleaner. Don't clean any component or intake with the wet cleanser though; that could harm it. Just clean the outside of the case with the cleanser and use a dry rag for the rest. Figure 3-3 shows what your air intakes should *not* look like.

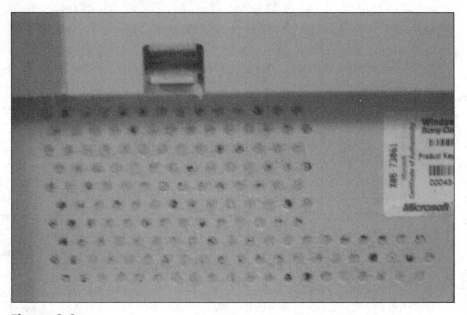

**Figure 3-3**
This is not what your computer's air flow area should look like.

---

*TIP: With everything currently removed from underneath your desk, you might consider skipping to Chapter 4, "Degunking and Configuring Your PC Work Area," and then return to this chapter when you're finished there.*

---

With the case clean, take a dry cotton swab and very gently clean the cables and connectors. Use compressed air to remove stubborn dirt. Don't forget to label everything with stickers or masking tape, even the electrical cords. Make sure you have a decent surge protector too. Don't plug anything back in yet; we're going to clean the inside of the tower next.

---

**TIP:** *Labeling everything as you work is really important. We can't emphasize it enough. You might think that you're certain of what everything is and feel you can save a step here, but resist the temptation. It's really easy to get confused when you are disconnecting a number of connections. If you get things mixed up, you could waste a lot of time trying to put your PC back together.*

---

## Cleaning the Inside of the Tower

Cleaning the inside of the tower is just as important as cleaning the outside and its connections. This is especially true if the back of your computer looks like the one shown in Figure 3-4. If your tower is dirty on the outside, you can bet it will be dirtier on the inside. No matter how hard we try to keep our PCs clean, they seem to attract dust and other gunk like a backyard woodpile attracts mice.

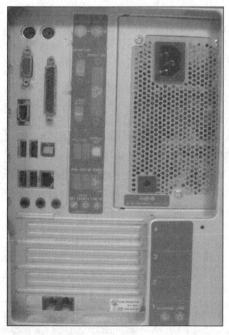

**Figure 3-4**
Dirty on the outside means dirtier on the inside.

When the inside of the case is not cleaned regularly (twice a year at least), the dust, grime, smoke, and pet hair particles build up around the components. This buildup can cause numerous problems, including computer lockups, memory errors, and more. Particles can also keep cooling fans from spinning properly, thus creating a hazard for the CPU and other components. And small dust particles can impact your media drives, which can create all kinds of problems. Therefore, it's important that these tasks make your spring and fall cleaning "to do" list.

## Opening the Case

Assuming you still have everything disconnected and sitting on a counter somewhere, take a look at the computer case. (If you've reconnected everything already, unplug it from the wall and disconnect the hardware and cables as detailed in the previous section.) See if you can find some way to open the case. (Don't open it yet though; you have a lot to learn about static electricity first.)

When looking for a way to open the tower, in most cases, there are four to six screws located on the back of the case and you'll use a Phillips head screwdriver to remove them. Once they're removed, the entire case usually slides off, from front to back. Sometimes, the panels move independently. You'll have to be patient while working your magic here. Not all cases open the same way, and it isn't always easy. If you can't find any screws at all, you'll need to search for the following:

√   See if the computer's faceplate pops off. If it does, chances are you'll find a couple of screws under there. If this is the case, you'll usually pull from the bottom of the faceplate outward.

√   Check for hex screws or bolts. These odd-shaped connectors require a specific tool such as an Allen wrench or a hex key to unfasten. You'll have to hope you received some with your computer and know where they are; otherwise, you'll need to take a measurement and head out to the local computer store to purchase a set of tools for that purpose.

√   If you still can't get in the case, see if the top of the case slides forward and off. Sometimes there are screws located underneath the top plate.

Okay, you have permission to take off the case. Unplug the power cord from the wall if you haven't already though. Listen carefully now: **don't touch anything inside the case until we tell you to**! We need to chat for a minute about ESD.

---

*TIP: Some people will tell you to leave the computer plugged in when cleaning the inside of the case. It has to do with electrostatic discharge (ESD), which we'll talk more about next. Most experts, though, including us, believe that unplugging and taking the appropriate precautions is the best choice.*

---

### Electrostatic Discharge

Electrostatic discharge, or ESD, describes the discharge of static electricity between you and your computer. When the case is open and you touch a computer component inside it, you can transmit ESD. An electric shock that you'd feel when touching a doorknob in winter is enough to kill a component and render the computer unusable. Any electric shock, though, even one you can't feel yourself, can damage the integrated circuits or computer components inside. Therefore, it's extremely important to know how to avoid producing ESD while working inside the case.

The best way to avoid zapping the components inside the case is to wear an ESD wrist strap. One end slips on your wrist and the other connects to the case's chassis (the metal frame) with an alligator clip. This device channels static electricity, or grounds you so to speak, so you can't damage the computer or components. ESD wrist straps are extremely inexpensive and are available online or at any computer store. In addition to ESD wrist straps, anti-static mats are available. They work basically the same way but are more expensive and less convenient.

If you do not have either of these items, you can ground yourself properly by placing one hand on the power supply and keeping it there during the entire process. Unfortunately, this leaves only one hand for working, and you may be tempted to remove your hand, if just for a second, to do something else. This isn't a good idea.

Finally, you can ground yourself by leaving the computer plugged into the wall (turned off, of course) and by touching the metal chassis before touching any computer part inside. When you touch the computer chassis while the computer is plugged in, any static buildup you might have yourself is discharged because the electrical circuit is grounded by the outlet. We prefer to use other options, though, because working with any plugged-in electrical component produces risks not associated with one that isn't.

### Cleaning the Inside

Whew! We're finally inside the case and grounded properly. Now what? Well, our best advice is to get a can of compressed air and blow short bursts onto the components. Position the can so it's as upright as possible, and blow the dust out of the case. There's no point in blowing the gunk from one area of the case to another. Make sure you're in a place where you don't mind dust flying about though; there will be a lot of it!

---

**TIP:** Before using the compressed air, make sure that no loose screws or other items have fallen into the case.

---

If you don't think the compressed air got all of the dust, grime, hair, pollen, and other contaminants, there are other ways to attack it. You can use a vacuum cleaner and a brush or other attachment to pull dust off the motherboard and components. This is a bit more dangerous, though, because you could pull components loose and damage the computer. If you do decide to vacuum, keep the attachment a few inches away from the motherboard. When moving a vacuum, use slow movements and take your time.

Finally, you can use a small paintbrush to remove stuck-on dirt and grime. Be careful not to leave any brush hairs inside the case or loosen any wires or other components, though. Use the brush as archaeologists do during a dig. If you are not careful, you'll have a hard time figuring out where a stray jumper or wire goes if one comes loose.

After cleaning the motherboard and components, take a look at the tower itself. The inside of the air vents may be just as dirty as the outside was. Use a vacuum or compressed air to clean these areas.

When cleaning the inside components, remember these tips:

√   Never use anything wet on any component.

√   Work slowly and deliberately. Working too fast will likely cause errors in judgment.

√   Don't leave anything inside the case when you're done. Stray screws can cause damage to components and cause problems that are really difficult to diagnose.

√   Perform these tasks twice a year.

## Putting It All (Back) Together

Once you've degunked inside and out, you can start putting the computer back together. Take these steps slowly and carefully or you'll create more problems than you solve. Most problems that occur during this process occur because a cable is plugged into the wrong connection (keyboard to mouse and mouse to keyboard), something isn't plugged in at all (the computer's power cable to the wall outlet), or something is plugged in incorrectly (network cable to wrong port of a hub, such as the uplink port).

Putting the computer back together is the opposite of taking it apart:

1.   Set cords aside that you no longer need or that don't go to anything. For instance, if you used to have a Web cam but no longer use it or own it, don't plug its cord back in. If you unplugged cords from the computer, like USB cables, but nothing was attached to them and you don't know what they do, don't plug them back in.

2.  Reconnect network cables, routers, modems, and phone line connections. Make sure the phone line is necessary; if you've moved to DSL or cable, you no longer need it. Label everything appropriately if it isn't already.

3.  Connect the monitor to the back of the computer. Label the monitor's power cord and plug it in.

4.  Connect speakers and the microphone, if they exist, and label the cords and connections. If you've gotten a new monitor and it has speakers, don't reconnect your old ones. Plug the speakers into the wall outlet.

5.  Connect keyboard and mouse.

6.  Connect all USB and FireWire hardware and cables. Use the pen and masking tape (or stickers) to make a note about what is connected and to what port. Label all cords and cables.

7.  Plug in the tower's power cord. Label it appropriately.

8.  Gently move the tower (with all connections intact) to an area away from dust and dirt, and preferably off the floor. Don't gunk up your desk with it though; if you have a cubby for it, put it there, but only if you can get a vacuum attachment back behind it.

9.  Turn on all components, and then turn the computer on. Figure 3-5 shows a before shot, and Figure 3-6 shows an after shot.

**Figure 3-5**
Before degunking the PC.

**Figure 3-6**
After degunking the PC.

If you have problems with any device, make sure it's plugged in correctly and turned on. Don't let something as simple as an improperly connected network cable cause you to reconfigure your network or a computer that's not turned on at the back cause you to take your computer to the repair shop!

*TIP: If you choose to set aside and store cords and cables to components you don't use, make sure you label them. There's nothing more frustrating than trying to connect a Web cam with your old digital camera's cable.*

## GunkBuster's Notebook: Make No Mistake. All that Dust under There Is Baaaaaad News...

And so are dogs, cats, stacks of papers, the inability to vacuum, temperature extremes, lightning storms, smoke, bugs and ants, and environmental catastrophes. When putting your computer back together, it's important to take all of this into consideration.

If your cat likes to curl up next to your warm computer or sleep on your keyboard, you should consider getting a keyboard drawer and placing the computer in a cubby so the cat can't shed all over them. If you regularly stack things beside or on top of your computer tower, find a new place for storing those items, like a bookshelf or drawer. Your computer tower needs a little ventilation. If you smoke, purchase an air filter or a smokeless ashtray; smoke collects on anything magnetic, including disks and tape drives, and will eventually damage it.

As for environmental issues, make sure you have solid and reliable power surge strips and that you turn off and unplug all components at the mere threat of a lightning storm. Make sure the room the computer is in has adequate temperature control (between 55 and 90 degrees Fahrenheit) and that there are no bugs or other critters lurking around looking for a warm place to live and hide.

Finally, position the computer so it's slightly away from walls and drapes so it can stay cool and ventilated, purchase and use antistatic spray, get a filtration system if necessary, and purchase some computer cleaning wipes. Use these items regularly. Keeping all of this in mind will not only help you set up your computer in a more productive environment for you, it will also help you create a safer environment for your computer.

# Clean Your Laptop

Cleaning a laptop is another task you may want to perform. Many people have more than one computer, especially those who travel or work outside a regular office. If you have started degunking your desktop PC and have a laptop to clean too, you may want to finish off the PC degunking before starting this one. However, if you're a pretty good multitasker, knock yourself out!

## Cleaning the Outside

The first step is to clean the outside of the unit. To clean the outside of your laptop, you can follow the general directions for cleaning towers presented earlier in this chapter. You'll want to get the grime, dust, and dirt from the case using a damp cloth or mild cleanser and use compressed air or a dry cloth to clean the connections and any air intakes or vents. You'll also want to clean the monitor as described earlier for LCD screens.

For the keyboard, you can use compressed air again. Just hold the keyboard upside down or at a downward slant and blow the compressed air onto it. There's no point in blowing those skin cells and leftover sandwich crumbs deeper into the unit! You can also use a toothpick to loosen stubborn particles if all of the dirt isn't removed. A note of caution though: Do not shake your laptop to loosen dirt or dust, and do not remove keys to clean and then reinsert them. You could cause damage. Oh, and did we mention that the unit should be turned off? Well, that only makes sense!

## Cleaning the Inside

The inside of a laptop will get dirty just as the inside of the tower will. All of this dirt can cause your laptop to run hotter than it should and can cause problems with its functionality. Problems can include what some call the blue screen of death (BSOD) or complete shutdowns. BSODs are complete meltdowns where the computer automatically shuts itself down and then pops up a nasty little blue screen with cryptic writing on it. It'll give you headaches for quite a while. You'll want to avoid these problems first, but if you're noticing problems now, dirt could be the culprit.

First, a quick note of caution before we go any further. Opening up the laptop's case can void the manufacturer's warranty. Additionally, if you don't have a clue what you're doing, you could cause problems yourself. If, after you read this section, you feel this may be over your head, please consult a qualified technician.

Here's how to clean a laptop from the inside:

1.  Gather up the required tools to open your laptop case. This may include a flat head or Phillips head screwdriver, an Allen wrench, or a hex wrench. You will also need cotton swabs, isopropyl alcohol, and tweezers.

2.  Remove the computer's battery by opening the battery compartment and following the instructions for removal found there. Unplug the computer from the wall and disconnect any connected hardware. Figure 3-7 shows a laptop with the battery removed and some of the tools you may need.

3.  Open the laptop using the necessary tools. You may have easy access to only the CPU and heatsink area. If that's the case, start there. Take all the precautions mentioned earlier regarding ESD and remain patient while you figure out how the case opens.

4.  Remove any large clumps of dust, and use canned air to blow out smaller pieces of dust.

5.  Use a cotton swab to remove stubborn dirt.

6.  Replace covers and the battery when complete.

Cleaning a laptop is a little more difficult than cleaning a tower, but it's still a task that should be performed a few times a year. Doing so will prolong the life of the unit.

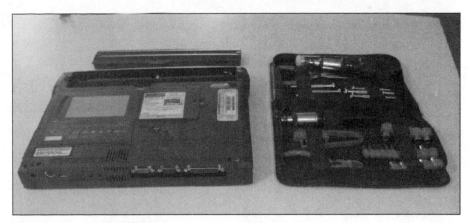

**Figure 3-7**
Remove the laptop's battery and gather up the required tools.

# Clean Your Keyboard and Mouse

Snacking while you compute, especially if you favor fried snacks like chips, will put grease on your fingers, and from your fingers it will travel to your keyboard keys, to the backside of your mouse, and to your desk surface. We've seen people literally dump a pile of chips on the desk next to their mouse pad, spilling crumbs and fragments onto the pad. This deposits grease directly on the pad, from which it is a short path indeed to the inside of your mouse. Even if you don't snack while you compute, the world is a greasy place. You may use hand cream, which is just more grease from your mouse's perspective.

The little rubber ball inside a traditional rolling-ball mouse picks up grease from the surface it runs on. It then deposits that grease onto three small plastic rollers that bear against the ball to sense the ball's rotation. The rollers become slightly sticky over time, and dust, cloth lint, and small animal hair will adhere to the rollers. Eventually you will have a thin layer of physical gunk, held together by grease, between the rubber mouse ball and the motion-sensing rollers. Grease being what it is, the ball will begin to slip against the rollers and the motion of your mouse pointer on the screen will become erratic.

## Cleaning Your Keyboard

For good or for bad, PC keyboards have a lot of moving parts and are exposed to even more potential gunk than mice. Most of this gunk comes directly from you. Pieces of potato chips or crackers can fall between the key tops, and a large enough piece can prevent a key from depressing completely. Drops of soda, even small ones, will dry into sticky spots that will attract dust, lint, and pet hair like magnets. The hidden spaces underneath a keyboard's key tops can hide a great deal of gunk (see Figure 3.8).

**Figure 3-8**
Gunk hiding underneath keyboard key tops.

Even if you manage to keep crumbs from falling into the keyboard, potato chip grease from your fingers will coat the key tops. Keeping food out of your computer room isn't a complete cure for greasy keys. Hand cream or natural skin oil will eventually cause dirt to adhere to key tops, forming dark deposits like those shown in Figure 3-9.

Grease deposits are harder to clean than you might expect because nearly all PC keyboard key tops are slightly textured, providing near-microscopic crannies for grease to adhere to. Counterintuitively, grease gunk will collect most heavily on lesser-used keys because your fingers tend to polish the tops of keys used frequently, like E and T.

If you have only a few grubby keys, it's possible to clean them in place by lightly wetting a round cotton pad (sold for removing makeup) with dish detergent or rubbing alcohol. Don't get the pad so wet that pressure forces liquid out of it to drip in between the keys. Some keyboards are well sealed against liquids, but most are not.

On the other hand, a venerable keyboard of many years' use may require some major work, and this work is best done one key at a time, by removing the key top. On nearly all keyboards (especially the better ones), the key tops are held in place by friction only, and by pulling upward on a key top you can remove it

**Figure 3-9**
Grease deposits on PC key tops.

from the keyboard entirely. Since the key top is just a piece of molded plastic, you can scrub it under running water with soap and a Scotch-Brite pad.

The trick, of course, is pulling the key tops when there's no room to get your fingers around or underneath them. In the '80s and early '90s, many high-end keyboards came with a small tool designed to make pulling key caps easy. (The tool was really intended more for switching the location of key tops than cleaning them.) Those rugged Northgate keyboards, much beloved by people who learned to type on a mechanical typewriter, came with a tool that consisted of a plastic handle with two wire loops on one end (see Figure 3-10).

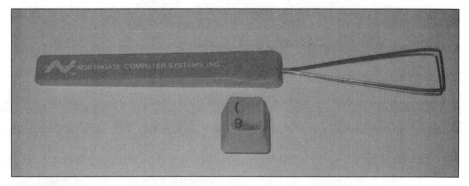

**Figure 3-10**
A key top puller.

Northgate puller tools turn up on eBay from time to time, and new "CapsOff" tools are available from Design Components, for under $5:

Design Components
19671 Descartes
Foothill Ranch, CA    92610
(949) 830-6797
(949) 830-6799 Fax
(888) 222-0435 Toll Free
**http://members.aol.com/capsoff/capsoff@aol.com**

It's *not* a good idea to simply hook a small screwdriver under a key cap and pry upward. If you exert too much sideways force on the key, it may separate the key switch from the underlying circuit board and the keyboard will be ruined.

Here are some tips on cleaning keyboard key tops:

√   Pull them and clean them one at a time. If you pull them all at once, you run the risk of losing a key top or putting them back in the wrong position.

√   Dry them thoroughly before putting them back. Blow loose water droplets from the underside of the key top, and pass it by a hair dryer for a few seconds.

√   After you pull a key top, inspect the area around the exposed key switch for cracker crumbs, pet hair, and dust. Remove any visible gunk with tweezers. Blowing will only force it under adjacent keys!

√   Avoid letting liquids (like soapy water) fall in between keys or onto exposed key switches while cleaning the keyboard. This will shorten the life of the keyboard, especially in damp climates, where slow-drying fluids allow mold to grow.

Note that some cheap keyboards do not have removable key tops. If you pull firmly on a key top and it won't come loose, don't force it or you may rip the key switch right out of the circuit board, ruining the keyboard completely.

## Cleaning Your Traditional Rolling Ball Mouse

If the motion of your on-screen mouse pointer isn't smooth and proportional to the movement of the mouse itself, and especially if the pointer seems to "stick" in one dimension or the other, it's high time to degunk. Here's how:

1.   Turn the mouse over and open the ball chamber. This is done by turning the little round retainer disk (with a hole at its center) to one side, usually counterclockwise. Look at the retainer disk itself for clues: There will almost always be an arrow or some other indication on the retainer disk of which way will open the mouse chamber and which way will lock it closed.

2.  Remove and inspect the retainer disk and mouse ball. Both may be washed freely with soapy water to remove any grease, dust, or lint. A Scotch-Brite scrubbing pad works well and will not damage plastic. Set them aside to dry.

3.  Blow any dust or hair out of the ball chamber. If there is anything down in the chamber that won't blow out, pick it out with tweezers.

4.  Look closely at the three spring-loaded plastic rollers that bear against the ball in the ball chamber. You'll typically see an irregular streak of gunk wrapping around the center of each roller. This is the gunk that needs to be removed, and you must remove it with a tool that won't scratch the plastic of the rollers. We've had excellent results with wooden Popsicle sticks or some other thin piece of wood with a sharp edge. Rub the edge of the stick back and forth against each roller until the gunk scrapes away. You'll need to rotate the rollers slightly every few scrapes so that you expose the entire roller. Keep rubbing the stick against the rollers until all observable gunk has been scraped away.

5.  Blow into the ball chamber to remove anything you might have knocked off the rollers down into the chamber.

6.  Reassemble the mouse and test it. If the pointer still sticks or moves erratically, you may have missed some gunk on one or more of the rollers. Repeat the process and test again.

If cleaning all visible gunk from the rollers and the ball chamber doesn't get the mouse pointer moving smoothly again, you may have a loose roller or some other mechanical problem inside the mouse. Such defects are not easily fixed, and you might as well grit your teeth and buy a new mouse. If you do, we powerfully recommend one of the new-generation optical mice, which do not have balls and for the most part do not require any cleaning.

If the body of your mouse has visible gunk on it, clean it with a round cotton pad (sold at drug stores to help remove makeup) wet with soapy water or rubbing alcohol. Don't get the pad so wet that water or alcohol gets inside the mouse body. Needless to say, don't immerse the mouse in the sink or hold it under running water!

### GunkBuster's Notebook: Are Optical Mice Better?

In the last few years, our dirtball mechanical mice have come in for some new competition. In 1999, Microsoft first marketed an optical mouse technology developed by Agilent. Today, many companies offer optical mice using the Agilent technology and with the appalling name Intellieye.

An Intellieye mouse literally takes pictures of the surface immediately beneath it using a CCD (charge coupled device) image sensor very much like the one in digital cameras, albeit smaller. A red LED illuminates the surface so that the image sensor can "see" it. Small imperfections in the surface over which you glide your mouse (the mouse pad's fabric weave, scratches in the Formica, wood grain, and so on) change position in the pictures taken by the CCD image sensor. A powerful embedded processor inside the mouse analyses the changes between one surface snapshot and the next to determine which way the mouse is moving and how quickly. It sends appropriate data to the PC mouse driver, which then moves your mouse pointer proportionately on the screen.

There are no moving parts in an Intellieye mouse. There is only a small slot in the underside of the mouse. Neither the illuminating LED nor the CCD sensor are ever in contact with the mouse pad or desk surface, so they are unlikely to pick up surface-based gunk. Dust may collect over a period of years on the LED and/or the image sensor, but one swipe with a dry Q-tips swab every few months should keep the dust from becoming a problem.

This sounds great—no more rollers or balls to clean!—but in our testing, optical mice have a downside: They're a little sensitive to the type of surface you move them over. Some surfaces work better than others, and a few common ones don't work at all. Here are some issues we have found with Intellieye mice:

√ Transparent glass surfaces and mirrored surfaces don't work at all, unless (ironically) they're filthy. The mouse pointer will twitch and jump, but not move consistently.

√ Polished stone (especially medium-grained granite) works poorly.

√ Wood surfaces with a deep gloss finish (like Behr Build 50) work poorly.

√ Iridescent surfaces with strange reflective patterns may cause the mouse pointer to jump or move in an odd direction every so often.

In general, flat or matte surfaces work better than gloss. Cloth-covered mouse pads work perfectly.

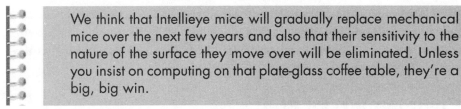

We think that Intellieye mice will gradually replace mechanical mice over the next few years and also that their sensitivity to the nature of the surface they move over will be eliminated. Unless you insist on computing on that plate-glass coffee table, they're a big, big win.

# Clean Your Printers. Nozzles. and Printer Heads

You've cleaned the gutters, vacuumed the cobwebs in the corners, swept underneath the refrigerator, and dusted off the baseboards. Now it's time to clean up the "extra" stuff (peripherals). If we were to extend our house analogy, we would need to defrost the mini-fridge in the bar, clean the oven or run its self-cleaning program, run vinegar through the coffee pot, that kind of thing. When talking about computers, we're talking about cleaning up printers, scanners, Web cams, and similar items.

As with anything, if you have the manufacturer's instructions you should read them first. There are lots of reasons for this, but some hardware manufacturers have specific rules for cleaning components, and doing anything that isn't documented will void the warranty. You'll also get the best results using their tried-and-true techniques. If you can't find the instructions, look on the Internet. Type in the brand, make, and model, and look for maintenance or cleaning tips. That aside, in this section we'll show you how to *generically* clean different types of printers.

## Preventing Printer Problems

Use it or lose it. That's a common phrase heard round the world that states if you don't use something regularly, its functionality will likely be lost. Muscle function, brain function—all kinds of things fall into this category. Your doctor will tell you that's the truth too; you have to use your muscles regularly or they will become weak and not work as well as you'd like. Your mechanic will say the same; you have to change the oil in your car regularly, even it it's running well, just to prevent problems down the road. All of this is true of printers too.

Turning your ink-jet printer on every few days, whether you use it or not, will actually prevent problems before they happen. Most ink-jet printers perform short mini-cleans and diagnostic tests when turned on. These mini-cleaning sessions keep ink from drying on the underside of the ink heads and thus keep print heads in good order. With laser printers, there aren't any jets of ink though;

instead, the printer uses a laser beam. Because of the complexity of a laser printer, you should not opt to turn it off and on regularly to prevent problems; instead, you should choose regularly scheduled home cleaning and one professional cleaning a year.

## Cleaning Ink-Jet Printers

Almost all modern printers come with a self-diagnosing feature that allows you to maintain them on a regular basis. Figure 3-11 shows an example. Here, you can see the status of the printer; perform a nozzle check, head cleaning, or print head alignment; or switch out cartridges. We suggest you perform each of these tests as needed, but at least three times a year. Table 3-1 shows when and why to use specific tests.

**Figure 3-11**

Printer maintenance tasks.

**Table 3-1**          **Preventative Maintenance**

| Problem | Solution | How Often |
|---|---|---|
| The print is light on the page and you think you may be out of ink. | View the status of the printer (using, for example, the Status Monitor feature shown in Figure 3-11). | As needed. |
| Gaps appear in the print or you believe the print nozzles are clogged with ink. | Perform a nozzle check. This check will force ink through the clogged nozzles, thus clearing any dried ink. | As needed or after the printer has been turned off for an extended period. |
| The nozzles are (or were) clogged and the nozzle check has been performed, or you believe the print heads are not clean. | Perform a head cleaning. | As needed, after the printer has been turned off for an extended period, or after a repair nozzle check. |
| Print is blurry or misaligned, or vertical or horizontal lines appear on the printout. | Perform a print head alignment. | As needed or after a cartridge replacement. |
| No ink appears on the page (black, color, or both), or the computer indicates that the ink cartridge is empty. | Replace the cartridge. | As needed. |

Usually, you can access these built-in options by doing the following:

1. Click Start, and then Printers and Faxes.

2. Right-click the printer's icon to troubleshoot or maintain and select Printing Preferences or Properties. In most cases, Printing Preferences is the appropriate choice. If you must use Properties, choose File and then Properties from the Printer dialog box that appears.

3. Work through the tabs until you find the maintenance tools.

### Cleaning the Outside of Your Ink-Jet Printer

Every time you change an ink-jet cartridge, you should clean the outside of the printer with a damp cloth. As with monitors and other devices, make sure nothing spills inside the printer. Moisten a lint-free cotton cloth with cleaner first, and then wipe the outside gently.

To clean any stray dust or lint in the paper path or tray, use a soft brush or a vacuum and small brush attachment. You can also use a feather duster or a hand vacuum. Just be careful not to jar anything loose or leave any remnants of the dust cloth or feather duster. Finally, use compressed air to blow dust and grime out of the ports, both the USB and standard parallel ports.

### Cleaning the Inside of Your Ink-Jet Printer

You can clean the inside of the printer and the cartridges, but if you do, do so carefully. Manually cleaning the inside of the case usually isn't necessary though, and it can cause more problems than it's worth. If you must though, you can clean the cartridges:

1. Turn the printer on, open the cover, and let the cartridges move to the center of the printer. If that doesn't work, you can get the cartridges to the desired position by choosing the option to change the printer cartridges in the printer's preferences dialog box. Most of the time, it's also okay to move them yourself if they don't move there automatically.

2. Turn off the printer and unplug it. Open the printer door to view the inside. Figure 3-12 shows an example.

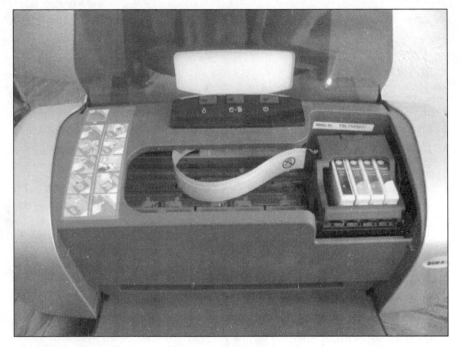

**Figure 3-12**
The inside of the printer holds the cartridges.

3. Remove the empty cartridges, being careful not to touch any working part of the cartridge or the printer. Place the cartridges on a piece of paper.

4. Run a cotton swab under water and squeeze out the excess.

5. Carefully clean each cartridge with the cotton swab, removing dust and dirt. Do not touch the nozzle plate or any of the circuitry.

6. Replace the cartridges, plug in, and then turn on the printer.

When cleaning a printer, keep these tips in mind:

√ Don't clean any part of the printer with alcohol, although people will tell you it's a good way to remove dried ink. It's too easy to mess up and damage something.

√ Don't remove the ink residue inside the case; this is normal.

√ Don't lubricate any parts with oil.

√ Don't work on the inside of the case with the printer plugged in.

√ Don't leave cartridges out for more than 30 minutes. They will dry up.

√ Do purchase a printer cleaning kit if all else fails. Cleaning cartridge kits contain special cleaning fluid that can solve most print problems inexpensively.

### GunkBuster's Notebook: Problems with Ink-Jet Printers and Print Cartridges Can Ruin Your Day

The ink-jet printer is one of the best and worst PC peripherals invented in the last 10 years. They are wonderful because you can print in color and create prints of your photos and perform all kinds of other printing magic. But the cartridges for these printers can get really expensive. We often think that the companies who make the ink-jet printers could actually give their printers away for free because they make so much money selling cartridges. Fortunately, you can save money on your cartridges by simply taking better care of them. Often you might think that you need a new cartridge when in reality you simply need to clean it.

First and foremost, don't use refill kits to refill your print cartridges. We know the manufacturer's ink is more expensive, but it's not as expensive as a new printer twice a year. Ink-jet refill kits cause all kinds of problems due to poor quality control. They'll leak, clog, and dry up. Refilling the already-damaged cartridge won't solve those problems either. Used cartridges (cartridges that come pre-refilled) are also of questionable quality. There's a huge black stain on my desk from a faulty refilled cartridge. If you've gone this route, remove the offending cartridges and purchase high-quality replacements. If you want to know more about refilling your own cartridges and the problems that you might encounter when refilling cartridges, read the GunkBuster's Notebook in Chapter 5.

If you've chosen a high-quality refill cartridge purchased at a reputable dealer, installed it, but are having problems printing with it, try the following:

√ Visit the manufacturer's Web site for help.

√ Run the print head cleaning utility several times. Sometimes the print heads get clogged, and running them once does not solve the problem.

√ Run the other maintenance checks available.

√ Remove the cartridge and put it back in. Sometimes something just doesn't click.

√ See if the cartridge has an expiration date.

√ Make sure that you removed the pull tab if one is added. These tabs are sometimes added to keep ink inside the cartridge until you need it.

√ Unplug the printer, and using a cotton swab with distilled water, gently clean the electrical contacts on the ink cartridge. If it doesn't void the warranty and is approved by the manufacturer, also clean the print cartridge holder assembly.

√ Check the printer properties and verify that no properties are set that would prevent a cartridge from working (Use Grayscale Only, Use Black Ink Only, etc.).

√ If you have a second cartridge, try it. If you have a second printer, see if the cartridge you are having problems with will work in that.

√ Consider purchasing a printer cleaning kit from the manufacturer.

Finally, visit **www.fixyourownprinter.com** and search the archives. You'll find a wealth of information there. As you'll find out, some printers are simply prone to failure after cartridge replacement, sort of the same way the water heater bursts a week after the warranty expires. Most problems, though, are due to clogged print heads.

# Cleaning Laser Printers

Laser printers are more expensive than ink-jet printers and don't work by laying ink down on the paper. They are much more complex, using a laser unit, toner, a toner hopper, a fuser, and a photoreceptor drum assembly. They also contain a corona wire, a laser scanning unit, a developer, and a discharge lamp. These things work together to put words on the paper. Because the hardware is so complex, cleaning is complex as well. Figure 3-13 shows an example of a laser printer.

**Figure 3-13**
Laser printers are more complex than ink-jet printers.

What this means is that you should be sure you're up to the task before taking on the cleaning procedure yourself. Are you ready to open up a high-dollar machine to try? If so, read the manufacturer's instructions and then return here for a few more pointers.

*TIP: If cleaning the laser printer yourself will void the warranty, we advise against it. Instead, purchase the manufacturer's printer cleaning kit and follow the directions there, or take the printer to a service center.*

### How Laser Printers Get Dirty

When a laser printer prints, the printer puts millions of tiny dots, which form words and images, onto the paper. Although many factors are at work, there are two that make the cleaning process a little trickier: toner, a messy black powder that can be a hazard if spilled, and a fuser roller, which can get very hot when in use. While printing, the printer emits small particles of toner dust, which forms gunk that sticks to everything it meets. This dust and the resulting gunk must be cleaned up occasionally or problems will occur.

## Laser Printer Cleaning Kits

Laser printer cleaning kits contain everything you'll need to clean your laser printer, along with detailed instructions. Most kits contain cartridge cleaning papers, cleaning solutions, swabs, cloths, and hand wipes. Going this route rather than gathering the materials yourself guarantees that the swabs are lint free, the cloths are antistatic, and the cleaning solution is the correct type for your printer. Your cleaning kit may also include a toner grabber, which picks up toner just as a magnetized screwdriver picks up screws. There's no trick to it, unless you don't want to use a cleaning kit and choose to use your own tools!

## Doing It Yourself

If you want to make a career out of cleaning laser printers, you should take a class, read a book, and purchase the required equipment. That's going to be about the only way to justify not using the manufacturer's laser printer cleaning kit, as least economically, when you want to clean your printer yourself. If you must though, there are some things you'll need to know and some things you'll need to purchase.

Toner is nasty stuff. You shouldn't inhale it, blow it into the air, or get it on your skin. You'll need to work in a room with minimal air disruptions and clean up any toner that you spill. You can't use a regular vacuum though; vacuums won't pick up such small particles. Instead, you'll need a *toner vacuum,* which can be had for a little under $300. Oh, and you'll need replacement filters too (about $25 each).

While inside the case, be careful of the fuser roller. It's hot. For safety, you should turn off the printer for a little while before you open it. There are also some extremely delicate and expensive parts you'll need to be careful not to break, like the corona wire. You'll need a few other things too, like a mask and gloves, and some experience with laser printers and how they work.

So, if you still have your nerve and are insistent on doing it yourself, here are all of the items you'll need and some advice on how to use them:

√ Paper mat to place the printer on and gather excess dust.

√ Toner mask to wear to keep particles from getting into your lungs.

√ Latex gloves to keep toner off your hands.

√ Brush to remove toner from crevices. You'll use the brush in conjunction with the vacuum and cloth (see the next two items).

√ Toner vacuum to vacuum toner from crevices and paper paths.

√ Toner cloth to clean up excess toner after vacuuming. Use the cloth outside the case in the paper path. Do not use inside the case because you could leave remnants of the cloth inside.

√   Lint-free cotton swabs to clean the corona wire. Use in conjunction with alcohol.

√   Isopropyl alcohol. Use pure alcohol to clean the corona wire. Gently, please.

It's our opinion that it's best to do a simple clean a few times a year with a cleaning kit (and use the manufacturer's cleaning kit) and then take the printer to a qualified technician for a deep clean once a year. There are a million things that can go wrong while cleaning a laser printer: breaking the corona wire, leaving remnants of a cloth inside the printer, or burning yourself on the fuser roller. It's best to take a more realistic approach, one that is safer for both you and your machine.

# Clean Your Scanners, Web Cams, and Camera Lenses

How long has it been since you cleaned the windows in your home? The glass door on your oven? Your reading glasses? Now, think about how long ago you cleaned the glass on your scanner. Oops. What about the lens on your digital camera or Web cam? Oops again. We've lumped all of these together because they're all sort of the same. Scanner glass, Web cams, and camera lenses (or LCD screens) all need to be cleaned, and for the most part, in the same way.

As with other components, you can use a soft brush, such as camel's hair, to brush away loose dust. And you should never spray cleaner directly onto any piece of hardware. Instead, use a lint-free cotton cloth and spray the cleaner you'll use onto it, and then wipe the device with the cloth. For scanners, you can use a gentle glass cleaner, although specialty optical-surface cleaning products are available and are a better choice. They keep streaking to a minimum and are designed for specialty equipment. If using a commercial glass cleaner, make sure to get one that's ammonia free.

For camera lenses, LCD screens on cameras, and Web cams, you can use the same specialty optical-surface cleaning products, although several are available just for digital camera lenses. Make sure what you choose will not scratch or harm the surface and that you choose a soft cloth. To be safe, we'll suggest that you purchase something from a camera store or from the manufacturer.

## More about Scanners

Scanners can accumulate a haze underneath the glass over time too. This haze will reduce the contrast of the scans, and if it's bad enough, will even affect the resolution. There's no solution except to take the scanner apart, remove the glass, and clean the underside of it thoroughly. In many cases, this sort of cleaning will void the warranty of the product, although in all fairness, the warranty is likely expired by the time such a buildup occurs.

Most manufacturers don't want you underneath the glass and don't offer much help. Therefore, it'll be up to you to figure out how to clean under the glass. At **www.photo.net**, there's some information on how to get into UMAX's scanner and clean the glass. There are two notches on the back of the scanner you can pop out with a screwdriver. With that open, you can then pop the glass out and clean it. Other sites, such as **www.technology-corner.com**, also offer assistance. Here, you can find out how to open an Epson case using the screws on the back.

As always, though, make sure the scanner is not plugged in and that you've read and visited the manufacturer's Web site for help first. There's a good chance you're not the first person to have the foggy-hazy-under-the-glass-scanner problem.

# Maintenance Schedule for Physically Cleaning the PC

Now that your computer is clean, the monitor is clean, the printers are clean, the keyboard and mice are clean, and the laptop is clean, how can you keep them that way? Table 3-2 offers a schedule for doing so; stick to it and you can be sure you're computer will be happier than it's ever been!

| Table 3-2 | Scheduling Tasks for Degunking Your PC |
|---|---|
| **Degunking Task** | **How Often** |
| Monitor | Anytime it's dirty, but at least four times a year. |
| Outside of the tower or laptop | Anytime it's dirty, but at least four times a year. |
| Inside of the tower or laptop | Two to three times a year. |
| Keyboards and mice | Anytime they are dirty, but at least four times a year. |
| Print nozzles and heads | Each time you change cartridges or anytime performance suffers. |
| Laser printers | Twice a year or anytime performance suffers. |
| Web cam, camera, and scanner glass and lenses | Anytime they are dirty, but at least four times a year. |

# Summing Up

In this chapter you learned just about all you need to know to physically clean your computer and peripherals. Cleaning inside is just as important as cleaning outside, and it's all about knowing how and when to do it. Keeping your computer physically clean will prolong its life, keep it from overheating, and make it more pleasurable to work with.

With a clean set of wheels then, let's move on to something a little different, physically cleaning your work area. By now, you should be able to *almost* vacuum under your desk, but you probably have a lot of gunk yet. In the next chapter, we'll start to take control of cables and cords, wires and speakers, and printers and other items you no longer use.

# Degunking and Configuring
# Your PC Work Area

## Degunking Checklist:

√ Remove clutter from your desk by using a flat screen monitor and hiding (or better arranging) speakers.

√ Hide the tower for your PC and still keep it safe and accessible.

√ Organize printers and scanners so they aren't in your way.

√ Go wireless with specialty keyboards and mice.

√ Remove some of the peripherals from your work area.

√ Choose reliable and safe surge protectors.

√ Use an uninterruptible power supply (UPS) to save the day if the power goes out.

√ Experiment with innovative tricks for hiding all types of cables.

√ Learn how to get organized if you use a wireless PC and you have a virtual workplace at home.

D egunking your work area and getting it configured expertly is similar to degunking your garage. You take everything apart, place it aside, and then rearrange everything so that you can work more efficiently. In this chapter you'll learn how to set up all your equipment on your desk (and underneath it) so it's organized and have plenty of room to work. We've already touched on that a little, by labeling the cords and cables you've already removed and cleaned, but we also have to talk about throwing stuff away, placing things (like scanners, printers, and speakers) in unconventional spaces, and storing items you don't use that often in a drawer or closet. We'll even talk about some stuff you can buy to make your life easier.

Gunk accumulates because almost all components must plug into an electrical outlet, peripherals must connect to the front or back of the computer tower, and cameras, Web cams, printers, and scanners must plug into USB or similar ports. These all require wires and cables. Even if you've purchased a wireless keyboard and mouse, you still need a base station or transceiver to transfer the data. It's now time for you to deal with the things you absolutely must have on your desk, under your desk, and/or connected to your PC and make the most (and get the most out of) of the gunk you have to keep.

# Choose a Flat-Screen Monitor

One of the best ways to degunk your work area, albeit a tad expensive, is to get rid of that monster of a computer monitor and spring for an LCD flat screen. By moving to a smaller, LCD flat-screen monitor, you can open up lots of room on your desk for other things. LCD (liquid crystal display) flat screens work differently than CRTs. They don't need to *project* light (in fact, they actually *block* it), and that's why they can be created in much smaller units. These smaller units will free up lots of valuable desk space.

## Making the Purchase

If you decide to buy an LCD monitor, be prepared to spend a few hundred dollars, and go ahead and spend the extra $50 to $100 for a 19 inch over a 17 inch. The jump to a 21-inch screen can be quite a bit more costly, though, and likely not worth it. In our experience, 19 inches is the perfect size anyway because 21 inches is just too big; it's like trying to read a Jeopardy! question on a 59-inch big screen TV. After a while, it gets uncomfortable having to move your eyes, neck, and sometimes even your head left and right to see what's on the entire screen!

While you're shopping, make sure the monitor has a 0.26 millimeter true dot pitch too, and a maximum resolution of 1280 by 1024 (although 1600 by 1200 is even better). Dot pitch defines the amount of space separating two adjacent pixels from one another; resolution details how many pixels are displayed horizontally and vertically. Of course, the more pixels you can show on a screen, the sharper the image; that's what resolution is all about.

Once you've decided on size, dot pitch, and resolution, take into account these other advantages that LCDs have over CRTs, especially if you're still not sure you're ready to make the investment:

√ They produce less heat.

√ They use less electricity (power).

√ They use digital signals (crisp and clean).

√ They generally have more onboard controls.

√ They generally have speakers included (meaning you can remove the ones on your desk).

Of course, LCDs do have some disadvantages:

√ They are more expensive.

√ Speakers in LCD monitors can be of poor quality when compared to stand-alone speakers.

√ LCDs can have "pixel defects," where a square or two on the screen remain black and do not show color (or show the same color all the time).

√ Sometimes, the required digital cables on high-end models are not included.

√ Lower-end models may not have an adjustable base.

√ Lower-end models may have poor color and more dead pixels than higher-end models

---

**WARNING!** *Newer models of LCDs may not come with the usual 15-pin connector; some come with DVI (Digital Video Interface) connections found on the latest HDTV (High Definition Television) and home theater equipment. If you're purchasing a high-end model for your PC, make sure to check this.*

---

You don't have to make the decision right away. You'll want to take your time and compare brands and prices. In the meantime, position your large CRT monitor on a corner of your desk, if you can. You'll be able to make more of your desk space that way.

# Hide (or Remove) Your Speakers

A girl can never have too many pairs of shoes; however, one *can* have too many pairs of speakers! If you've recently upgraded to an LCD monitor that has its own speakers, you may be able to get rid of the extra ones on your desk. If you must have separate speakers though, and you don't use them for listening to music or for a home theater type setup, they will work just as well under the desk, beside the printer, or behind the monitor. There's really no reason to have them front and center in your work area. You can also purchase extremely small speakers or go wireless for a few bucks more. In the following sections, we'll discuss all of the things you never thought you needed to know (and more) about degunking speakers.

## Hiding Separate Speakers

If you use separate speakers and you're not worried about the quality of the sound, you can hide them. Often, simply setting the speakers behind your LCD display works, but they will still be on your desk. Another option is to put the speakers on a shelf below the desk, thus removing them from the work area. Speakers can also be hung on a wall or in a corner if space exists.

---

**TIP:** Don't turn the dials (if you have them) on your speakers all the way to the right. Set Tone and other options in the middle, and then experiment with the options to get the best sound from them. Turning the sound and tone all the way to the right "peaks" them out, and you won't get the best possible sound.

---

## Getting an LCD Monitor's Speakers to Work

Newer LCD monitors often come with speakers built in. Figure 4-1 shows an example of what most people should *not do*. Look closely and you can see speakers built in to the monitor and larger speakers sitting beside it (and turned on).

Although this is obvious gunk on most people's desks, there are a few reasons why you may opt for this setup:

√ You use your PC as a media center to listen to music and watch DVDs. You need high-quality speakers.

√ You don't know how to make the speakers in your monitor work, or you haven't made the appropriate connections.

√ The speakers in the monitor do not work at all or haven't worked since you upgraded to Windows XP.

---

**TIP:** If you're into high-quality sound, skip to the next section. You shouldn't be using the speakers that came installed with your LCD monitor; you should be using higher-quality hardware.

---

**Figure 4-1**
This is not a quadraphonic speaker system; this is just gunk.

If you just can't get your monitor's speakers to work, follow these steps:

1. Turn the monitor around and look at the back of it. You should see a power cord and a display cable. The display cable should be connected to the display input on your computer's tower.

2. On the back of the monitor, look for Audio In. There should be a cable that connects that to the Audio Out or Speakers output on your tower. If that is not connected, make that connection using the appropriate cable.

3. Unplug any other speakers connected to the back of the tower.

4. On the front of the monitor, look for a volume dial, an adjustment button, or some other way to verify that the sound is on and at an appropriate volume.

5. Click Start and click Control Panel.

6. Open Sounds and Audio Devices on Windows XP. Other operating systems have similar applets.

7. Click the Audio tab. Under Sound Playback, choose the default device. Figure 4-2 shows an example.

8. Click the Hardware tab and locate the default device. Select it and choose Properties.

9. Verify that the device is enabled. If not, select Enable This Device. Click OK.

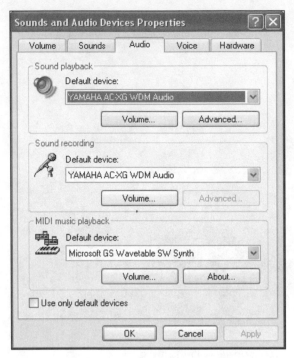

**Figure 4-2**
Choose a default device for sound.

10. Click the Volume tab. Verify that Mute is not selected, and if desired, select Place Volume Icon in the Taskbar.

11. Click the Sounds tab. In Program Events, select Asterisk.

12. Click the play arrow to hear the sound. Set the volume appropriately.

13. Click OK to close.

If the monitor's speakers still don't work, or if they haven't worked since you upgraded your operating system, visit the manufacturer's Web site for the newest drivers. Once the newest drivers are installed, reboot and repeat the preceding steps.

---

*TIP: The Web site **www.driverguide.com** has just about any driver you could ever need. If you don't have any luck at the manufacturer's Web site, try there. (Be prepared to work your way though a rather lengthy registration process.)*

---

## Specialty Speakers

If you think there wouldn't be much more to say about speakers, you'd be wrong. There are all kinds of specialty speakers, from stereo to quadraphonic, from surround sound to wireless. You can spend as little as you want or as much. Purchasing a set of $1500 speakers won't help audio quality that much, though, if you don't install a high-end sound card along with it. Your computer will also need a solid backbone—meaning a high-end motherboard and CPU and plenty of RAM.

So the problem is, if you have a plain or mediocre system, just how much should you spend on speakers to get the best possible output for what you have without going overboard by spending money on speakers that can't be used to their potential? That is the question, and the answer isn't simple.

If you're in the market for speakers, consider the following:

√   For most users, a standard pair of speakers is fine. If you want to spend money on speakers, make sure you really need them, and decide what you need them for.

√   If purchasing a two-speaker set, make sure they are brand-name speakers.

√   If purchasing more than two speakers, make sure the system is at least 5.1 Dolby compatible with a subwoofer and that your audio card supports it.

√   If you have an average sound card that does not have specific capabilities, like 3-D sound or 5.1 or 7.1 Dolby, don't spend money on speakers with that capability until you upgrade your card.

√   Think carefully before purchasing a 10-speaker system. Imagine the gunk from all of the wires and cabling!

√   If you can afford it, go wireless.

## Hide the Tower

Every kitchen needs a refrigerator, but you don't put it in the middle of the room. You put it in its perfectly created space—a space of the correct height and depth, and you make sure it has wheels just in case you need to get behind it to clean or to hook up an automatic icemaker. A computer tower is a necessary component just as a refrigerator is and, similarly, doesn't need to be right in the middle of everything to be functional. As with a refrigerator though, you sometimes need to access its backside, so it has to be placed conveniently in the room.

The tower contains all of the computer components and is what the keyboard, mouse, monitor, and other hardware plug into. The tower can go on the desk, the floor, in a special desk cubby, or in the corner, but it should be in a safe place. It should also be accessible, and you should be able to get to the CD and DVD drives easily and to the back of the tower in case a component stops working.

Getting the tower off of the desk will save lots of space, and the room will look less crowded and be more functional. Unfortunately, many towers only allow for USB connections from the back, and if you often switch out components, you'll be in a fine mess if you place the tower in a cubby. You'll likely need access to other parts of the back of the tower too. So, when considering a place to hide the tower, either under your desk, in a cubby, or on a shelf, take into consideration all aspects of your choice:

√ Does the place you've selected to hide the tower offer access to the USB ports, FireWire ports, and other ports?

√ Will the tower be safe if you spill something?

√ Will you be able to vacuum or dust around the tower weekly?

√ Will the display cable, power cord, and other components reach the tower?

√ Is there access to the CD and DVD drives?

√ Can you access the power button?

√ Is air flow allowed in and around the computer?

√ Is the tower in a place where cats and other pets cannot shed on it?

√ Is it near an air filter unit if you smoke?

√ Is it away from your backup unit?

The idea is to find a place for your tower that hides it enough to free up desk space while at the same time allow easy access, a safe environment, and access to all drives. Figure 4-3 shows a tower in a cubby. Although it looks good, it isn't very functional if you need access to the back of the tower often.

# Organize Your Printers and Scanners

Printers and scanners are a must-have for today's savvy computer users. Unfortunately, they are bulky and can be problematic. Printers can stop working after a cartridge change, and scanners can cause computers to hang while trying to complete a high-resolution scan. Unfortunately, because of the generally low expense to replace them, this hardware can often contribute to the gunk-factor of a work area.

**Figure 4-3**
Although you could put the computer in a cubby created for it, it will be difficult to
connect USB and other devices when you need too.

How many times have you done this: You replace the black cartridge in your
one-and-only printer and realize that no matter how many times you clean the
heads or remove and reinsert the cartridge, it just isn't going to ever print in
black again. These things happen. So, you run out, purchase a new $49 printer,
hook it up, and figure you'll keep the other one until you use up its color
cartridge. As it turns out, the printer just sits there, taking up room on the desk
because you really *do* like the newer one better and you use it instead. Maybe, at
some point, you remove the old printer from your work area, but chances are
you don't throw it out. We're betting it's in a closet or the garage, or even stored
in the attic for some unknown reason to both you and us. (Do you think you'll
need a part someday?) Whatever the case, if you only have one printer, you're
likely not the norm.

---

*TIP: Appendix A in this book details various ways to get rid of old equipment, including
printers.*

---

# Dealing with Multiple Printers (Including Fax Machines)

Do you need multiple printers? Professionals use all kinds of printers, from ink-jet to laser to sublimation and more. If you need multiple printers, by all means, don't get rid of any. However, if you use and keep more than one printer, look for ways to organize them more appropriately.

One way to organize multiple printers is to purchase (or build) a printer stand. Several companies make stands for multiple printers, and they are quite convenient. Using a stand, you can organize the printers in one area and keep them off of your desk. They are also easily accessible by others who need to use them.

If you only have one printer and your desk has a printer shelf or something like it underneath, you can use that too. Just make sure you can easily reach the printer and that it's convenient when you need to add paper or cartridges. You may even want to consider a separate, rolling cart for your printer. Figure 4-4 shows a large set of gunked-up printers.

**Figure 4-4**
Someone needs to learn some organizational skills.

*TIP: If your printer comes with two types of ports, parallel and USB, use the USB port to connect it to your computer. Information travels faster across USB cables than through parallel cables, and you'll see better performance. (Don't forget that wireless printers are now available.)*

## Hiding Scanners

If you can't remember the last time you used your scanner, chances are it's just gunking up your desk. While genealogists and scrapbook enthusiasts use scanners often, with the convenience and price of digital cameras, in general, most home users aren't doing much scanning these days. If you aren't using your scanner, remove it from your desk. If you just can't bear to do that, remember that scanners are flat and can be placed on low-lying shelves and in other interesting places.

## All-in-One Units

The best way to degunk all of that hardware sitting on your desk is to get rid of the whole shebang and replace it with a single all-in-one machine. These machines can do it all, and a single machine can replace all of the following:

√   Ink-jet printer

√   Fax machine

√   Scanner

√   Copier

√   Telephone

√   Answering machine (or it may offer an answering machine interface)

√   Memory card reader

You can shop for these machines online or at your local computer store. Make sure your all-in-one machine will connect to your personal PC and that you have the appropriate connections available. Most connect through a USB port. Also, consider a device that can replace the telephone, answering machine, and/or a fax machine. You'll be glad you did when you see the additional space you create in your work area. Figure 4-5 shows one kind of an all-in-one machine.

# Get Organized with Wireless Keyboards and Mice

One of the easiest and least expensive ways to degunk your work area is to purchase a wireless keyboard and mouse. Doing so will get rid of lots of cables

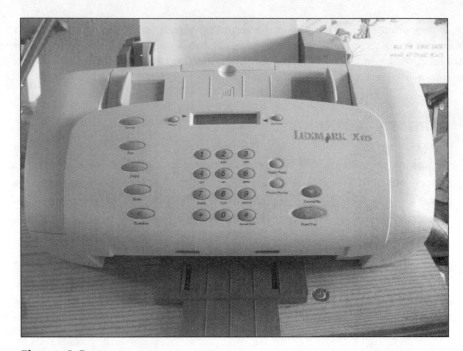

**Figure 4-5**
This is an example of an all-in-one machine.

and wires. It's an inexpensive fix for gunk too, as far as fixes go anyway. You can get a wireless set for around $50, or you can spend a couple of hundred. Either way, getting rid of excess cords and cables is well worth it.

## Choosing the Perfect Wireless Equipment

Not all wireless equipment is created the same. Some use the newest technology, Bluetooth, while others use radio frequency (RF). Although it's more expensive, Bluetooth has several advantages over RF:

√    It has a longer range, sometimes five times longer than RF.

√    It turns your PC into a Bluetooth-compatible computer (you can now connect a Bluetooth-compatible PDA or cell phone).

√    Once it's connected, you can communicate with up to seven Bluetooth devices.

Bluetooth keyboards and mice are not much more difficult to set up than RF hardware. RF wireless keyboards and mice have a base station that simply plugs in to a USB or PS/2 port. Data is sent to that station and transmitted to the computer through it. Bluetooth technology is a little more complex. As with

RF, you plug the wireless transceiver into the USB port, but you can then communicate with up to seven compatible devices at one time. (This means if you have a Bluetooth printer, you could put that printer in another room and get it off your desk completely!) Bluetooth is definitely the way to go if you can afford the extra expense.

---

*TIP:* *With any wireless keyboard or mouse, keep extra batteries handy, and remember, when something goes wrong with either, that's probably the cause.*

---

### GunkBuster's Notebook: Use the Software That Comes with the Keyboard

Just about any wireless keyboard and mouse set you'll purchase will come with software. Take advantage of it! This software lets you configure both just about any way you want. For instance, you can configure the mouse for lefties, change the speed of the double-click, and change the mouse pointer, speed, and visibility. You can even configure how fast the scroll works if there is one. For the keyboard, you can configure specific keys, in some instances the Function keys, the media keys, and other included specialty keys.

Here's how to access the software in Windows XP (the process is similar in other operating systems):

1. Click Start, and choose Control Panel.
2. If you're in Category view, select Printers and Other Hardware.
3. Select Keyboard to make changes to the keyboard functions; select Mouse to make changes to the mouse functions.
4. If you don't see the advanced controls listed in these areas, click Start, point to All Programs, and search for your keyboard manufacturer's name. Figure 4-6 shows a sample interface. Here, you can control every aspect of your keyboard and/or mouse. (This was opened using Start, All Programs, Logitech, iTouch, and iTouch Configuration.)

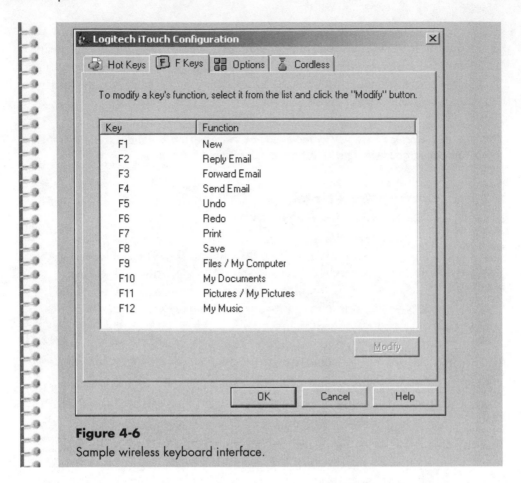

**Figure 4-6**
Sample wireless keyboard interface.

# Using TweakUI for More Control

There are a few really good programs available from the Internet that are free, useful, easy to download and install, and well written (translated: not buggy). One of those programs is TweakUI. TweakUI is a PowerToy, an add-on to the operating system, that allows you to tweak your system in ways that you never thought imaginable. As you would suspect, in this section, we'll look at TweakUI's keyboard and mouse options.

First, you'll need some version of Windows XP, and then, you'll need to obtain TweakUI:

1. Connect to the Internet and locate **www.microsoft.com/windowsxp/ downloads/powertoys/xppowertoys.mspx**. (There are other places to get it, but this page also contains additional PowerToys you might enjoy.)

2.  Scroll down to locate and click the download link: TweakUI.exe.

3.  When prompted, click Save. This is shown in Figure 4-7.

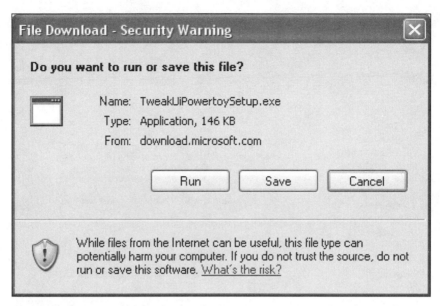

**Figure 4-7**

Save the download to your computer so you'll have it in case you ever need to reinstall it.

4.  Save the application, and when the download is complete, click Run. Proceed through the wizard to install the program.

To use TweakUI to manage keyboard and mice settings, follow these steps:

1.  Click Start, point to All Programs, point to Powertoys for Windows XP, and select TweakUI for Windows XP.

2.  Click Mouse. Notice that you can change the speed and sensitivity.

3.  Under the Mouse tree, click Hover. Notice that you can change the hover time and sensitivity. Continue experimenting with other options.

4.  Expand Explorer. Click Command Keys. If you have a specialty keyboard, you can make changes to any of the keys on it. Just select a key from the list, click Change, and make changes as you desire. Figure 4-8 shows TweakUI.

*TIP: Take a look at the other TweakUI options. You can disable annoying balloon tips, enable Autologon, remove items from the Start menu, and more.*

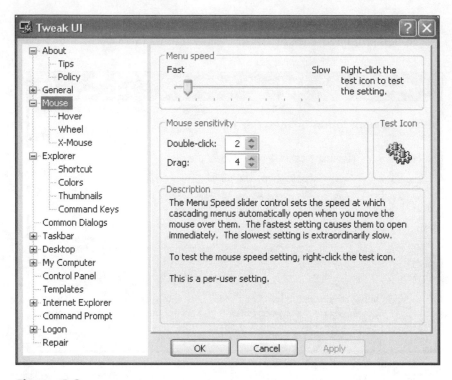

**Figure 4-8**

TweakUI is freeware and is reliable and quite useful.

## GunkBuster's Notebook: When Good Mice Go Bad

The only problem we've seen that's common among wireless mouse and keyboard users is that they sometimes behave erratically. Not the users, the mice and keyboards! This can be due to any number of things and is sometimes difficult to troubleshoot. To prevent these types of problems, you can be proactive by making sure to do the following:

√ Use the USB port instead of the PS/2 port if possible.

√ If the transceiver or base station is disconnected, turn off the computer, reconnect transceiver or base station, and then turn the computer on again.

√ Keep fresh batteries available and replace them as needed.

√ Enable the low battery reminder in the software.

√ If erratic behavior occurs, press the Connect button on the transceiver or base station and the mouse or keyboard to make a new connection.

√ If you upgrade your operating system, search for updated drivers for your wireless equipment.

√ Always use the most recent software for your equipment.

√ Keep wireless equipment within the recommended range.

√ Occasionally clean the wireless keyboard with compressed air.

√ Leave automatic updates for your wireless software enabled.

## Get a Gel Pad and Other Equipment

There are a few other ways to degunk your work area, and this time around it means adding stuff instead of taking stuff away. Gel pads, mouse pads with wrist rests, keyboard drawers, and armrests are all simple and inexpensive ways to make your work area more comfortable. Footrests are even available, as are specialty chairs. You wouldn't believe the things you can purchase online! For a sneak peak, check out **www.keyboardtray.com**. This site offers quite a bit of equipment and it's all really neat stuff.

## Remove Peripherals

Let's look for a moment at some plain and simple degunking techniques that don't involve throwing stuff away or purchasing new equipment. Throwing stuff away is painful for the packrat, and not everyone has the budget to spend $500 on an all-in-one print-fax-scan-copy-phone unit or $15 for a gel pad. Let's look then at some other ways to degunk that don't involve either.

Take a final look around your desk. Do you see any digital cameras? What about Web cams, PDAs, chargers, smart card readers, or other items? Do you have unnecessary pencil holders, hole punches, microphones, or headphones you don't use? There's no need for any of these items to remain connected to the PC or on your desk if you aren't using them.

Here are a few final ideas for degunking your work area:

√ Put unused PDAs and their chargers in a desk drawer or closet.

√ Put unused Web cams away.

√ Store your digital camera, cables, and power cords together and off of your desk.

√ Move chargers for cameras or PDAs to an area underneath the desk if you use them often.

√ Purchase a plastic drawer unit for your closet to hold extra peripherals and hardware.

√ Install shelves above or below your desk for additional equipment.

√ Get a file cabinet and use the top drawer for filing papers and another for holding equipment. Store cables for equipment together in plastic bags.

√ Label all cords and equipment before putting them away.

√ Get rid of unnecessary knick-knacks on your desk such as figurines, pictures, and coffee mugs.

√ If you aren't using the microphone connected to your PC, remove it.

---

*TIP: If you work in a room that is tight on space, here's a great storage idea to help you get clutter off your desk and into an organized area: Purchase plastic organizing drawers for storing unused or lesser used items. These organizers come in small, medium, and large, and can be placed in a closet or in a corner. They can hold extra power cords, digital cameras, PDAs, chargers, and all of the other items that either clutter up your desk or end up being difficult to locate when you put them somewhere else. Figure 4-9 shows plastic drawers converted into a handy gadget storage area.*

---

**Figure 4-9**
Use plastic drawers to organize extra equipment and hardware.

# Use Power Strips, Surge Protectors, and UPS Devices

Just as a seat belt can protect you in case of a car accident and a safety harness can protect you when mountain climbing, the proper equipment can protect your computer in case of a mishap. Lightning strikes, power surges, and power outages can all wreak havoc on your computer and connected equipment. One good lightning strike can render an improperly protected computer useless. Because of that, all computers and peripherals should be connected to a surge protector (at the very least), which come in the form of a power strip.

## Purchasing the Best Equipment

When deciding on what equipment to buy to protect your computer, don't just run out to your local hardware store and pick the least expensive one. You may end up with a simple power strip. Power strips don't offer protection by themselves. They are uncomplicated devices that only offer additional electrical outlets.

Surge protectors, on the other hand, offer those additional outlets and more. Surge protectors, as you would guess, protect the computer from power surges. Surges are unexpected increases in the voltage of an electrical current. They can and will damage sensitive electrical equipment. (Sags, a drop in electrical current, are the opposite of surges and are also dangerous.)

Beyond the basic surge protector are the advanced protectors. Advanced surge protectors (translate that to mean more expensive too) have additional inputs for modem and fax protection. Some even offer coaxial cable inputs for video equipment protection. They also often offer warranties, and the company will pay for damage up to a specific amount if the protector fails.

Figure 4-10 shows the difference between a surge protector and a simple extension. Notice that the surge protector has a switch for resetting after a surge and inputs for a phone line. The extension, like a power strip, only offers additional outlets.

**Figure 4-10**
Surge protectors offer more protection than simple power strips.

# Hiding Surge Protectors

The only time you'll need access to your surge protector is to unplug something, plug something new in, or reset it after a power surge. You'll need easy access, though, in case there's a lightning storm and you want to unplug the entire shebang. With that in mind, there are several more options for hiding the strip than there are for hiding hardware you must have access to every day. You'll need access to the strip, but not *everyday* access.

Almost all power surge strips can be hung on the wall. Hanging the strip waist high on a wall not only gets it off the floor, it also offers the access you need. No more bending over or crawling underneath the desk, and no more searching for the reset button after a surge.

Having the surge protector readily available makes unplugging and plugging in devices simpler too. Some items like digital cameras and PDAs go with you on your treks out of the house. If you have to take your DV camera on a family outing, to a wedding, or to another long-lasting event, for example, you're going to need its power cord. Crawling under the desk to locate that plug does get tiring after a while. Figure 4-11 shows an example of a surge protector attached at the wall. You can also see the cords are organized with cable ties.

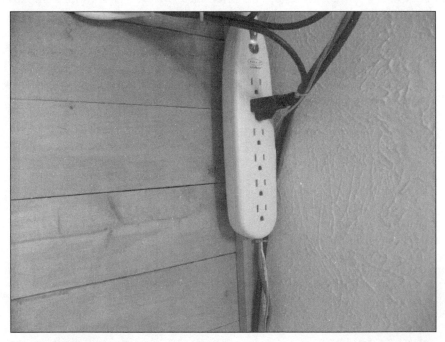

**Figure 4-11**
This is a nice place for a surge protector.

If you don't like the look of having a big power strip attached to your wall (or in view), consider attaching it to the inside of a desk or on a shelf near the floor. Of course, you can always leave it *on* the floor, but that sort of defeats the effort we're making to eventually vacuum under there. You'll have quite a few plugs attached, we're guessing.

Whatever you decide, keep in mind that you want easy access, although not everyday access as you need with a printer. The strip can be hidden away quite nicely and kept out of the way with minimal effort.

## GunkBuster's Notebook: Don't Let a Lightning Storm Ruin Your Good Time

If you live in a lightning-prone area, or if you don't take special care during the rare lightning storms you get once a year, you'll likely be the next unsuspecting lightning victim. Don't let yourself believe that a surge protector, even an advanced one, can protect you from such a powerful force. Lightning strikes can be several miles long, and they can certainly pack a powerful punch!

The cost of protecting your equipment from lightning strikes ranges from free to hundreds of dollars. The free way? Unplug *everything* at the first sign of a storm. Lightning can't travel through telephone lines, cables, and electrical outlets to harm your equipment if nothing's plugged into them. Unplugging everything at the drop of a hat (or the drop of a raindrop) isn't very convenient though, and it's impossible if you aren't home at the time of the storm. Although there is no fool-proof plan other than unplugging everything, you can give yourself a sense of security and a pretty good edge by doing the following:

√ Purchase a lightning arrestor and install it at the breaker box. These arrestors run about $50 and are easy to install. Some manufacturers claim a 100-percent success rate.

√ Make sure your surge protectors have options for phone and fax and for video or Ethernet.

√ If you depend on a surge protector, make sure there's a warranty, that you have the proper documentation, and that you've registered with the company.

√ Purchase surge protection from a reliable and well-known company such as Delta Surge Protectors.

√ Invest in a UPS device, detailed in the next section.

# UPS Devices

An uninterruptible power supply (UPS) device is a fancy piece of equipment that has its own internal battery that supplies power to the computer. There are two types: standby and continuous. Outside power is filtered through a *continuous UPS* device, so it also protects against power surges and sags. This type of UPS also gives you some time to safely shut down your computer in case of a power outage. Having this extra time allows you to shut down safely as well as save any work in progress.

A *standby UPS* device doesn't switch on until there is an interruption in the power supply. It kicks in and switches on immediately, giving you a short amount of time to safely turn off your PC. You can purchase a good UPS for under $200. The UPS should protect the computer and its peripherals—monitors, modems, routers, and the like.

## GunkBuster's Notebook: Label Your Wall Warts!

It seems like every small-to-middling PC gadget comes with yet another wall-outlet power supply (which we've come to call "wall warts"). If you're like most PC enthusiasts, you probably already have quite a collection. The problem is that they are *not* interchangeable. The voltage provided by wall warts varies all over the map, and even the polarity of the cylindrical power connector at the end of the wire isn't standardized. Most wall warts call the outer sleeve negative—but some go the other way, and if you plug the wrong wall wart into the wrong gadget, the wall wart, the gadge (or both) can go up in figurative (if not literal) smoke.

This is a special hazard on those uncommon occasions when you pull your entire PC setup apart and reassemble it, perhaps on a new desk in a new room, or when you set up an entirely new PC. Many wall warts look alike (apart from some very small print summarizing their voltage, current, and polarity), and it's very easy, when crawling around under a desk with wires in your teeth, to match a wall wart with the wrong peripheral.

The solution is simple: Every time you buy a new PC gadget with a wall wart, label the wall wart clearly with the name and model of the gadget to which it belongs. We recommend using a tape-based labeler rather than felt markers because most wall warts are shiny black plastic from which even permanent marker ink is easily rubbed off (see Figure 4-12).

**Figure 4-12**
A labeled wall wart.

Be sure to include both make and model number on the label. "Linksys" isn't enough—you may have several Linksys products in one room, even if they're not all connected to the same PC. Pull the room's PCs apart to move, for example, and all the parts are typically tossed in a box. By the time you arrive at your new abode and go to reassemble your PC (absent labels) you'll have long forgotten which wart goes with what!

# Clean Up Your Hubs, Switches, and Routers and Ensuing Gunk

There are some things you have to have but almost never need access to. Your water heater is one example, and it's hidden away in the back of the closet, in the basement, or in the laundry room to keep it out of sight for just that reason. Just like a water heater, a network hub and its components are also necessary. Once the network hub is installed, you'll likely never need access to it unless you need to replace it or troubleshoot it. Thus, you'll want to hide it as well as you possibly can. There's no need for you to have to look at network cables, and there's no reason you need to have the network hub, router, or switch on the desk or anywhere underneath it in view.

## Hiding Hardware

Once the network is functioning properly, you can hide the hub (or switch, or router, or modem) just about anywhere. A network hub can be attached to the back of a desk with two-sided tape or screws too. If you're feeling especially techie, you may even want to attach the hub to a wall with an attachment plate that comes with higher-end hardware.

---

**TIP:** *Hubs and similar hardware must be available for troubleshooting purposes if a problem occurs. Keep that in mind when hiding the hardware.*

---

Figure 4-13 shows a well-placed router. With the network router out of the way, it's time to tackle the cables that go along with it.

**Figure 4-13**
A well-placed router is out of the way but still accessible.

## Cable Ties and Stapling

There are lots of ways to hide cables. The tips and tricks here apply to more than Ethernet cables, though; these ideas apply to all kinds of cables: USB, power cords, printer cables, HDTV cables, and any other type of cable you have to deal with. One of the easiest ways to manage cables is to use cable ties.

Cable ties come in all shapes and sizes. Plastic, colored, cable ties that can be pulled tight (cinched) to the desired size are probably the most popular. You can purchase a hundred 4- to 10-inch ties for less than five dollars. The downside to this solution is that the cable ties must be cut if cable reworking is necessary; however, their inexpensiveness generally makes this a non-issue. Cable tie guns are also available and offer a quick and neat way to cut the ties once they are tightened. Cable tie guns are not a necessary purchase, though, because any old pair of scissors will do. Figure 4-14 shows a sampling of cable ties.

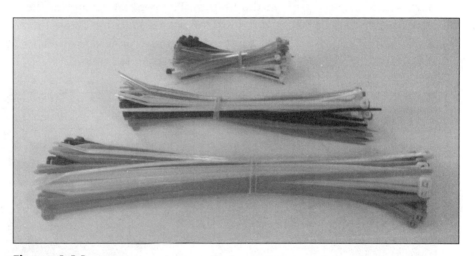

**Figure 4-14**
Cable ties often come in hand.

---

**WARNING!** *It's pretty easy to cut the cable when cutting cable ties to remove them. Be very, very, careful!*

---

Velcro ties are better than plastic cable ties because they can be used and reused as often as needed. Because they are Velcro, they can be easily adjusted too, making them a perfect solution for users who expect their network (or cable nightmare) to grow, or those who routinely add and remove or organize cables for travel.

Cable tie mounts and cable clips are available. Clips and mounts are self-adhesive, plastic hardware that you attach to the back of your desk or on a wall; you then insert the cable into the clip. This is a nice solution because cables can be mounted behind a desk or otherwise hidden and can be easily removed if troubleshooting of the network is needed.

## Split Tubing Flexible Conduit

Another option for managing the Ethernet, power, and USB cable nightmare is to use split tubing flexible conduit or similar materials. Split tubing flexible conduit is just that—a flexible plastic tube with a split down the center where the cables and wires are inserted. They come in almost any color and can be round or flat.

If you shop around you'll notice that some of the flat split tubing options also have a self-adhesive strip on the bottom. This type of tubing can be placed against or on baseboards, under doors, or even around and above them. With those in place, you can then route wires around or under doors or above baseboards for a cleaner look. Figure 4-15 shows an example.

**Figure 4-15**
Split tubing can help hide cables around doors and other public areas.

## How *Not* to Treat Network Cables

Now that you know what you should do, it's time to learn what you shouldn't. There are lots of ways to mistreat a network cable (or any cable for that matter) and hurt the integrity of the wires inside. Here's a list of things you should keep in mind:

√  Don't use *long* Ethernet cables; just use cables that are *long enough*.

√  Avoid running ethernet cables parallel to power cables.

√  Do not bend the cables at angles; instead, gently curve them.

√  When bundling lots of cables together with cable ties, don't overcinch them. Tightening them too much can harm them.

√  Never try to stretch a cable.

√  Keep cables away from things that produce electrical noise, such as televisions, copiers, and electric heaters.

√  Keep cables out of reach of children and pets.

√  Don't place cables or conduit in an area that will get stepped on often.

So, it's off to the store for you! While you're there, check out the other cabling options too. There are wire looms and all types of hooks and clips to browse through, and the available merchandise changes often.

# Media Centers and the Cable Mess They Produce

Media center PCs are completely different from regular desktop computers. Media centers are souped-up computers with souped-up operating systems. Microsoft's Media Center 2005 is ultimately Windows XP on steroids. Figure 4-16 shows a media center with all of its cables and cords appropriately hidden.

Media centers can be used to do the following (and while reading this list, think about all the wires and cables that come along with each):

√  Connect to a cable TV signal, or cable or HDTV box, for watching, recording, and pausing live TV.

√  Watch one TV show while recording another.

√  Burn CDs and DVDs of your personal pictures, music, and videos.

√  Connect analog hardware such as LPs and cassette players, and then convert analog to digital data.

√  Access Internet radio and local radio.

**Figure 4-16**
Media centers are nice, but they ultimately add to your wiring nightmare.

√  Connect to other PCs in the home, or output to other TVs or monitors.

√  Connect to an HDTV.

√  Upload video and pictures from digital and DV cameras.

√  Perform any computing task possible with Windows XP Home, and then some.

Knowing that, if you don't own a media center PC but plan to purchase one, you've got some planning to do. If you already own a media center, you've got some gunk to clean up!

*TIP: Microsoft recommends a wired network (not wireless) for best media center performance across a network. Yay, more wires!*

## Extra Connections and Cables

One look at the back of any media center PC and you'll understand why these specialty computers acquire gunk so much faster than other computers. There are audio and video in and out connections, TV out, an S video connection, HDTV connections, and coaxial connections, just to name a few. If you're running HDTV cables from a cable box to the media center, have a wired network, want your PC's output to run through your home theater system, and want to run an S video cable and an output cable to another TV or monitor in the room, you're going to have quite a few cables. These cables can really add up quickly and produce quite a mess.

The same strategies mentioned in this chapter and in this book apply to this scenario too, only on a larger scale. Your split tubing conduit will have to be longer and wider, your cables will need extensions, and you'll want to have a wireless keyboard and mouse. If you didn't purchase a flat-screen monitor with your media center, you'll want to consider getting one to free up some space on the table or desktop. Figure 4-17 shows a pretty good setup with a media center.

**Figure 4-17**

The best you can hope for when setting up a media center in a family room or kitchen is shown here.

To tame the other cables, especially when using a media center in a family room, game room, or even a small apartment, consider the following:

√  Use self-adhesive cable clips to attach and run wires across a wall near the baseboard.

√   Use flat split tubing conduit to hide cables under doorways and around doorjambs or run cables under couches or chairs.

√   Run wires under the couch if possible.

√   Use colorful, plastic cable ties when cables must be out in the open. Pick your favorite color or one that matches the room's décor.

√   Choose colored Ethernet cables if the cables are in the line of sight.

√   Attach the surge protector to the wall behind a couch or chair.

√   Understand that longer cords encounter more data loss than shorter ones, and they cost more. Position equipment close to each other for this reason.

√   Position the media center so you can access it with the remote control easily.

√   Use the media center's speakers if they are of high enough quality; otherwise, run cables to a home theater system or to the TV if it's connected. Try to avoid a separate set of speakers for the PC.

√   If you must run wires up a wall, use a staple gun created specifically for that purpose. Do not use a simple office stapler.

## Extra Peripherals

In addition to wires and cables, you'll have a myriad of peripherals all over the place if you don't plan ahead or take control now. The media center is the ideal tool for uploading and editing video, downloading music and burning CDs, and creating DVDs of your video creations. You'll need some way to back up data too, and that may take the form of an external device. You'll want to print and maybe scan, and you may even have a cable or HDTV box to deal with. There could be a Web cam. You'll have to figure out how to manage these peripherals.

Although it isn't the perfect solution for everyone, putting the media center on a network is an ideal solution for many people. With the media center on a network, printers can be placed in another room and connected to another computer and then shared. The media center user can print without having to have the printer in the family room. Internet access can also be shared across a network, relieving you of yet another cable.

You can go wireless too—there are wireless printers, wireless speakers, and wireless-anything-else-you-can-imagine. Again, although not a solution for everyone, a wireless Web cam allows you to get that particular peripheral off the table and somewhere more convenient. You might even mount it on the wall!

You should also create a place just for peripherals you'll always use with the media center. A drawer, a closet shelf, or a trunk for your digital camera, DV camera, PDAs, blank CDs and DVDs, and other devices can hold items when you aren't using them. They are also easily accessible. Keep the chargers for all your devices in another room. The maxim "Everything has a place and everything in its place" will keep your play area neat.

## Distance and Placement Issues

Finally, if you're still planning your media center setup or aren't happy with how it's set up now, take one last look at its placement. What do you want to use the media center for? If you want to be able to use the TV features, you're going to have to make sure you place the computer near a cable connection. If you want to watch what's saved on the media center on your big screen plasma TV, you're going to have to place it near that television set. Cables that connect media centers to TVs are only so long.

On the other hand, if you're going to work at the computer quite a bit, you'll also want to place it on a desk—and having a desk in the family room might not fit the decorating bill. And then there's Internet access. If you have a network and have Internet Connection Sharing set up for dial-up, or broadband set up for the entire home, this won't be an issue. However, if that's not the case, the media center will have to be close enough to a connection to be able to reach comfortably. And, you'll have to deal with that wire.

Remember while placing your computer you also need to take into account how far cables will have to run. You'll encounter signal loss over long cables, and this will cause problems with media transmissions. Chances are that you also have an infrared receiver for the remote, the keyboard, and the mouse, and generally can't wander too far off the 10-foot beaten path.

Whatever you decide, the ideas are clear. You want to neaten up the place, you want to make it a better environment for working or playing, and you want the best system performance possible. Everyone has gunk. It's up to you (and us) to figure out how to deal with it!

# Degunking Your Virtual Work Area

If you are like many PC users these days, you might be using the latest and greatest wireless technology and thus, you are able to freely roam around your home or office and use your PC. At first, this is the greatest feeling because you can work wherever you want—on the dinning room table, on the couch, on the patio outside (if your wireless connection is strong enough), and even in bed. But the problem with all of this is that as you move around, so does your office. All of the gunk you normally collect on your desk where your desktop computer resides can start to follow you around your house, and before you know it, you won't be able to find something important, such as your mouse or your digital camera. If you are experiencing this type of clutter, here are some tips to help you manage things:

√   Even though you have a wireless system, try to designate a work area in your home or office. In this work area, you should keep your main peripherals such as your printer, fax machine, scanner, and so on.

√   You might want to consider purchasing a wireless printer or wireless connection for your printer so that you can print from other areas of your home or office while you are using your laptop PC. This can add a new dimension to being able to sit on the couch watching the evening news while and working on a report for work for the next day, and then being able to send it to the printer without having to get up and miss the news.

√   Try to set up your desktop work area so that you can easily detach your laptop to work in other areas of your home or office.

√   Designate a drawer in your kitchen, where you'll often find yourself work-ing, for items you use a lot. Make this drawer a small second office, holding pens and pencils, CD+R and DVD+R disks, a calculator, a mouse, and other necessities.

√   Purchase a large tote bag with pockets to carry with you when you're mobile. Keep paperwork, manuals, books, and other large items in there.

√   Always choose a safe place to work. If your toddler, cat, spouse, or guest can reach the laptop, it's a disaster waiting to happen.

# Summing Up

In this chapter, we focused solely on how you can clean up and best configure your work area. Degunking your work area gives you more space, more room to work, and a nicer and more effective area in which to work. It's been proven that people work better in uncluttered environments, so you can expect a pro-ductivity boost to come out of all your hard work.

We covered several ways to degunk: You can remove printers and scanners, get rid of multiple copies of hardware, and replace wired keyboards and mice with wireless ones. You can also replace larger monitors with smaller ones and fur-ther degunk with all-in-one units. This mostly involves throwing stuff away, purchasing less-gunked-up replacements, and putting things away you don't use often. You should now be able to vacuum under your desk, put your feet under your desk, and get under your desk yourself without sneezing from the dust and grime. You shouldn't be tripping over cables or cords in your office or in your family or game room. Everything should be well-hidden and well-organized. If it isn't, take two aspirin and start this chapter over in the morning!

In the next chapter, we'll move away from the physical degunking and on to the virtual. You'll learn how to configure your monitor, keyboard, and mice for the best performance possible, how to choose a good CD and DVD burning program, and how to do those seemingly impossible printer tasks like getting a professional quality print. It's time to see just how far we can take it!

# Degunking Your Main PC Components

## Degunking Checklist:

√  Fine-tune your monitor settings by changing resolution; icon size and type, color schemes, font size, type, and color, and dpi settings.

√  Discover the truth behind screen savers and themes and how to use them without hurting the performance of your PC.

√  Configure your PC so that you regularly receive service packs and updates.

√  Set up the software you should have—adware and spyware checkers, registry checkers, and cleanup updates—and get rid of files and software you don't need.

√  Degunk your CD and DVD software and learn what software is necessary for proper performance.

√  Set up your printer to get the best possible performance for what you own.

√  Learn why you shouldn't use refilled ink cartridges or try to refill your own unless you're ready to deal with the problems that come along with it.

Whathat we've done so far by way of degunking your PC (and what we're going to do next) is not that much different from how you'd take control of an unorganized house. First, you'd throw away stuff you didn't need, then you'd physically clean it, and then you'd rearrange and organize what's left. After that, you might purchase new furniture or even install shelves in the garage. You'd probably even do your once-a-year tasks like clean the gutters or defrost the refrigerator. That's what you've done so far with your PC and work area—you've cleaned it.

With the house clean and organized, the next few steps are to make the house more livable. Perhaps you'd have an exterminator get rid of any bugs or termites (and schedule them to come every three months), you'd install gutter guards so leaves couldn't collect there again, or you'd purchase a refrigerator that didn't need defrosting or a self-cleaning oven to eliminate those tasks forever. Maybe you'd get a wireless phone and a DVD player as an upgrade, paint the walls a new color, or put a pair of reading glasses in every room so you wouldn't have to always search for a pair when you need them. All of these things make the place nicer and more livable, and even the tiniest improvements go a long way. That's what we're going to do next regarding degunking your PC. We're going to tweak it for better *livability*.

With that in mind, consider this: If we had organized this book into sections, we'd be starting a new one. The first section you've already worked through— the *physical* degunking of the computer and its peripherals. This section would thus be the *virtual* degunking—configuring the monitors, setting up CD and DVD burners and their software, degunking the virtual mess inside the tower, and tweaking your printers for best performance and usability. Let's start with the monitor.

# Degunk and Configure Your Monitor

Maybe you don't think much about your monitor, but the monitor is what you use to see what you're doing at your PC and it should give you the best performance possible. A monitor is the equivalent of your eyes; there's no other option for perceiving the visual.

Because of this, you should personalize the monitor and the monitor's output to suit your own preferences. You can configure the monitor's display settings from inside the operating system, including resolution and color schemes, but you can also configure much more. You can change the icons and their sizes, the dots per inch (dpi) settings, and the fonts and font sizes. Beyond that, you can override Internet Explorer's (IE's) default settings so that they are suited to your tastes and needs for reading e-mail and surfing the Web. (If you have over-40 eyes, you know what we're getting at here!) Finally, there are things that can actually hamper performance, like screen savers and themes. In the following sections, we'll eliminate the things you don't need and set up important features to help you be more productive.

## Configuring the Correct Resolution for Your Needs

Monitor resolution is how many pixels are used to show data on a monitor's screen. A pixel is a small dot of color data (which can be only one color at a time), and images you view on your computer screen are formed using thousands and thousands of them. Since pixels are units of color data, the more pixels you use, the less noticeable the pixels are and the better the image. Figure 5-1 shows an example of an image both in its regular state and enlarged so you can see the individual pixels that make it up. You can see that each pixel is only a single color.

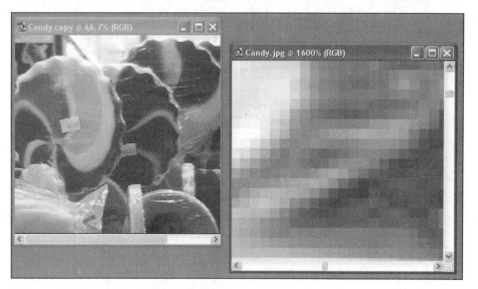

**Figure 5-1**
Pixels are small units of color data.

When choosing a screen resolution (to decide just how many pixels you want on your monitor), you have several choices. The choices will differ from monitor to monitor and video card to video card. To see what options you have, follow these steps:

1. Right-click on an empty area of the Desktop and choose Properties.

2. In the Display Properties dialog box, select the Settings tab.

3. Select Advanced.

4. From the resulting dialog box, select Apply the New Display Settings Without Restarting. Click OK.

5. Back at the Display Properties dialog box, under Screen Resolution, move the slider all the way to the left and click Apply. Move the slider to the right one notch and click Apply again. Continue in this manner until you've viewed all available resolutions. You may have to choose Yes or No from a dialog box to accept or reject the resolution, depending on your operating system and monitor.

6. Figure 5-2 shows an example of one setting you may choose. Leave the Display Properties dialog box open and don't click OK yet; after reading the next paragraph or two you may want to choose a different one.

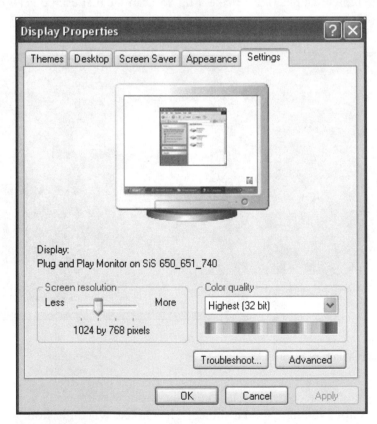

**Figure 5-2**
Configure screen resolution in the Display Properties dialog box.

MORE INFO: A screen resolution of 800 by 600 pixels would offer almost 500,000 pixels, while a screen resolution of 1024 by 768 pixels would offer almost 800,000.

You may have noticed that as you went up in resolution, the dialog box became much clearer, but much smaller. You probably also noticed that the icons on your desktop became smaller too. In fact, while more pixels offer a clearer image, as you increase the number of pixels shown on a computer monitor, you also decrease the size of all of the information shown. The size of the data decreases because the monitor displays more pixels in the same screen space.

So, when choosing a screen resolution, you'll need to balance several things: the condition of your eyes, the distance you sit from the monitor, the size of the data you need to see, and the physical size of the monitor. Your best bet now is to take another look at the resolution choices you have and choose one you think will work for you. Then, visit a Web page, read a document, and edit a photo. If you don't like the setting you chose, you can always go back and change it to something else.

---

TIP: *If you own a media center PC, you'll probably want a lower resolution. That's because these particular PCs are usually in a family or recreation room and are positioned farther away from users than regular PCs do.*

---

## Changing DPI Settings, Default Icons, and Color Schemes

From the Display Properties dialog box you can also change a number of other items. You can change the icons used for default Desktop icons like My Computer or the Recycle Bin, make tweaks to the Windows color schemes or create your own, and even change the dpi settings for the monitor. Dpi stands for dots per inch—which means how many dots appear per inch on your computer monitor. If your screen resolution makes data too small to view comfortably, you can increase the dpi to compensate.

To change the screen's dpi, follow these steps:

1. Right-click on an empty area of the Desktop and choose Properties.
2. In the Display Properties dialog box, select the Settings tab.
3. Click Advanced.
4. In the monitor's dialog box that appears, under DPI Setting, select Large Size. Click OK to verify that you'll need to restart the computer. Click OK again to close this dialog box. Close the Display Properties dialog box by selecting Close.

Once your PC has rebooted, open Internet Explorer to see the difference. You'll notice that the toolbars are larger and the words and icons are larger but the data on the Web page is not. (You'll learn to make the data on Web pages larger in a later section in this chapter.) Next, right-click on the Desktop to see how much larger the menus are. Figure 5-3 shows an example.

**Figure 5-3**
Increase the dpi settings to make almost everything a little larger.

---

*TIP: Again, making a change to the dpi settings is a good choice for those with media centers that are positioned farther away from the user than regular monitors, for the elderly who have trouble with their eyesight, or for anyone who'd just like everything to be a tad bigger.*

---

To change the default icons on the Desktop, follow these steps:

1.  Right-click on an empty area of the Desktop and choose Properties.

2.  In the Display Properties dialog box, select the Desktop tab.

3.  Click the Customize Desktop button.

4.  In the Desktop Items dialog box, select an icon to change. (Notice that you can also add or remove Desktop icons in the first section, Desktop Icons). We'll choose My Computer, the first choice. Click the Change Icon button.

5.  In the Change Icon dialog box, select a new icon to represent My Computer. The choices are shown in Figure 5-4.

6.  Click OK three times to close all open dialog boxes.

**Figure 5-4**
Windows offers several icons you can use to replace the default ones.

---

**TIP:** *If you know how to create your own icons or download icons others have created, you certainly can. The Browse button is available in the Change Icon dialog box for just this reason.*

---

To make changes to the Windows color scheme, follow these steps:

1. Right-click on an empty area of the Desktop and choose Properties.

2. In the Display Properties dialog box, select the Appearance tab.

3. Under Windows and Buttons and Color Scheme, note the choices. To see any theme or color, select it and click Apply.

4. To make your own specific and personalized changes to the color scheme, click the Advanced button.

5. The Advanced Appearance dialog box allows you to select a specific part of the Windows theme you're using and make changes to it. Click the down arrow under Item to see what is available. Choose Active Title Bar. In this example, we'll change how the title bars appear.

6. Use the up and down arrows to change the active title bar's size and color(s), as well as the type, size, color, and other attributes of the font. Notice that you can preview the changes without clicking OK.

7. Once you've decided on any change, continue selecting items from the Item list and making additional changes as desired. Click OK when finished and OK again to chose the Display Properties dialog box.

---

*TIP: Making a change to the color scheme and/or fonts used is a good choice for those who are color-blind or have other visual impairments. It's also for anyone who just wants to add a little spice to the old and tired Windows colors.*

---

You can make additional changes to the display properties by working through all of the available options. For instance, from the Appearance tab and the Effects button, you can choose Large Icons, perfect for media centers since they're usually farther away than other monitors are, and you can apply effects to menus (or remove them). Now that you're aware of the options, take a few minutes to browse through them.

## Overriding IE Defaults

If you have had trouble viewing Web pages because the text was too small, you might have already tried various ways to remedy that, including lowering the resolution on the monitor. Lowering the resolution does make the text on Web pages appear larger. If you wanted the text smaller so you'd have to scroll less while viewing a page, you may have increased the resolution of the monitor. Raising the resolution makes everything smaller. However, this technique also has ramifications for everything you view on your computer, and this may or may not have been an acceptable change.

Some of the changes noted in this chapter, such as changing the monitor's dpi settings or changing the icon size from smaller to larger, don't have any effect on the size of the text shown on a Web page anyway. While changing both does increase the size of IE's toolbar, it does nothing for the size of the text on the Web page itself. If you want the text shown on a Web page to change, what can you do that won't affect the rest of the computer?

Well, there are a couple of options. First, you can open IE, and from the View menu, point to Text Size and choose Smallest, Smaller, Medium, Larger, or Largest. Doing so almost always changes the size of the text shown, but it doesn't work for all Web pages. Choosing Largest doesn't actually make the text as large as it really could be either. Some Web pages have a specific font size, color, and type, and the size won't change just because you've selected Largest or Smallest from the View menu.

To make sure that your changes apply to all the pages you view, you'll have to tell IE to override Web page defaults:

1. Open IE. IE is available by clicking Start, pointing to All Programs, and choosing Internet Explorer. It may also be available from the Desktop or the Quick Launch area of the Task bar.

2. From the Tools menu, select Internet Options.

3. On the General tab, near the bottom of the Internet Options dialog box, select Accessibility.

4. In the Accessibility dialog box shown in Figure 5-5, check Ignore Font Sizes Specified on Web Pages. Click OK twice to close all dialog boxes.

**Figure 5-5**
Use the Accessibility dialog box to override IE's defaults.

5. From the View menu in IE, point to Text Size and select Smallest, Smaller, Medium, Larger, or Largest. Notice that these options are now actually applied to the Web page. Figure 5-6 shows a Web page your grandmother could read from 15 paces! (Notice that overriding a Web page's font size could distort the page some.)

---

**TIP:** *If you use Internet Explorer and come across a Web page that has a lot of data, press F11 to increase the viewing area. Pressing F11 again toggles out of this mode.*

---

Besides text size, as shown in Figure 5-6, you can also override default font styles and the colors shown on Web pages. Open IE and choose Tools, Internet Options as detailed earlier. From the General tab of the Internet Options dialog box, click Colors or Fonts to configure settings for overriding the defaults. Click Accessibility again, and then click one or both of the remaining choices.

**Figure 5-6**
Now this is a large font!

This could be a good option for those who are color-blind, or for you creative types in the audience. Figure 5-7 shows a new font and color scheme created from the same Web page used in Figure 5-6.

## The Myth about Screen Savers

A long, long time ago, in a land far, far away, people used screen savers to actually save their computer screens from what was then referred to as burn-in. Burn-in occurred when an image was left on the screen for an inordinate amount of time and the image became "burned in" to the monitor. It was possible to burn the phosphors out of a CRT by leaving items displayed. When high-resolution screens became available, those initial, boring screen savers that were used for an actual reason (remember the flying Windows and the flying toasters?) got a facelift. Programmers started creating really cool screen savers, ones you could lose your job over because you stopped working and simply stared at them all day.

Now, screen savers aren't generally necessary. For the most part, monitors these days don't "burn in." You have a better chance of winning the lottery than of

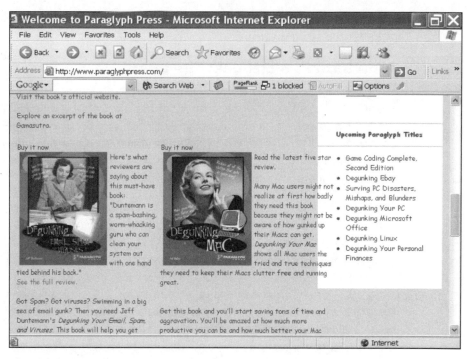

**Figure 5-7**

Overriding Web page defaults can be functional as well as fun.

burning an image into your monitor. The only real use for a screen saver is if you use it to password-protect your PC when you're away from it. (Open Control Panel, open Display, select the Screen Saver tab, and check On Resume, Password Protect.)

There are problems in using intricate screen savers though, and you should be aware of them before you decide which screen saver you will apply:

√  Screen savers hog resources. If you're trying to render a movie overnight in Movie Maker 2, disable your screen saver so all of the available resources are actually available to the program.

√  If you have an older operating system like Windows 95 or Windows 98, choose a screen saver that doesn't use many system resources.

√  Most screen savers require you have at least 64 MB of RAM and a graphics card that can display 256 colors.

√  Freeware and shareware screen savers you download from the Internet are usually not created by large companies. Therefore, you can expect that the code is not up to par. Poorly written code can crash an otherwise healthy machine. Stick with trusted sites and manufacturers.

√  If you download shareware screen savers, be prepared for registration pop–
ups each time you use them.

### GunkBuster's Notebook: The Unknown Danger of Themes

If you have Windows XP, you no doubt know about themes; if you're not aware of them already, skip this section and forget you ever read this sentence. If you use themes or are thinking about using them, though, read on. Themes are a huge resource hog, much more so than the innocent-looking screen saver.

Themes are set in the Display Properties dialog box, available from the Control Panel or by right-clicking on an empty area of the Desktop and choosing Properties. While the Windows XP Theme and the Windows Classic Theme are safe, the ones you acquire from third-party software or from the Internet have is-sues. As with a resource-intensive screen saver, you may encoun-ter a drain on your system when using them. Unlike with a screen saver though, the drain on available resources will be huge and noticeable on almost any low-end or mid-range computer.

Each of a theme's features need and use resources from RAM and the CPU. Depending on the theme selected, you could be using a large amount of available resources. If your computer's RAM is filled up with instructions for the mouse pointer, screen saver, and sound effects, and the CPU has to make calculations for those as well, those resources won't be available when you want to view media, edit an image, or render a movie. With that in mind, here is a list of what themes usually offer:

√  Screen saver and screen saver effect settings such as frequency, speed, or sound

√  3-D rendering for screen savers and a required 16-bit or 32-bit monitor setting and compatible graphics card

√  Themed mouse pointers, including pointers for Normal Select, Busy, Text Select, Unavailable, Move, Link Select, and more

√  A high-resolution background image, or multiple images that change

√  The theme's colors in all windows, and new icons for the Recycle Bin and other Windows icons

√ New sounds for all system events, including Asterisk, Critical Stop, Default Beep, Exclamation, Exit Windows, Maximize, Minimize, Program Error, and more

Of course, each theme is different, so you can expect various levels of features and their attributes. However, the message here is clear: If you don't want to gunk up your machine, don't use themes!

# Configure Your PC

You've already learned from the previous chapters that there are certain precautions you must take to keep your desktop PC or laptop safe and in good working condition. You know you must clean the inside of the tower and the air intakes and vents a few times a year, and that the tower must be placed somewhere where there's adequate airflow and where it can remain safe in case of a broken water heater or spilled cup of coffee. You also have to be careful to keep pet hair, smoke, and dust particles from accumulating there too. These are all physical things. As you would guess, there are important configuration tasks that you should perform, such as regularly downloading service packs, updating device drivers, and cleaning out other gunk.

## Getting Service Packs and Windows Updates

Have you ever purchased a new car and then had to return to the dealership because you received a notice about a recall? Automobile manufacturers don't always get everything right the first time around. Recalls are the manufacturer's way of fixing something that has proven to be faulty or dangerous. You, the consumer, don't have to pay for the parts or the labor. Recalls are issued to replace poor-quality tires, to repair unreliable brakes or oil leaks, or even to replace a latch that is compromised. Just as cars are recalled due to dangerous or faulty hardware, software is recalled too. You don't take you PC back to the store for service, though; instead, you have it serviced using service packs that are sent via the Internet. In fact, the service happens behind the scenes so that you might not even realize what is taking place.

Setting up your PC so that it can receive service packs on a regular basis is important because this is one of the best ways to keep your PC safe from hackers. Microsoft, just like an automobile manufacturer, can discover defects after the fact, such as faulty code or dangerous holes in the operating system. If you don't get your PC serviced, you are not fully protected against hackers and poor performance. Service packs also allow you to improve how your PC operates by performing certain tasks:

√   Fixing known bugs with internal operations

√   Speeding up and automating critical tasks

√   Fixing faulty device drivers

√   Improving user interface features

√   Installing updates to applications included in the software, such as Media Player and Movie Maker

√   Installing proactive protection for communication tools such as Outlook Express, Internet Explorer, and Windows Messenger

√   Repairing compatibility problems with third-party software and hardware

√   Adding pop-up protection and firewalls as they are created and deployed

√   Adding support for new technologies such as DirectX, Bluetooth, and more

To make sure you're getting the required updates, log on to the Internet often and verify that Automatic Updates is configured to run:

1.   Open Control Panel and open System. (You can also right-click My Computer and select Properties.)

2.   Select the Automatic Updates tab. Figure 5-8 shows the recommended setting for Automatic Updates. We suggest you configure it to get updates automatically.

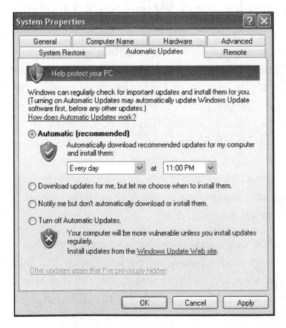

**Figure 5-8**
Preferred settings for Automatic Updates.

3.  If you want to have updates downloaded but not installed automatically, choose Download Updates for Me, but Let Me Choose When to Install Them. This gives you more control over what time an update is installed. If you want to only be notified of updates and choose and install them manually, select Notify Me but Don't Automatically Download or Install Them. Finally, to turn off Automatic Updates, choose Turn Off Automatic Updates.

4.  Click OK.

## Updating Device Drivers

A device driver is a software program that lets a specific device communicate with a PC. Device drivers are needed for digital cameras, printers, scanners, modems, video cards, sound cards, and Web cams, just to name a few. Device drivers can be "signed" or "unsigned." A device driver is signed if it has been fully tested by Microsoft and found to be compatible and working properly. A device driver is unsigned if it has not undergone this testing or has failed it. As you would suspect, signed drivers are better and more reliable than unsigned ones.

Just as Microsoft issues updates to its operating systems, so do manufacturers of device drivers. A device driver update may be issued if a driver was unsigned originally and is signed now. A device driver update may also be issued if a device driver is deemed faulty and the fault has been corrected. You'll want to keep up with the latest drivers, just as you want to keep up with the latest updates.

Microsoft issues signed driver updates for your specific devices through Automatic Updates. However, it only issues driver updates that are signed. If you want to check for an update for a device that is not signed, you'll have to go to the manufacturer's Web site.

If you're unsure if a driver is signed or not, check Device Manager. There, you can also install a new driver you've downloaded or roll back an installation of a new driver that didn't work as expected:

1.  Open Control Panel and open System. (You can also right-click My Computer and select Properties.)

2.  Choose the Hardware tab and click Device Manager.

3.  Expand any tree and double-click any device entry.

4.  From the device's Properties dialog box, click the Driver tab. If the digital signer is Microsoft or any form of it, such as Microsoft Windows Publisher, you have a signed driver that will be updated as updates are available. If the digital signer is not Microsoft, you'll need to visit the manufacturer's Web site to see if a more reliable driver has been published.

5. Once a new driver for a device has been located and downloaded, click Update Driver to install it. Work through the wizard to locate it on your hard drive and to install it. Close all open dialog boxes by clicking OK.

If the driver does not work properly, work through these steps again and choose Roll Back Driver. The previous driver will be used.

---

**TIP:** *If you download and install a new driver and it doesn't work, and then you download and install another one and it doesn't work either, and if you then decide to use Device Driver Roll Back, you'll get the first non-working driver. Device Driver Roll Back only rolls back one driver. So, if you're testing drivers, download and install, then test, and then roll back before trying another one.*

---

## Additional PC Configuration Gunk

Keeping your PC updated will help it perform better and keep it safe from hackers who have learned to exploit known holes in the software's code. What's been detailed in this section on configuring your PC isn't even the half of it, though. Keeping your Windows-based desktop or laptop PC functioning at its best requires lots of thought and lots of work. The following list contains other degunking tasks you'll have to tackle, and each is outlined in depth in the first book in the Degunking series, *Degunking Windows* (Joli Ballew and Jeff Duntemann). To avoid duplicating that book, we'll mention only a few of the tasks here:

√   Get rid of unnecessary files and programs stored on your hard drive.

√   Organize remaining files and folders.

√   Tweak programs you want to keep using Program Compatibility Mode and System performance settings and by locating and installing upgrades.

√   Install adware and spyware checking programs and monitor suspicious activity.

√   Install a registry checking program and run it monthly.

√   Remove unnecessary freeware and shareware.

√   Take control of spam, and delete unnecessary saved e-mails.

√   Organize your e-mail by creating folders and message rules.

√   Use NTFS instead of a FAT file system if available.

√   Configure security zones in Internet Explorer and firewalls in Control Panel, and purchase and configure antivirus software.

√   Use System Restore, Msconfig, and sfc /scannow. Change BIOS settings, and use other not-so-well-known tricks to solve computer problems.

√   Add RAM if your pocketbook and spouse allow it.

There's more, certainly, but these basic tips are required for keeping your PC running smoothly. A computer is like a house; it's going to acquire gunk, and you have to clean it out occasionally. You have to take out the trash. You also have to lock the doors, repaint, and clean out the gutters. You may choose to purchase upgrades to dishwashers or ovens too, or add another room if you have the money. But one thing is for sure: You must always remember to lock the doors and windows! So if you take only one piece of advice from this paragraph: Get some antivirus software and keep it up-to-date, get adware and spyware checkers, enable a firewall, and keep good backups!

# Set Up CD and DVD Burners

CD and DVD players and burners come with device drivers, as all devices do. Device drivers are necessary. They can also come with software. While some of this software is good, an equal number of programs are not necessary, or worse, completely useless.

## Software That's Needed and Software That Isn't

If you have Windows XP and a CD burner, you don't *have to have* CD burning software. You don't *have to have* a slide show program, or a program that organizes your images for you. Windows XP already has all of that built in. These unnecessary applications just take up extra room on your hard drive. They may also kick in when you don't want them to, overriding the computer's defaults, and they can be difficult to use. If you find that this is the case, uninstall those unnecessary programs or at least tweak them so they don't take over.

DVD burners come with multiple software programs too. But unlike the programs that come with CDs, you'll need most of these. You'll need the programs that convert your Windows media files to other formats for VCDs and DVDs, programs for copying one DVD to another DVD, and a DVD decoder to play DVDs on your computer. However, if you just want to create data DVDs, you can often do that by simply dragging and dropping to your DVD disk drive icon. If you're only in the market to copy data DVDs, don't mess around with the complicated software if you don't have to.

# Degunk Your Photos (and Printers)

A printer is just as much a computer component as a mouse or keyboard. Almost everyone with a PC has one, needs one, and uses it often. In fact, most PC retailers have made deals with printer manufacturers to give you a free printer with the purchase of a new PC. That's *not* because the printer manufacturers want to get their name out there or because the retailer appreciates your business; it's because the printer manufacturer knows you'll spend the rest of your days purchasing their (expensive) ink cartridges!

In these sections, you'll learn how to get the most out of your ink-jet printer and the photos you print on it. We'll degunk the entire printing process by first talking about what you can do to improve performance, starting with taking the right picture and then moving on to acquiring the proper inks and papers and, finally, setting printer defaults. We guarantee you can degunk your printer with these tips and tricks!

## You May Have (or Have Had) Several Printers

Among us, we have had (and still have) several "professional photo printers." Our favorites accept digital media cards from digital cameras and produce professional-quality prints on various sizes of paper. Some printers offer more than quality ink-jet prints though; some also print images onto sublimation papers (using sublimation inks), and the prints are used for adhering the images to coffee mugs, mouse pads, and similar promotional items with a special heat press. You know if you have one of these high-end printers that you can get great results, but you should know you can get professional-looking prints from the others too.

It has been our experience that you don't have to have an expensive printer to get high-quality prints, and that's what we'd like to talk about here. You can get really good prints from the cheapest of ink-jet printers if you know a few tips and tricks. It's all about using the right papers and the right inks and configuring the correct options. You just have to know how.

## Start with a Good Image

First, it's important to note that you can't get a good print from a bad image. A printer isn't going to add the top of your cousin's head to the photo, it won't sharpen a blurred image, and it won't remove your thumb from the photo. You'll have to take a good picture. Before printing them, you should also enhance your images with purchased or free image-editing programs. The point is, you'll want to have a good image in hand before attempting to create a professional photo from your ink-jet printer!

Besides shooting an eye-pleasing image, you'll also need to shoot at the correct resolution. Table 5-1 shows the basic guidelines for resolution and print size. If you plan to print an 8x10 of the picture you're taking, you'll need to have your camera's resolution set at its highest setting. If you have unlimited memory card space and unlimited hard drive space, consider shooting at the highest image resolution all of the time. You can always modify the images later.

**Table 5-1  Image Resolution Guidelines**

| Image Resolution | Print Size |
| --- | --- |
| 800x600 or less | 4x6 or smaller |
| 1024x768 | 4x6, although sometimes 5x7 produces a good print |
| 1152x768 | 5x7 |
| 1600x1200 | 8x10 |

*TIP: Make sure your digital camera is at least a 2-megapixel camera if your goal is professional-looking prints.*

# Choosing the Most Reliable Inks

With your best photo edited, enhanced, cropped, and ready to print, you'll need to change your focus and concentrate on your printer. Your ink-jet printer probably came with the most basic of ink-jet cartridges, and you most likely installed them without thinking that there were better choices for printing photos. Although you can use the default ink-jet inks when printing your digital images, you'll get the best results if you purchase a photo cartridge and substitute it for the black cartridge in the printer. The inks in this cartridge will create more vibrant colors and, thus, better prints.

Photo cartridges are better than the regular black ink-jet cartridges because instead of putting down black ink that must mix with the color cartridge, the photo cartridge offers multicolor output and works in tandem with the existing color cartridge to create brighter, more vibrant prints. Photo cartridges offer faster drying times too, making them more efficient and less likely to cause smears before the photo is completely dry.

*TIP: Gray photo ink-jet cartridges are also available, and these cartridges contain special light and dark gray photo inks, plus a photo black ink. These cartridges work together with the existing color cartridge to offer exceptional color prints, but they are especially suited for black-and-white prints.*

# Choosing the Best Papers

After acquiring the best inks, you'll want to look around for the best paper to print your images on. Papers created specifically for ink-jet printers and for printing photos are generally smoother and brighter, which makes the image appear more vibrant than it actually is. Because the paper is smoother, it reflects light better than rough paper does, thus enhancing the print to the viewer's eye.

Papers created for ink-jet printers also have different absorption rates than regular papers, and when the ink is sprayed onto the paper by the printer, it stays where it should and is not absorbed by the surrounding parts of the paper. When the surrounding areas of the paper absorb ink they aren't supposed to, it's called *feathering.* Good-quality papers, the ones with a coating on the surface, keep this from happening by allowing very little absorption and thus very little feathering. This reduces the chance the image will blur, smear, or otherwise look less than perfect. This is why photos look best when they are printed on glossy photo paper, although regular (non-glossy) photo paper offers a good print too.

## Setting Printer Defaults

Almost all ink-jet printers these days come with software that allows you to tweak advanced settings, including quality settings, picture orientation, and color management options. You can tell the printer what kind of paper to expect too. Making this declaration in the printer settings dialog box helps the printer make some choices on its own regarding how much ink should be used when printing, as determined by the paper you've chosen to use. As with anything, these settings can be tweaked for getting the best prints possible.

When configuring the settings, you should first verify that you are using the highest number dots per inch (dpi) the printer allows. Never print less than 200 dpi. You can configure a printer's dpi settings from the software that came with the printer, just as with anything else.

Most times, getting the perfect settings requires a little trial and error. You'll try different paper brands and different color management controls, and you may even learn that the printer you have always seems to print a little darker than expected and subsequently raise the brightness in the advanced settings before printing. Most printers offer hundreds of ways to configure print settings.

Notice in Figure 5-9 that we've selected Glossy Photo Paper , we've chosen the Best Photo option, and we deselected High Speed (to let the printer work on the picture a little longer). Digital Camera Correction was also deselected because we'll do all the corrections in an image-editing program. You can experiment with your printer too and find what works best for you.

To sum up, no matter what kind of ink-jet printer you have, even if it's a low-end printer, you'll have a myriad of options to choose from to get better prints than you're getting now. The changes may require you to purchase photo inks and photo papers or manually configure the color settings, but improvements are certainly available. Experiment to find what settings provide the best image output for your printer, monitor, camera, and tastes.

**Figure 5-9**
Most printers offer lots of configuration choices.

### GunkBuster's Notebook: Refilling Your Own Cartridges and Buying Pre-Refilled Ones

We've both done it, and maybe you have too. We purchased refilled cartridges and tried to refill our own and ended up with a printer with clogged heads, an ink stain on the desk, or a completely useless printer that could only muster up the lowest quality of prints. Worse, though, we've ended up with printers that wouldn't print at all. Although pre-refilled and refilled cartridges sometimes work just fine, in our experience, they cause more problems than they are worth.

Our advice is to purchase cartridges from the manufacturer, even though they are more expensive. They're quality-controlled, have warranties, and best of all, they work! If your budget doesn't allow it though, or if you're the daredevil type and want to take the risk, you can save quite a bundle on your printing costs by going the other way.

If you insist on second-hand cartridges or refilling your own, at least follow these guidelines:

√ Refill cartridges over newspaper or an old towel to avoid making a mess.

√ Run the printer's cleaning routine after replacing or refilling a cartridge and print a test page. If the test page produces streaks or lines, run the program two or three more times.

√ Clean the printer's circuitry after replacing a cartridge to remove any spilled ink or residues.

√ Print something once a week to keep the heads and ink from drying or clogging.

√ Align your print heads with the printer's alignment program after replacing or refilling any cartridge.

√ Don't install a refilled or used cartridge if it is leaking ink, is too full, or has ink on the outside of it. Wipe all cartridges clean before replacing.

√ Don't use a sharp object to open or clear the air or vent hole, if one exists. If the refill kit requires it, use the plastic squeeze bottle included to repressurize the cartridge.

√ Don't let an empty cartridge sit very long without refilling it. If you wait too long, the empty cartridge can be ruined.

# Summing Up

In this chapter, you made the move from physically cleaning your equipment and environment to actually configuring your main PC components. You configured your monitor by setting the best resolution, changing the icons, and overriding IE's default font, font sizes, and colors. You also degunked your desktop or laptop PC, not physically, but virtually. There are lots of tasks to keeping the hard drive running properly, and you learned a few here. Finally, you learned about DVD and CD burners and players, and about printers. There are lots of ways to degunk those, including uninstalling unnecessary software and tweaking the software you use. Next, we'll dive deeper into the peripheral world and take on cameras, scanners, PDAs, and more.

6

# Degunking Your Peripherals

## Degunking Checklist:

√ Make sure you are using the best connection options for your cameras and Web cams.

√ Get together extra batteries, memory cards, and even cables to ensure you don't have problems with your cameras.

√ Avoid gunk by deleting images from your camera before they are transferred onto your hard drive.

√ Use the correct resolution to produce the best scan, taking into account your computer's resources.

√ Keep your scanner drivers updated, and let the scanner have all the resources it needs.

√ Recognize that unused peripherals are gunk; if you don't need that PDA, give it to a charitable cause.

√ Learn how to keep Pocket PCs and PDAs out of the way, and learn when and why you really need to synchronize.

√ Understand that smart displays are almost always gunky, and learn what you can do about it.

Think about all of the peripherals you have in your kitchen. You could have a blender, a toaster, an electric can opener, a pasta maker, a coffeemaker, and a food processor all on your countertop. If you use each of these items on a daily basis, that's just fine. However, if you use only the electric can opener, coffeemaker, and toaster every day, then the blender and food processor are gunking up your valuable countertop space. If you don't use the pasta maker at all, then it is gunking up your house! Your PC peripherals operate in the same manner; you need to take inventory and seriously consider what you use every day, what you use rarely, and what you no longer use at all.

The peripherals we'll be covering in this chapter include Web cams, digital cameras, scanners, PDAs and Pocket PCs, and smart displays or similar devices. Degunking these devices can be tricky, and there's an art to it. Beyond physically degunking, you have to make sure you are using the best connection options and the best settings, and if you have various wireless equipment, learn to avoid interference and disruption of your wireless or wired network.

---

**TIP:** Getting rid of peripherals you don't need or use is the truest form of degunking. Peripherals that don't exist can't gunk up your work area, your PC, or the area underneath your desk. So, before going any further, take a look around and see if there's anything you don't need, and get rid of it.

---

# Degunk Your Cameras and Web Cams

There are several ways to degunk cameras and Web cams, including making the proper connections, keeping your cables and cameras organized, and keeping extra cards, batteries, and tapes on hand. If you have the choice between a serial connection and a USB connection, choose the faster USB connection. But you can also take precautions against gunking up your hard drive by not letting unwanted pictures get there in the first place. Finally, you can organize the pictures you want to keep by uploading them to your hard drive responsibly; namely, creating folders beforehand, creating descriptive names for your images, and enjoying your pictures at your computer instead of just storing them there. What's the point in taking all of those pictures if you can't enjoy them?

## Make the Proper Connections

Most devices come with several ways to connect them. For instance, printers and scanners often come with a parallel port connection and a USB connection. Digital cameras used to come with a serial port and a USB port, but most newer models now come with USB or FireWire, or both. Wireless equipment, of course, comes with access points and wireless hardware, but some wireless equipment like PDAs also come with a USB port to connect to the computer for synchronizing. Because there are multiple options, it helps to know which connections do what in terms of transferring data so that you can make the best choice possible.

Since you're mainly concerned with speed and reliability when transferring data, we've included Table 6-1 to compare the connection types.

**Table 6-1   Connection Types for Peripherals**

| Connection Type | Speed | Reliability | Use For |
|---|---|---|---|
| Serial | One bit at a time, extremely slowly. | Good, but it's just too slow. | Older cameras, scanners, and mice. |
| Parallel | Eight bits at a time, relatively slowly. | Good. | Older printers, scanners, and fax machines. |
| Wireless LAN | Eleven megabits per second, fast. | Varies, depending on access point location and interference. | Any hardware with a wireless card and the capability of connecting to a wireless access point. |
| USB | Twelve megabits per second, fast. | Good. | Audio players, joysticks, printers, cameras, scanners, PDAs and Pocket PCs, and keyboards. |
| Ethernet | Ten to one hundred megabits per second, fast. | Good. | Anything with a NIC capable of connecting to a network. Computers, printers, hubs, routers, and switches are examples. |
| FireWire | Four hundred megabits per second, extremely fast. | Good. | DV cameras and any other device with a FireWire connection. |

Using this table, you can now make an informed decision regarding your hardware. If your digital camera has a serial port and a USB port, by all means, use the USB port. If you have the option of getting to your cable or DSL modem via a 100-Mbps Ethernet router versus a 12-Mbps USB connection, choose the Ethernet router.

# Have Extra Memory Cards, Batteries, and Tapes

There's nothing worse than running out of gas while driving down the road. Similarly, there's nothing worse than missing the greatest shot ever because your batteries are dead or you don't have any room left on your memory card. While it may be a little expensive, it can't hurt to have extra supplies around. With that in mind, here are a few things you might want to gather up, along with a few degunking tasks you should consider:

√    Always have extra DV tapes on hand.

√    Always have an extra battery or at least an available power cable for the camera on hand.

√    Carry one extra memory card, even it it's only 16 MB.

√    Keep the manual or instruction guide with the camera, especially if you have a camera that offers a number of settings.

√    Clearly label all used tapes.

√    Clearly label all cords and connectors.

√    Keep all camera peripherals in a padded camera bag with lots of pockets for extras.

√    Bring several extra batteries on long trips, when filming weddings or graduations, or when filming a sporting event.

Every time you purchase a new peripheral, such as a camera, it is a good idea to purchase a padded bag to hold the device and cables, memory cards, extra batteries, the manual (or at least a quick reference guide), and any other support items that you might have. Keeping these items together will always ensure that you have what you need and it will help to keep you from losing anything.

## GunkBuster's Notebook: Keep Cables and Cameras Organized and Safe

You must also take precautions to keep your cameras, cables, and other items safe. Figures 6-1 and 6-2 show what you shouldn't and should do, respectively.

Organizing this drawer took only a few minutes. Viewing each of the tapes and labeling what was on each took the rest of the day. If you're into degunking, you'll want to perform these tasks as soon as possible. You may even find you have a few tapes you can reuse, or some you haven't uploaded and archived on your computer. (If you own a laptop and work in various areas of the house, you should also designate a drawer like this in each room you work in.)

**Figure 6-1**
Don't do this to your cameras and cables.

**Figure 6-2**
It's much better to keep your peripherals organized and safe.

# Uploading Images Responsibly

Windows XP has a system in place to help you upload images sensibly. By that, we mean you can create folders for sets of images and number them descriptively and sequentially, which helps you keep track of the images you want to keep. However, XP can't do it alone; it needs your help.

When uploading pictures, you can regularly perform some preventative degunking as listed here:

√   Delete pictures from your camera that were blurry or didn't turn out as you expected. Don't let those images have a chance of surviving any longer than necessary, and don't copy them to your hard drive. Once they get on your hard drive, you'll likely forget about them and collectively they can take up much more space than you might realize.

√   Create a subfolder in the My Pictures folder each time you want to upload pictures. Then, choose that folder when uploading. Name the folder with either the date or subject matter.

√   When uploading pictures to your hard drive, use Microsoft's Scanner and Camera Wizard. It'll walk you through the process and give you an opportunity to organize the pictures as you see fit. Figure 6-3 shows this choice.

**Figure 6-3**
Microsoft's Camera and Scanner Wizard is a good tool for uploading digital images.

√ When using Microsoft's Scanner and Camera Wizard, also choose to delete the pictures from the camera after copying them. This way, you'll never run out of space on your memory card.

With the images uploaded and in folders, you can now enjoy your pictures at your PC. Many people forget about this part; they upload their pictures, print the ones they want, e-mail a few others, and then burn the images to a CD or DVD for archiving and backing up. All of that results in gunk if you aren't enjoying the images.

Windows XP comes with an application that allows you to watch a slide show of your images from inside the My Pictures folder. Just look for View as a Slide Show in the left pane. While that's all well and good, there are a couple of free PowerToys you may be interested in too: the Slide Show Wizard PowerToy and the Wallpaper Changer PowerToy.

The Slide Show Wizard PowerToy lets you create a slide show of your digital images and show them on a Web site. The Wallpaper Changer PowerToy lets you specify a group of images to be wallpaper on your Desktop and changes those images after a certain amount of time. Whatever you decide to do, make sure you're enjoying the pictures you took so much time to obtain, upload, and organize!

## Keep Track of All Your Photos by Labeling Them

Once you upload your photos, you might find it difficult to keep track of all of them and to remember important details such as when and where a photo was taken, camera settings that might have been used to take the photo, who took the photo, who was in the photo, and other notes such as lighting conditions or where you might have been traveling. When you upload your images to your PC, many of the these details might be clear in your mind, but after many months you'll likely forget them. This is especially true if you accumulate lots of photos. As part of the degunking process, you'll want to know what your photos actually are so that you can easily decide later if you should later keep or discard them.

Fortunately, Windows XP provides an easy-to-use feature so that you can add comments to your photos. To do this, follow these steps:

1. Right-click the photo to add information and select the Properties option.

2. In the dialog box displayed, select the Summary tab.

3. As Figure 6-4 shows, you can then add any comments that you want in the

Comments box. You can also give your photo a title and enter other information, such as subject, author, and category, to help you keep track of it.

4. When you are finished entering information, click the OK button.

The best part about this feature is that you can easily view the notes that you have assigned to a photo at any time by simply opening the folder where the photo is stored and moving the mouse pointer so that it touches the image. Now, you'll never have to wonder who was in a photo, where or when it was taken, or what event it represents.

**Figure 6-4**

Using the file properties feature to provide important notes for a digital photo.

**GunkBuster's Notebook: Don't Let Those Pictures Just Sit There—Create a Slide Show for Your Web Site**

As mentioned before, if you've gone to all of the trouble to take, edit, store, and archive photos of your family and friends and then you never use them, share them, or view them yourself, that's gunk! If that's the case, consider downloading a free application that lets you create a slide show of your images for a Web page.

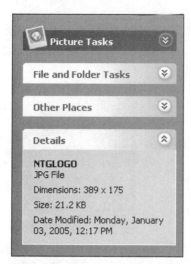

**Figure 6-5**

Viewing the notes assigned to
a photo.

The HTML Slide Show PowerToy, available from Microsoft's PowerToys Web site, is awesome and will help you turn your picture gunk into something useful and enjoyable. Using the wizard, you add images, create a name for the slide show, and configure the image options to create suitable image sizes for the Internet.

When creating a slide show for the Internet, keep in mind that you will want to keep the images small; larger images will take longer to download. To be on the safe side, select 320x240, the smallest option, or 640x480. You'll have some other options too; you can create a simple or advanced slide show or configure it to run full screen. The options are easy to understand and are shown in Figure 6-6.

When the wizard completes, select View the Slide Show Now to see your creation. By default, the slide show will be saved in My Documents\My Slide Show, but you can change that while working through the wizard. (If you have a pop-up blocker, you may have to disable it or hold down the appropriate key.) The only thing left to do is to upload it to your Web site.

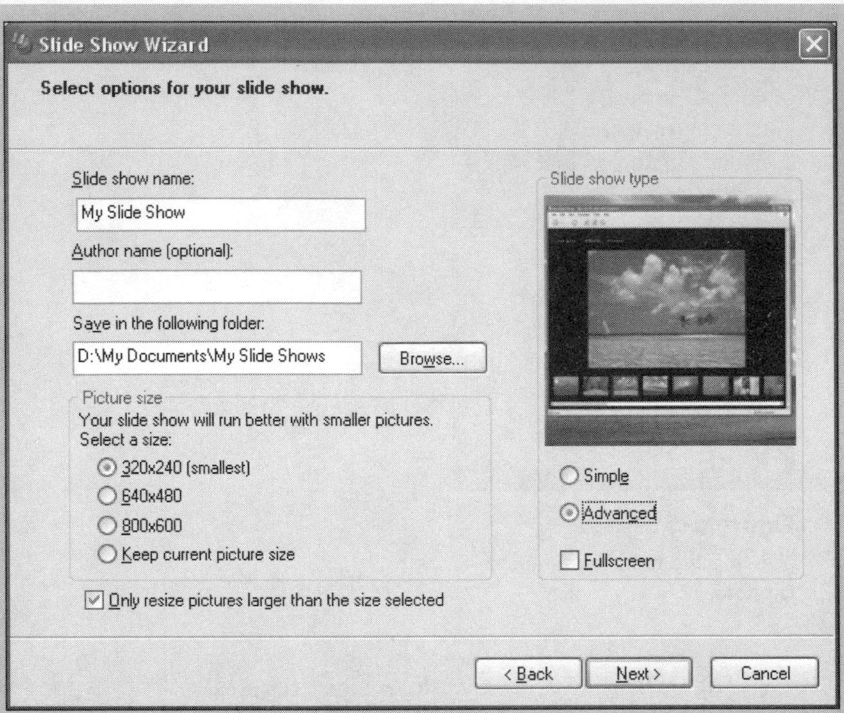

**Figure 6-6**
Make good use of your photos; don't let them become gunk.

# Degunk Your Scanner

Scanners seem like such simple objects. You think you should be able to clean the glass, pop in a picture, and scan the image without any problem. As you know though, the art of scanning isn't always that straightforward. Scanners use a lot of system resources and tend to hang, scanned files can be quite large and unmanageable, and the quality can be less than stellar. Lines in images are common, as is the inability to make out what's been scanned, especially if it's a newspaper clipping or something similar.

In the following sections, we'll teach you how to get better performance and better scans. We'll talk about resolution, keeping drivers updated, and allowing the scanner to have enough system resources to function properly.

## It's Not Always about the Resolution

Most people new to scanning think if they scan at the highest resolution their scanner will allow, they'll be getting the best output possible. That's not necessarily true; you should consider why you're scanning first and then configure the resolution based on those needs. If you're scanning for printing, you'll be concerned with image size; if you're scanning for output to a computer monitor, you'll be concerned with your screen size and its resolution. Either way, choosing the highest resolution only guarantees you'll produce a huge file; it doesn't necessarily mean you'll get the best image.

Consider this: you scan an image at the highest resolution your scanner will allow, and when you open it to view it on your monitor, it's way too big for the screen. You have to use the scrollbars to view the entire image. That's not the best output possible. Additionally, if your goal is to scan an image and e-mail it, you're not going to make the recipient very happy if it takes an hour to download the picture to their PC. So resolution is a compromise between size, quality, and how you'll output the image once it's scanned.

---

**TIP:** *The quality of an image improves with a higher resolution, but only to a point. Increasing the resolution after that only makes the image unwieldy and too large to work with effectively. If your goal is to scan in an image so that you can e-mail it, make sure that you scan the image in a lower resolution, and before you e-mail the image file, make sure you double-check the file size. The last thing you want to do is gunk up a friend's computer by trying to e-mail them a 10 MB file. Believe it or not, this happens to us quite frequently.*

---

The math and science involved in choosing the right resolution for an image is intense. If you'd like to learn the steps for choosing the correct resolution for the correct scanned image and desired output, there are plenty of Internet sites devoted to it, as well as a myriad of books. You may also want to brush up on some of the math involved if you plan to get serious! For now though, keep the following guidelines in your head when scanning:

√ If you're scanning an image to print, scan at 300 or 600 dpi.

√ If you're scanning a document you want to fax, scan at about 200 dpi and choose Line Art.

√ If scanning an image for a Web site or for e-mailing, scan at 72 dpi.

√ If you need to enlarge a small picture, scan at between 600 or 800 dpi.

√ If scanning to view on your computer monitor, try first scanning at 300 dpi, then 600 dpi.

These tips should help you produce scans that are better suited for your specific applications. If you still aren't getting the output you want though, visit **www.scantips.com**; it's fantastic. At this Web site, you'll find a number of tips and insights for scanning images.

## Make Sure the Scanner Has What It Needs

There's nothing more frustrating than waiting for the scanner to finish and later finding out the whole system has hung up and isn't doing anything. While this can be due to scanning at an abnormally high resolution, it can just as well be a corrupt or outdated driver. You can see if it's the latter by going to the manufacturer's Web site and checking for a newer one. Scanners aren't like a lot of PCs; with a scanner you can actually look right on the scanner case or lid and see the model number, the company name, and often even the Web site address. A quick check at the manufacturer's Web site will let you know if your scanner problems are driver-related.

Finally, for better scans, let the scanner have all of the resources it needs. This means refraining from rendering a movie in Movie Maker or performing resource-intense image editing in Photoshop while you're trying to scan an image. Your scanner will thank you.

# Degunk PDAs and Pocket PCs

If you have a PDA or Pocket PC you never use, get rid of it by giving it to a charitable cause (or selling it on eBay). Don't forget to include the charger, its base, your synch cable, your travel kit and travel case, the USB and power cord, and the software. If you keep all of this stuff and don't need it, it's the same as keeping a disabled car in the back yard. It's just gunk and chances are you'll never use it; eventually, it'll be too late for it to be of use to anyone. If you do decide to give away or sell your PDA, make sure that you first delete all of your personal data from the device.

If you still use your PDA or Pocket PC, at least follow the guidelines in previous chapters for hiding it, keeping it in a drawer, and labeling and managing the cords that come along with it, and use the guidelines in this chapter for choosing the best connection. You can organize your PDA and accessories the same way you organize your digital camera. Designate a drawer or an area of the closet for it. You'll be happier (and so will your spouse).

## Quick Tips for Improving Your Experience with Your Handheld Device

So how can you improve the performance of your PDA or Pocket PC? Well, you can check for updates often and regularly degunk what you stored on it. If you copied a 30 MB movie of your kid's graduation to show your relatives and you won't be showing it again, delete it. You'll still have it on your hard drive and archived on CDs or DVDs. In addition, regularly degunk unwanted pictures and downloaded media, music, and outdated information. There's no need to waste valuable space and resources on things you won't use or don't need.

You can also make sure you have the programs you need. If you need an office program, get one; if you need a money management program, get one; if you use your handheld device to keep track of your medical progress or health issues, make sure you have a reliable program for that, one that also synchronizes with your PC easily and one your doctor or personal trainer understands.

Finally, make sure you have enough RAM and an acceptable battery, and that you have wireless capabilities with Bluetooth technology. Make sure you keep your handheld charged too; you don't want it to lose valuable data or not be available when you need it. You should also become familiar with the various PDA, Palm, and Pocket PC newsgroups. There's a wealth of information there.

## Data and File Synchronization

Data and file synchronization is the subject of many a book and Web site. There's so much data, so many devices, and so little time. You may have to synchronize a laptop, PDA, cell phone, or portable e-mail device, just to name a few. All of this synchronization can become quite a hassle, and quite hard to keep up with.

While synchronization is straightforward if you connect directly to your PC using a physical connection, it's much more complex when looking for a solution to synch up over the Internet. When physically connected to the PC, you simply use the software that ships with the device itself, based on your configuration. (You may want to tweak this configuration to make sure you're synching up what you need to, while not synching unnecessary data.) You'll have to train yourself to synch up every day, or as often as data changes, but that's pretty easy. Figure 6-7 shows an example of a possible configuration.

What's not so easy is taking synchronization a step further and doing it wirelessly and over the Internet. The setup is more difficult, but the rewards are great. You can synch up anywhere, anytime. If you have a Microsoft Pocket PC, you can set up your PC to accept incoming calls and then set up ActiveSync to dial into your PC while you're out. If you have a Palm or Windows CE device, you can use programs such as AvantGo and Mazingo to synch up your PDA over a broadband connection. There are many other programs and companies to check out: PCsync by LapLink, PCAnywhere by Symantic, and QuickSync by LinkPro. Figure 6-8 shows a synchronization in process.

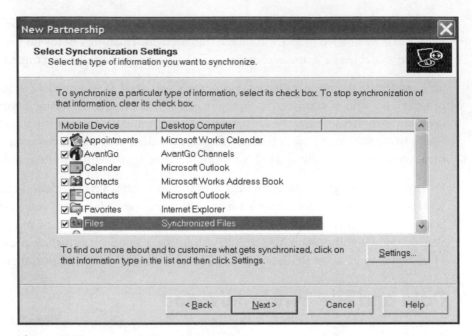

**Figure 6-7**

Synching options.

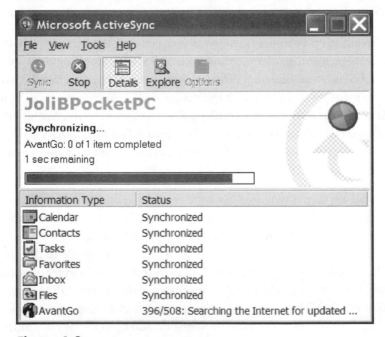

**Figure 6-8**

Synchronization in process.

## GunkBuster's Notebook: Be Smart when Saving Media to a Mobile Device

If you've made movies on your PC of your family's outings, weddings, camping trips, recitals, or other interesting family events, you can take those movies with you on your PDA or Pocket PC. You'll be able to show your movies on the go, at parties, family reunions, office events, and other galas. If you've already done some of that (or if you haven't), we're sure we can help you improve the quality, display size, and physical size of those videos so that you get the best bang for your buck with the resources available on your mobile device.

Generally, you'll create Windows Media Files (WMVs) when creating movies, and you'll drag and drop them from your PC's hard drive to the appropriate folder on the connected mobile device. However, WMV files can be created with a myriad of settings for bit rate, display size, aspect ratio, and frames per second. It's hard to know what each term means and certainly what settings are best.

Let's look at the terms first, and then you can decide, from Table 6-2, what choices are best for you:

√ Bit rate: The rate at which bits of data pass through a given transmission medium at any time. Kbps, kilobits per second, describes the number of kilobits passed through a given point per second. For media, you'd want to have as many bits per second as your mobile device could manage while staying within file size limitations.

√ Display size: The physical size of the movie as it is configured to show on the device. Larger display choices create larger file sizes.

√ Aspect ratio: Describes the proportional relationship between the width and height of an image. Most computer devices display images at a 4:3 aspect ratio. Media centers may display at a 16:9 aspect ratio.

√ Frames per second: Movies are created using frames, and a frame is a still image. Displaying frames in succession gives the illusion of a movie. The more frames per second you can have, the smoother the movie will look.

**Table 6-2    Compare Settings for WMV Files**

| Video for Pocket PC | Bit Rate | Display Size | Aspect Ratio | Frames per Second | Advantages over Other Choices | Disadvantages Compared to Other Choices |
|---|---|---|---|---|---|---|
| 143 Kbps | 143 Kbps | 208x160 pixels | 4:3 | 8 | Smallest file size | Least amount of fps, resulting in the lowest quality |
| 218 Kbps | 218 Kbps | 208x160 pixels | 4:3 | 20 | Relatively good file size | Small display size |
| Full screen 218 Kbps | 218 Kbps | 320x240 | 4:3 | 15 | Relatively good file size, good display size | Lower fps, than most other options |
| 2003 348 Kbps at 24 fps | 348 Kbps | 320x240 | 4:3 | 24 | Good file size, good fps rate | Large file size |
| 2003 348 Kbps at 30 fps | 348 Kbps | 320x240 | 4:3 | 30 | Good file size, good fps rate, best quality | Large file size |

Compare the physical file size when selecting bit rate, display size, and frames per second. Your movie software will tell you how large a file each choice creates. You'll give up quality when choosing smaller file sizes, but you may have to make that choice if you have a limited amount of space on your mobile device.

# Avoid Smart Displays

A smart display is a device that allows you to access your PC from another room in the house. It is a flat touch-screen device that you control with a stylus, and it's wireless. Think of it as an extension of your monitor, only wireless and flat and easy to carry around. Figure 6-9 shows an example.

Whatever you can do at your PC's monitor, you can do from the smart display. For instance, if you can surf the Web from your PC, you can also surf the Web from your smart display. You can download recipes in the kitchen, show media on the porch, or burn a CD from the comfort of your couch. Unfortunately, because it uses 802.11 technology, you don't get that much bandwidth, and you won't get great media or Internet performance.

Even though the smart display *can be* a great convenience, more often than not it becomes a gunk magnet. You'll need a wireless access point for it, a wireless adapter for your PC, and you'll have to configure it as a network device. You'll also need Windows XP Professional. To store it requires a stand, and the smart

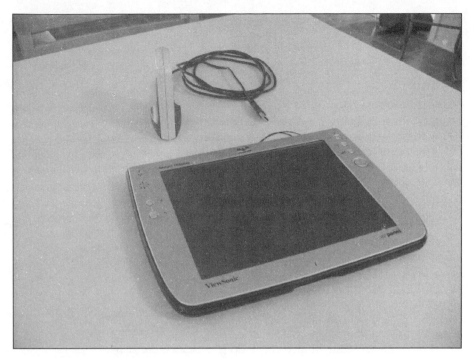

**Figure 6-9**
Smart displays are flat and wireless.

display, like any wireless device, must be charged. You'll need to organize this hardware as detailed for other peripherals earlier.

In addition to all of the hardware you accumulate, when you're using the smart display, your PC becomes inaccessible. The smart display uses "remote desktop" technology, a technology that allows you to work while away from the actual PC. To make this a secure and viable option, the PC must be locked and un-available to anyone else who may have access. Finally, like any wireless device, if improperly configured, it can wreak havoc on your existing wired or wireless network.

## Degunking Tasks for Your Smart Display and Other Options

Unfortunately, smart displays often end up in the "I like this but I don't use it" pile of hardware you keep on or underneath your desk, or in the closet. That's because of the aforementioned problems: they can be difficult to configure, they can mess up existing networks, and your PC is unavailable when you're using it. Besides, after a while, it just gets a little boring. (It's like a new Web cam;

you probably go crazy with it for a couple of weeks, and then it just sits there, taking up desk space.)

Since smart displays are wireless equipment though, you can improve performance. You can optimize their access points, learn how to troubleshoot a wireless network, and understand how fast a wireless network is capable of transmitting data. All of this is detailed in Chapter 11.

On the other hand, if you can sell your $1400 smart display for $700, you can purchase a cheap laptop and install a wireless networking card. Chances are the screen will be larger, and you can be sure you won't have the networking problems you'll have with the smart display. You'll also be able to use your PC while using the laptop, a real advantage. So, if you're looking for the best way to degunk your smart display—get rid of it!

# Summing Up

In this chapter, you learned about degunking peripherals, including cameras and Web cams, scanners, PDAs and Pocket PCs, and smart displays. As you saw, there's always something you can do to enhance performance, improve output, and store data more effectively.

With cameras and Web cams, you can choose better connections, and with scanners you can learn about proper resolution. You can learn how to better synchronize handheld devices, and you can be smarter when it comes to using the data you collect. As usual, you can and should get rid of gunky hardware and unused peripherals and store the ones you use efficiently.

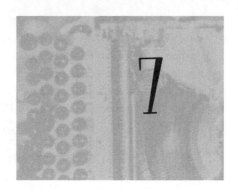

# 7

# Untangling Your USB and FireWire Connections

## Degunking Checklist:

√ Understand how you can use USB to speed up the transfer of data from your PC to other devices.

√ Determine if your PC is fast enough to use USB; don't try to install a USB 2.0 add-in board on a PC slower than 1 GHz or so.

√ Don't kink your USB or FireWire cables.

√ Make sure you have a USB 2.0 port before buying a USB 2.0 peripheral.

√ Be careful what devices you plug into a bus-powered hub.

√ Be mindful of the total bandwidth required by all the devices plugged into a USB hub or (especially) nested hubs.

√ Don't attach more than eight devices to a single USB port via hubs.

√ Don't plug a USB 2.0 hub into a USB 1.1 port. Odd things may happen.

√ Don't force USB or FireWire plugs into their ports if they won't easily insert.

If you have followed the PC business through its infancy and adolescence (as your humble authors have), you may recall the horror that was DOS-era serial port support. The cables were fragile, nonstandard, bulky, and stiff. The connectors were huge and had 25 pins, of which only 3 were in some cases "live." Serial protocols varied all over the map, involving hardware and software handshaking, ACK, NACK, and wire jungles we called "breakout boxes" because when we finally decided to use them, we were on the verge of breaking out in hives. (Or, as a Greek friend said more than once, breaking out the ouzo.)

Fast-forward to the Windows era, and life has gotten *way* better. Although nearly all PCs still carry those ancient "legacy" serial ports that gave us such grief in 1987, nearly all serial connections are now made through one of two vastly better technologies: the Universal Serial Bus, or USB, and IEEE 1394, better known as FireWire. As easy as they are to use, USB and FireWire are still subtle, and there are ways to go wrong when you attempt to use and configure them. Worse, it's not always obvious how (and where) you went wrong. In this chapter, we'll help you degunk your PC by putting this technology to work, and we'll provide some tips on using them both at peak speed and reliability.

# Understand How USB Works

Data passes *serially* through a USB cable, hence the name. Inside the cable, data bits travel one bit at a time, in single file, nose to tail. (Needless to say, they travel *very* quickly.) A single hardware USB port on the back of your PC can connect to a maximum of 127 different devices if you split the port using hardware devices called *hubs*. In practice, however, it's not a good idea to put more than three or four separate devices on a single USB port. (We'll talk about why a little later in this chapter. There are no free lunches, and there is no free bandwidth, either.)

USB is a *master-slave* technology. This means that in virtually all cases, one end of a USB connection is to the PC (the *master*) and the other end is to a peripheral, like a printer, scanner, or digital camera. These peripherals obey the commands of the master side of the connection (the PC) and hence are known as *slaves*. USB cables have entirely different connectors on their two ends, making it impossible to connect the wrong end to the wrong type of port. The master end of a cable will only go into a master port, and the slave end will only go into a slave port. You can't connect them the wrong way!

The master USB ports on your PC have another interesting capability: They can provide modest amounts of electrical power to a slave device on the other end of a cable. This means that some low-power USB devices, like USB mice and some Wi-Fi networking adapters, can be operated from the power that comes down the cable, eliminating the clutter of another wall wart. Of course, large devices like printers and scanners require too much power to draw on the meager current (500 milliamps or less) available through the USB cable. In the last year or two, PC accessories for USB ports have appeared that are not computer devices at all but simply use a USB cable for power. Some of these are brilliant, like a small reading light that plugs into your laptop and runs off the laptop battery—while others, like a USB-powered electric toothbrush, make you wonder if some engineers somewhere don't have quite enough to do.

USB cables can only be so long. The maximum recommended length of a USB cable is 5 meters, which is about 16.5 feet—and the best practice is to use the shortest cable that will reach. You can work around this distance limit to some extent by using powered USB hubs, which we'll discuss later in this chapter.

USB's maximum speed at the current time is 480 million bits per second (Mbps). The related FireWire technology, in its 2.0 version (often called FireWire 800) can move bits at 800 Mbps, almost twice as quickly. FireWire (discussed later in this chapter) is thus preferred for devices like digital camcorders, which require very high data transfer speeds. FireWire hardware is significantly more expensive than USB hardware, so inexpensive devices will almost always use USB.

# Understand the Four Flavors of USB

Many of the problems that people have with USB stem from the little-known fact that there are four distinct "flavors" of the USB technology, and telling them apart can be a task akin to sexing baby chicks—definitely for experts, as the signs are small and subtle. The four flavors are these:

√  USB, version 1.1. This is your basic USB technology.

√  USB, version 2. As you might guess, this is just like USB, only faster.

√  USB On-The-Go. This brand new USB flavor connects peripherals to one another in a peer-to-peer fashion.

√  Hi-Speed USB On-The-Go. This flavor also connects peripherals to one another in a peer-to-peer fashion, only faster.

Note while that at this writing, the two USB On-The-Go flavors are so new that very few products incorporate them, and we will treat them only briefly in this book.

## USB 1.1

USB ports have been routinely built into Wintel PCs since 1997 or so. Prior to 2003, virtually all USB ports were of the original USB 1.1 standard. USB 1.1 ports can run at two different speeds: 1.5 Mbps (megabits per second) and 12

Mbps. Industry jargon about these speeds is confusing: USB 1.1 running at 1.5 Mbps is sometimes called "USB" without qualifiers, and USB 1.1 running at 12 Mbps is often called "Full Speed USB." Simple peripherals like mice and keyboards can run very well at 1.5 Mbps. Most common peripherals like scanners, printers, and external USB Wi-Fi adapters require 12 Mbps to work well.

USB support is generally poor in Windows versions prior to Windows 2000. If you're still running Windows 98 or Me, you can expect to have at least occasional problems. (We don't recommend attempting to install USB devices on PCs running Windows NT4 or 95.) Windows 2000 and XP have excellent built-in support for USB 1.1. Windows 2000, however, appeared prior to USB 2.0, so you must upgrade your copy of Windows 2000 to Service Pack 4 before attempting to use USB 2.0 on a Windows 2000 installation. Windows XP handles USB 2.0 with aplomb.

---

**TIP:** *Microsoft released a special version of Windows 95, called Windows 95B, which contains USB 1.1 support. If you're running Windows 95B, you'll have some (slim) chance of getting USB devices to work. However, this early support was not bug free, and if you're stuck using an older PC, upgrading to Windows 98 is your best bet for reasonably reliable use of USB 1.1 peripherals. It's very likely that any PC that came with Windows 95 will not be fast enough to handle USB 2.0, so don't try!*

---

# USB 2.0

In 2001, the USB 2.0 specification was finalized, and USB 2.0 ports began to appear in PCs and peripherals in 2002. If you purchased your PC before 2002, you can be quite sure it does not include USB 2.0 ports. Even if your PC was purchased in 2003, its USB ports may still be V 1.1. Only by mid-2004 were USB 2.0 ports to be reliably found in consumer-class PCs. The formal name for USB 2.0 is Hi-Speed USB, though you won't hear that very often.

The main benefit coming with USB 2.0 is the new Hi-Speed data rate of 480 Mbps (million bits per second). That's a *lot* of data per second; more, in fact, that just about any minor peripheral really needs. Keep in mind that peripherals designed to run at USB 1.1's data rate of 12 Mbps still run at 12 Mbps when connected to a USB 2.0 port. To use that greater speed, a USB peripheral must have been designed to use it. Most peripherals requiring USB 2.0 Hi-Speed data rates fall into three general categories:

√ High-speed Wireless-G Wi-Fi network adapters

√ Professional quality digital camcorders and other digital video peripherals, including a few Web cams

√ External disk drives, including both hard drives and CD or DVD burners Devices like these often require USB Hi-Speed to work well, or even to work at all. A Wireless-G Wi-Fi adapter will fall back to Wireless-B data rates (11 Mbps) when connected to a USB 1.1 port. Digital video peripherals may not work at all when connected to a USB 1.1 port. Make sure you understand the requirements a USB peripheral has before you buy it!

## USB On-The-Go

As we explained earlier, USB is a master-slave technology. One end of any USB connection must be to a PC, which acts as master of ceremonies, controlling all aspects of data transfer across the USB cable. FireWire, on the other hand, is a peer-to-peer technology, meaning that any port can connect to any other port and the port on the PC has no special privileges. This proved to be very useful for doing things like connecting digital cameras to photo printers, where the PC's presence isn't really necessary. Recognizing that direct connections among peripherals would be a good thing (and wanting to bring USB to feature-parity with FireWire), the USB standards group created a new standard in 2001, called USB On-The-Go. USB OTG was designed to allow non-PC devices to connect to peripherals and other non-PC devices, as FireWire has always done.

At this writing, USB On-The-Go is extremely new, and products for it are few and far between.

# Determine If Your PC Is Fast Enough for USB 2.0

Before we go a whole lot farther, we have to expose the dirty little secret about the very fast USB 2.0 ports and about fast I/O ports generally, including both FireWire and Ethernet network ports. *Fast ports require fast PCs.* If your PC is old and slow, it will not have a USB 2.0 port in it, and installing a USB 2.0 port will likely swamp the machine and either cause it to malfunction or bring its speed down to a crawl.

The problem is simple and easy to explain: Your PC has to manage the passage of data to and from peripherals through a USB (or any other) port. The faster the data moves, the more work the PC has to do to keep everything on track. This work requires CPU cycles, and the faster data moves through a port, the more CPU cycles the PC must spend managing the process. Slower PCs just don't have enough available CPU cycles to do the job.

Ignore manufacturers' recommendations. After all, they want to sell you hardware. There's a rule of thumb born of much bitter experience: Your PC's clock speed in megahertz should be, *at minimum,* twice the bit rate in megabits of any port you use. USB 1.1 has a bit rate of 12 million bits per second. Any modern PC can comfortably handle that. (24 MHz PCs haven't been sold in over 15 years.) USB 2.0, on the other hand, has a bit rate of 480 million bits per second. Twice that is 960 million bits per second, which is just short of a billion bits per second. For USB 2.0, therefore, your PC should run at a clock speed of a billion clock cycles per second, or one gigahertz. Go much slower than that and you *will* have problems.

This problem also applies to FireWire ports. FireWire 400 requires a 600 MHz PC to work well, though for technical reasons, FireWire is a little more forgiving of slower PCs.

There's no free lunch, in PCs nor anywhere else: Fast ports require fast PCs.

## How Fast Is Your USB Port?

Clearly, much depends on knowing whether the USB ports on the back panel of your PC are standard USB or Hi-Speed USB. There's absolutely no way to tell by looking at the physical ports themselves. The connectors are absolutely identical. To determine whether your USB ports are USB 1.1 or 2.0, you have to look in the Device Manager window of the System Control Panel applet. To do this, follow these steps:

1. Bring up Control Panel.

2. Open the System applet.

3. Click the Hardware tab.

4. Click the Device Manager button.

5. At the very bottom of the window, click the plus symbol by the item labeled "Universal Serial Bus controllers."

What you'll see is a list of USB root hubs and controllers. A typical example is shown in Figure 7-1. What you're looking for is the word *Enhanced* on a line describing a USB controller, as you'll see in the highlighted line item in the figure. You should also see something labeled "USB 2.0 Root Hub."

---

**TIP:** *If you add a USB 2.0 port board to a Windows 2000 PC that has not been brought up to Service Pack 4, the board will not necessarily show you an enhanced controller or a USB 2.0 root hub. Windows 2000 must be brought up to Service Pack 4 to get the full use of a USB 2.0 hardware port!*

---

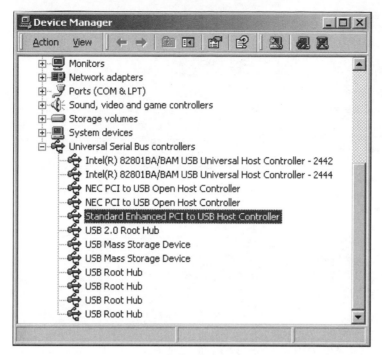

**Figure 7-1**

USB controller and hub displays in Windows Device Manager.

# What Windows Can Tell You about Your USB Ports

The USB section of the Device Manager window from the System applet in Control Panel can tell you quite a bit about the USB ports in your system:

√   What devices are currently connected to your PC's USB ports

√   How much power each device is allowed

√   How much power each device is actually using

This information can be very useful in deciding how to make the best (and most gunk-free) use of the USB capabilities of your PC.

To read this information, follow these steps:

1.  Open the USB section of the Device Manager window, as explained in the previous section.

2.  Right-click on any of the lines labeled "Root Hub."

3.  Select Properties.

4.  Click on the tab labeled "Power." You'll see a dialog like the one shown in Figure 7-2.

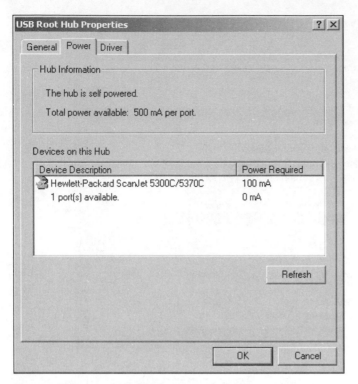

**Figure 7-2**
The Power tab of the USB Root Hub Properties dialog.

The first thing you'll notice in Figure 7-2 is that an HP 5370C scanner is connected to one of the two ports in the selected root hub. You can tell that there are two ports in the root hub because all connected devices are listed in the dialog's list box, and if any ports are still open, the dialog will indicate how many ports remain available. In this case, there is one available port and one occupied by the scanner, for a total of two.

The list also shows how much power each device is drawing from its port. The HP scanner shown is drawing 100 milliamps (mA) from the port. In the Hub Information box above the device list, the maximum power available per port is also given. In this case, that is 500 mA, which is the most you'll ever see as available from a single USB port. The scanner is only drawing 20% of the power available from its port, so it's comfortably within bounds.

Figure 7-3 shows the Device Manager Power tab display for another root hub. This time both ports are occupied, each by a USB thumb drive. (A thumb drive is a small device that provides data storage on a Compact Flash memory board built into a housing the size of your thumb, hence the name.) Each thumb drive is shown to be drawing 200 mA.

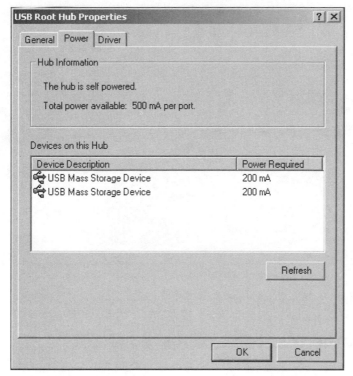

**Figure 7-3**

The Power tab display for two thumb drives in a root hub.

The Power tab displays are useful because they tell you which devices are connected to the same root hubs. As we'll explain in detail later in this chapter, root hubs must split their bandwidth among their several ports. Some USB devices are fussy about bandwidth and need to be alone on a root hub. The Power tab displays allow you to be certain that the devices attached to a root hub are not swamping the root hub's capability to provide power or bandwidth. This is especially important once you begin attaching external hubs to your PC's USB ports, as explained later in this chapter.

## Testing USB Ports with Dedicated Hardware

If you're a gadget freak and like to test and tinker with your own PC hardware, there are good tools available to test USB ports. The ones we recommend come from PassMark Software. Its $49 USB 2.0 plug product (see Figure 7-4) will tell you how fast your USB port (either 1.1 or 2.0) is running, its error rate, and several other things. It's a small, mouse-shaped device that connects to your USB port via a shielded USB 2–compatible cable. Unfortunately, they only support Windows 2000 and XP, but for those versions of Windows they work beautifully.

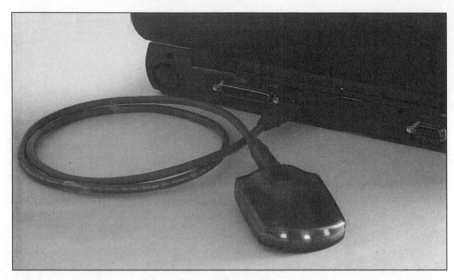

**Figure 7-4**
The PassMark USB loopback plug. (Photo courtesy of PassMark.)

## USB Peripherals: Look at the Box!

It's a lot easier understanding the USB requirements of a given peripheral. The USB standards group has created a set of four logos that manufacturers may print on their product packaging to indicate which of the four basic USB technologies are built into the product. The four logos are shown in Figure 7-5. From left to right they are USB, Hi-Speed USB, USB On-The-Go, and Hi-Speed USB On-The-Go.

For a product that is a USB port add-in board, the logo indicates what sort of ports are on the add-in board. For a product that is a peripheral, the logo indicates what sort of port the peripheral requires to work at its best—and sometimes, to work at all. Compatibility between USB 1.1 and USB 2.0 is subtle and deserves a section all to itself.

# Know the Details of USB 1.1 and 2.0 Compatibility

Great pains were taken during the design of the USB 2.0 technology to be sure that USB 2.0 and USB 1.1 are compatible. There are really only three possible speeds in a USB port, and in fact, each speed is supported by a separate digital logic block, often implemented on separate silicon chips inside the PC. The USB master port will detect what speed the connected USB slave device requires and will connect to the slave device through the appropriate logic block.

**Figure 7-5**
USB product packaging logos.

Here are some simple rules describing compatibility between USB 1.1 and 2.0 master ports:

√ USB 1.1 slave devices will work perfectly in USB 2.0 master ports. They will run at the speed they were designed for, of course. A 1.5 Mbps USB keyboard or mouse will still run at 1.5 Mbps when connected to a USB 2.0 port.

√ A USB 2.0 slave device will connect to a USB 1.1 master port, *but it will only transfer data at USB 1.1 speeds.* This means that a USB 2.0 digital camcorder will connect to a USB 1.1 port at only 12 Mbps, which is only 1/40 the maximum speed of a USB 2.0 Hi-Speed port. The camcorder may not be able to operate correctly at that slower speed and will malfunction or abort the connection. Read camcorder or other digital video device documentation carefully before connecting the device to a USB port!

√ A USB 2.0 slave device may not install or work correctly if connected to a USB 1.1 master port on a PC running Windows 95, 98, or Me. The vendor of the device may provide additional software to allow its products to run under an older Windows version, but in our experience most do not. It's best to assume that USB 2.0 devices will *not* work under Windows 95, 98, and Me *unless* you install a USB port add-in board with drivers designed for those languages. The excellent Adaptec USB2Connect add-in boards work this way, and we recommend them, with the important caveat that *USB 2.0 Hi-Speed peripherals work poorly on slow PCs.*

As always, for best results with USB 2.0, we recommend Windows XP and a PC faster than 1 GHz.

# Understand the Problems of USB Hubs

In a sense, we told you all of that to tell you this: Most of the gunk involved with using USB lies in the concept of a USB *hub.* A USB hub is basically a way of splitting one USB port into several. This is sometimes necessary to expand the number of USB peripherals you can connect to your PC. (Most PCs have only two USB ports, though some have four.) USB hubs can be either internal to the PC (and are called root hubs, more on them shortly) or external to the PC and connected to a USB port on the PC by a USB cable. An external USB hub has

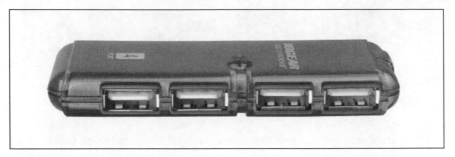

**Figure 7-6**
The IOGear GUH274 Multi-TT USB 2.0 hub. (Photo courtesy of IOGear.)

several USB ports, and a USB device—or another hub—may be plugged into each. A very good external USB hub is shown in Figure 7-6. The IOGear GUH274 is a "multi-TT" USB 2.0 hub, which is important, as we'll discuss shortly.

Physically, an external USB hub is typically a small plastic box with one USB slave port and several USB master ports. A few USB keyboards also contain built-in hubs and provide one or two "extra" USB ports. These keyboard hubs are mostly intended to accept USB mice and cannot accept peripherals demanding high bandwidth or significant power.

Theoretically, a single hub can be split to support 127 separate USB devices. *Theoretically.* In reality, you should never split a single port more than about eight ways. Let's talk about why.

## USB's First Big Hub Gotcha: Splitting Bandwidth

Somewhere inside your PC there is a chip (on the motherboard or on a USB port add-in board) called a USB controller. The controller chip manages communication between your PC and one or more USB devices connected to that controller through USB ports. The controller chip can provide a certain amount of data transfer per second to the USB ports that are connected to it. This data transfer is called *bandwidth,* and it is expressed as bits per second. Here's a fundamental truth that you must keep in mind:

*All ports connected to a USB controller share that controller's block of available bandwidth.*

Read that again. It's crucial. Here's an example: A USB 1.1 controller can provide a total of 12 megabits per second in bandwidth. If it is connected to 4 ports, each of those 4 ports can provide a maximum of only 3 megabits per second when all ports are connected to peripherals. A USB 2.0 controller can provide a much larger block of bandwidth: As much as 480 megabits per second. However, split that block 8 ways and you're down to 60 megabits per second for each port. Split it 16 ways and you're down to 30 megabits per second, and so on. The more devices you connect through USB ports to a USB controller, the less bandwidth each device can have. If one of your devices is a digital camcorder, it may demand all 480 Mbps that the controller provides in order to function. Try to split that same port with other USB devices and your camcorder may no longer work correctly.

## USB's Second Big Hub Gotcha: Root Hubs

If you look at your PC's front or rear panels, you may notice something: USB ports rarely appear alone. In nearly all cases, you'll see two USB master port connectors (often called "A connectors") side by side. Each of those ports can provide a full block of bandwidth to a peripheral, right?

*Wrong.* In every single case we've seen, when two (or more) USB ports are stacked side by side, those two ports are part of a *root hub.* A root hub is a USB hub connected to a USB controller. Root hubs are always located inside your PC or laptop. A hub connected to your PC by a cable is not a root hub. (We'll talk about that sort of external hub shortly.)

Root hubs must share the bandwidth provided to them by the USB controller inside your PC. This means that if you plug two devices into the two ports of a root hub (typically on the front or rear panel of your PC), those two devices must share the bandwidth provided by the controller. Those two ports cannot each provide the full bandwidth supported by the USB 1.1 or 2.0 spec.

This is mostly a problem of less-than-full disclosure. Your PC may come with four USB ports built right into the case, but behind those four ports are only two USB controllers, and hence only two full blocks of USB bandwidth. You do not have four completely independent ports. Keep that in mind as you decide where to plug your USB slave devices. (More on this later.)

## USB's Third Big Hub Gotcha: Isochronous Devices

So all devices connected to a USB hub must share the bandwidth entering the hub from the USB controller (as in a root hub) or from the "upstream" USB port into which an external hub is plugged. But wait: It gets worse. Some USB devices won't gracefully accept their even-steven divided share of bandwidth from a hub. There is a class of USB devices that are called *isochronous.* They are things that handle video and sound, but especially video, like Web cams and digital camcorders. An isochronous (from the Greek for "same time") device must be able to send data to the USB port at a specified, consistent rate. A Web cam may require 70 percent of a USB 2.0 port's maximum bandwidth to successfully transfer 30 frames of video per second. Plug a second Web cam into the same hub and both Web cams will demand 70 percent of the hub's total bandwidth. They won't get it. Both will transmit garbled, incomplete data, or they may throw an error message.

This gotcha is poorly understood, especially by nontechnical people using Web cams and USB speakers. (Professional videographers understand bandwidth limitations only too well.) Read the documentation of any video- or sound-related USB peripheral very carefully. If the peripheral is described as "isochronous," it may demand the entire bandwidth block of a USB controller. Isochronous devices do not play nice. To be safe, each isochronous device should be the sole device on a USB root hub. (To learn how to determine which ports are on which root hubs, see the next section.)

## USB's Fourth Big Hub Gotcha: USB 1.1 Devices on USB 2.0 Hubs

One of the gnarliest of all USB problems (and the toughest to explain easily) lies in the difference between external hubs that meet the USB 1.1 and USB 2.0 specifications. Most common, inexpensive external USB hubs are USB 1.1 hubs. That is, all ports on the hub can only provide USB 1.1 bandwidth, *even when the hub is plugged into a USB 2.0 port*. Newer hubs are available where all ports on the hub meet the USB 2.0 specification. These cost a little more than USB 1.1 hubs, but they can divide the larger bandwidth of a USB 2.0 port among several USB 2.0 devices.

Most people assume that you can plug (say) four USB 1.1 devices into a four-port USB 2.0 external hub and have all four devices running at the maximum USB 1.1 bandwidth of 12 Mbps. After all, you can plug four USB 2.0 devices into a four-port USB 2.0 hub, and the four USB 2.0 devices will happily share in that abundant 480 Mbps bandwidth.

Not so. The USB 2.0 hub must include at least one chip-level device called a *transaction translator,* or TT. The TT translates data traffic from a USB 1.1 device to the USB 2.0 format and vice versa. If you plug a USB 1.1 device into a USB 2.0 hub, all data coming from and going to the USB 1.1 device must pass through a TT.

Now, follow closely here: Each USB 2.0 hub must have at least one TT. It may have more—the best ones have a TT for each port on the hub, so that a four-port USB 2.0 hub can have as many as four TTs. However, the minimum is one. A four-port USB 2.0 hub with only one TT forces that one TT to serve all four ports on the hub. If you plug four USB 1.1 devices into such a hub, all four of those devices must work through a single TT. That TT can only provide, at best, 12 Mbps of bandwidth. So even though the hub is plugged into a 480 Mbps USB port on your PC, each USB 1.1 device plugged into the hub can at best access 3 Mbps of bandwidth through the single TT.

If the four-port USB 2.0 hub had four TTs, each USB 1.1 device would have its own TT and all would work at maximum USB 1.1 bandwidth. Therefore, when you buy a USB 2.0 hub, make sure you're getting a *multi-TT* hub. Read the fine print. Multi-TT hubs cost a little more because of the extra TT chips needed to manufacture them. However, if you're going to bother with a USB 2.0 hub at all, you might as well make sure it has *complete* compatibility with USB 1.1 devices!

## USB's Fifth Big Hub Gotcha: Powering Devices from Hubs

From a power standpoint, there are two kinds of USB hubs: bus-powered and self-powered. A self-powered hub has a separate power supply (usually a wall wart) and can provide power to devices plugged into the hub as though each port in the hub were an independent port on the PC. A bus-powered hub has no power supply. All it can do is pass along a fraction of the power provided to the hub by the PC's USB port into which the hub is plugged.

A bus-powered hub is thus of very limited use, and only low-power devices (like USB mice) should be plugged into bus-powered hubs. (Most USB thumb drives are *not* low-power devices, as we'll explain a little later in this chapter.) If you insist on using a bus-powered hub, be aware that plugging power-hungry devices into it can overload the USB port the hub is plugged into on the PC, triggering a "USB Power Exceeded" error message and causing all devices connected to the hub to shut down.

---

*TIP: Unless you can't possibly avoid it, don't use bus-powered hubs!*

---

## The USB Thumb Drive Power Problem

Apart from printers, thumb drives are probably the most widely used USB peripherals. They're small and simple, and so people sometimes assume that they require almost no power to operate. Not so—and the worst of it is, the power requirements of USB thumb drives are all over the map. Some require *much* more power than others, and that can become a problem when you attempt to use a thumb drive in an unpowered USB hub.

Here's a rule of thumb: Unless you *know* that a given thumb drive is low-power, don't try to use it in a bus-powered hub. The kicker is that it's sometimes difficult to tell whether a USB hub is self-powered or bus-powered. As described earlier, if a hub comes with its own wall wart power supply, it's self-powered. If no power supply comes with the hub, it's bus-powered. Where most people get in trouble is with USB keyboards. Some USB keyboards have USB ports built into them for sharing the keyboard's USB port with other peripherals, typically mice. The USB ports built into USB keyboards are bus-powered, assuming that the keyboard itself draws its power from the USB port on the PC or laptop. For this reason, it's not always a good idea to plug a USB thumb drive into an open USB port on a USB keyboard. The keyboard may be taking as much power as the master port can supply, and the addition of a power-hungry thumb drive may trigger a "USB Power Exceeded" error message and shut the port down.

### GunkBuster's Notebook: Don't Buy "Fat" USB Thumb Drives!

If you've looked at a number of PCs and their USB ports, you may have noticed that USB ports often come in pairs and are "stacked"—that is, set side by side with very little room in between them. The A plugs on the large ends of USB cables are standardized and cannot be so thick that two plugs wouldn't fit side by side in a pair of stacked ports.

Unfortunately, the same can't be said about USB thumb drives. They come in all shapes and sizes (including drives built into small plastic ducks!), and most of them are too thick to allow a pair of thumb drives to be plugged simultaneously into a pair of stacked USB ports. A thick thumb drive plugged into one of a pair of stacked ports may prevent you from plugging *anything* into the second port. Figure 7-7 will give you an idea of how thin a pair of thumb drives must be to fit side by side in a pair of stacked ports.

For this reason, we recommend being careful about the brands of USB thumb drives that you buy. Don't use thumb drives thicker than 11/32" (.343") thick. How wide they are is much less important. We recommend the SanDisk Cruzer Mini thumb drive

**Figure 7-7**
Two thin USB thumb drives in a pair of stacked ports.

product line because the drives are only a hair more than 5/16"
thick and are available "off the peg" at a great many retail stores.
They use relatively little power as thumb drives go, and their only
downside is that they are not bootable, but bootability is a deep
geek feature that most people won't need—or at least won't need
as much as the use of that second stacked port!

# Avoid USB Hub Problems

Our experience has been that USB hubs are pretty random creatures, and the
best way to introduce instability or other puzzling behavior into your PC is to
add a USB hub to it. As we've shown in the previous section about USB's five
big hub gotchas, hubs are involved in almost every sort of USB problem. In this
section, we'll provide several tips that will allow you to avoid certain common
USB problems:

√ Some peripherals just don't like hubs. Often the product documentation will
come out and say so ("Do not plug our BoogaVision Web cam into a USB
hub!"), but sometimes it won't. If a product malfunctions when connected
to a hub, try it in one of the ports built into your PC. If it works, you may
have to give the product a port on the PC itself rather than on a hub.

√ Do not plug an isochronous USB device into a hub. Isochronous devices
require constant bandwidth, and usually lots of it. For best results, plug
isochronous devices into a root hub on the PC and leave the other port or

ports in the root hub empty. If you need another root hub, install an add-in USB port board to your PC. Most such boards provide two additional USB root hubs.

√ Don't plug a USB 2.0 hub into a USB 1.1 port. This is supposed to work, but experience has shown that weird things can happen when a USB 2.0 port is "downstream" from a USB 1.1 hub.

√ Be careful using bus-powered USB hubs. A bus-powered hub can only deliver a portion of the power available from the port into which it is plugged. Attach a couple of power-hungry devices to it (like USB thumb drives, which can consume 300 mA of power or more all by themselves) and the upstream port will overload and shut down. Attach only low-power devices into bus-powered hubs. To determine how much power a USB device consumes, plug it into one of the PC's built-in ports and then display the Power tab in the Device Manager window for USB devices. (See the section "How Fast Is Your USB Port?" earlier in this chapter for instructions on how to do this.) Sometimes a very small gadget can suck a *lot* of power!

√ Only plug USB 1.1 devices into "multi-TT" USB 2.0 hubs, like the IOGear GUH274. Single-TT USB 2.0 hubs will starve your USB 1.1 devices for bandwidth.

√ Divide a single USB port on your PC no more than eight ways. This is a rule of thumb, but a strong one: Count the devices attached to a built-in PC USB port, either directly or through hubs. Eight devices is the limit. If you have more USB devices than that, buy an add-in PCI card that provides additional USB ports and spread the load around.

√ Daisy-chain USB hubs only when all hubs are the same type. In other words, do not daisy-chain a USB 1.1 hub with a USB 2.0 hub. Make all hubs in a chain either USB 1.1 or USB 2.0. Don't mix them. (Better still: Don't daisy-chain hubs at all! Buy and install an add-in board providing more ports for your PC.)

# Use the Correct USB Cables and Cable Length

USB peripherals almost always come with their own cables, so there's rarely any need to buy your own. If you do, buy the best cables that you can, ideally those certified as compatible with USB Hi-Speed and shielded. The maximum length of a USB cable is 5 meters, or about 16.5 feet. One caution: If you buy a peripheral that comes with a shorter cable, don't swap in a longer cable, even if it connects physically at both ends. Some peripherals are designed to connect via short cables for timing or other reasons. (USB Wi-Fi network adapters are the best example of this.) Putting them at the end of a longer cable may cause them to malfunction.

## Active USB Extension Cables

If you must connect to a USB peripheral that is farther than 16 feet away from your PC, you can use an active USB extension cable. Such a cable has a "Type A" (master) plug on one end and a "Type A" jack on the other end. The jack end has a bulge containing a USB repeater, which electronically strengthens the data stream passing through the cable. Active USB extension cables are almost always 16 feet long. They are basically single-port USB hubs. Although some vendors claim that you can daisy-chain them five deep (giving you 80 feet of extension!), we advise against that. Each active USB extension cable requires a little bit of current to power its repeater electronics, and once you stack them five deep, you're using over half the current available from the USB port on your PC. As with true hubs, two of them daisy-chained is the practical limit.

## Shielded Cables and USB Cable Care

The best USB cables are shielded. The shielding is actually more to keep the data flowing smoothly inside the cable than to keep interference from radiating into radios and stereos. If you buy USB cables, go the distance, spend the money, and buy shielded cables certified for use with USB 2.0. Ordinary non–shielded USB cables will work fine with USB 1.1 peripherals, but if you intend to work with peripherals that need the high bandwidth of the USB 2.0 specification (like video cameras and Web cams), shielded cables are a must–have.

You may note that when you buy USB 2.0 cables, they're packaged in an elliptical or round coil, *not* folded back and forth and cinched in the middle with a twist-tie. This is important: If you store or travel with USB cables, roll them in a circular bundle no smaller than six inches in diameter. Do not fold cables back and forth so that the cable contains a number of 180° bends. These sharp bends introduce electrical disturbances into high-speed signals passing through the cable and can cause lost data or data slowdown. Figure 7-8 shows the right way (left) and the wrong way (right) to store USB cables. The general rule: *Never* kink a high-speed data cable!

## What If a USB Device Doesn't Install?

Typically, when you plug a USB device into a PC running Windows 2000 or XP, Windows Plug and Play detects the presence of the new device and pops up a dialog indicating what it found. Sometimes you have to give Windows a

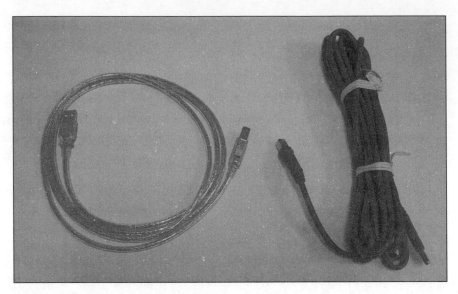

**Figure 7-8**
The right and wrong way to store USB cables.

little guidance on where to find drivers, but most of the time, if drivers are already tucked away on your hard drive somewhere, Windows will find them and your USB device will install without any trouble. Follow the instructions in the Windows wizard that pops up when Windows Plug and Play detects the new USB device.

If you have a hard time making a USB device install, here are some trouble-shooting tips:

√ *Did you fail to follow directions?* USB devices usually come with instructions on how to install them. *Follow those instructions to the letter.* Some USB devices (like thumb drives) are so standard that Windows 2000 and XP will identify and install them without forcing you to install drivers first. (This is *not* true for Windows 9x and Me!) Many USB devices require that you install Windows drivers and support files from a CD before plugging in the USB cable to the device. If you plug the device in before you install its drivers, Windows may misidentify the device as something else.

√ *Does the device require a separate power supply?* Some small USB devices can be powered from the ports they plug into, but large devices like printers and scanners almost always require their own power sources. Is the power source plugged in? Check to be sure that a device with its own power supply is getting power.

√ *Are you attempting to install the device through a USB hub?* Some USB devices just don't like USB hubs and will either refuse to install or, once installed, will misbehave. Digital cameras are notorious for this, as are certain classes of scanners. Usually, devices that require faster data connections are less tolerant of hubs than slower devices like keyboards and mice. In general, hubs are a bad idea. If you need more USB ports than your PC provides, consider installing (or having installed; many computer retailers like Best Buy will do this) a PCI add-in board with additional ports.

√ *Could your PC have a defective or disconnected port?* We've seen PCs with front-panel USB ports that have never been connected to the motherboard, or have been connected incorrectly, with the wrong ribbon cable, conductors in the wrong order, and so on. Most PCs that have front-panel USB ports also have back-panel USB ports. Try the device in one of the back-panel ports. Back-panel ports are almost always mounted directly on the motherboard, and thus the chances of the port being disconnected or incorrectly connected are much less. If you buy a PC with front-panel USB ports that aren't connected or are connected incorrectly, take the PC back to the retailer and complain.

√ *Are you using Windows NT4?* Windows NT4 does not contain native Windows USB support. Some USB devices will install under Windows NT4, but you must install software to support the device before attempting to install the device itself. If you're still running Windows NT4 and wish to make wide use of USB peripherals, consider upgrading to Windows 2000, which will install on nearly all PCs that will run NT4.

√ *Is the device itself defective?* It's always possible that "infant mortality" caused your USB device to be DOA. If it won't install on one PC, try to install it on another PC, especially a PC on which other USB devices have been successfully installed. If it won't install on a second PC, the USB device is probably defective.

# Use FireWire Effectively

USB's main competition is FireWire, a similar and slightly more upscale method of connecting peripherals (especially fast peripherals) to a PC using a serial data stream. FireWire was developed by Apple Computer in the early 1990s and was established as the IEEE 1394 standard by 1995. For a while, only Macintosh computers had FireWire ports. Apple tried to get FireWire established in the PC world toward the end of the 1990s, but once again, the folks at Apple assumed that the world would pay a higher price to use its obviously superior technology. Apple's royalties for using the FireWire patents added a dollar per port to the cost of manufacturing each FireWire-equipped PC (in addition to a $7500 one-time charge to the manufacturer), and in the razor-thin margins of the PC business, that was a cost that many manufacturers chose not to pay, especially with USB available as a royalty-free alternative. This meant that FireWire ports were basically unknown in PCs until Apple caved on the royalty issue in 2000. Starting in 2002, FireWire ports began to be popular on PCs, especially PCs used in connection with digital video.

Until very recently, FireWire data rates were limited to 400 Mbps, which, while high, was not as high as USB 2.0's 480 Mbps. In 2002, the IEEE 1394b standard was approved, which defined FireWire speeds of both 800 Mbps and a breath-taking 1.6 and 3.2 Gbps. At this writing, FireWire 800 peripherals are just beginning to appear in quantity, and FireWire 800 ports have not yet made it into any mainstream PCs to our knowledge. To use FireWire 800, you must buy a PCI add-in board and install it to your PC's expansion bus. FireWire 800 requires completely different cables and connectors from FireWire 400, so it may justifiably be considered a completely separate connection technology.

FireWire 800 peripherals are very expensive, and we will not discuss them further in this book. From here on, when we say "FireWire" we mean FireWire 400.

---

**TIP: Many technical gurus in the industry claim that FireWire 1600 and 3200 will never be implemented in real products. For serial data transfers at those rates, especially on external disk drives, most people are pointing to Serial ATA (SATA) which already works at 1.5 GHz and will soon (with the SATA II spec) work at 3 GHz.**

---

## FireWire vs. USB

FireWire differs from USB in a number of very basic ways. USB is a master-slave technology, which requires that one end of a connection be to a PC running special USB drivers. (This will change in the future with USB On-The-Go, but we're not there yet!) In contrast, FireWire is a peer-to-peer technology. Each FireWire peripheral does not require a separate connection to the PC host. Instead, FireWire peripherals can daisy-chain, one after another, from a single port on the PC. All such daisy-chained peripherals must share the bandwidth available from the PC's FireWire port, but the clutter of hubs and cables required by USB are not an issue with FireWire.

For reasons involving the underlying technology that are difficult to explain, FireWire requires less computing power from the PC to work well. Also, while the USB 2.0 data rate of 480 Mbps seems higher than FireWire's 400 Mbps, due to more efficient implementations, FireWire is actually a little faster (in terms of moving actual data over a cable) than USB 2.0.

## Power Struggle: FireWire, USB, and I-link

Like USB, FireWire can source modest amounts of power through its ports. The precise amount of power that peripherals can draw from a PC's FireWire port is not as standard as USB's and has been the cause of some problems. Some technical documents claim that FireWire can source 45 watts (W) of power through a single connector, but no one has ever implemented a port with that much power potential. Apple Computer's ports source a maximum of 15 W of DC power, compared to a USB port's 2.5 W. Unfortunately, 15 W isn't quite enough to power large external disk drive units, so most FireWire peripherals still supply their own power from an external power supply.

To make things even messier, Sony developed its own variation of FireWire called I-Link, which can be found on certain laptops, especially Sony's. I-Link ports, while in other ways identical to FireWire, do not source power at all. Some peripherals expecting to draw power from the FireWire port will thus not work on laptops or PCs containing I-Link ports.

---

**TIP:** If you try to use a bus-powered FireWire peripheral in a PC or laptop and it won't function for lack of power, check to see if the port is an I-Link port.

---

## Tips for Using FireWire Effectively

FireWire isn't used nearly as much on PCs as USB, but it has the advantage of being a better engineered and faster (along with more expensive) technology. So to close out this chapter, we'll provide a few FireWire tips in case you're in that elite user base:

√   FireWire and Windows XP Service Pack 2 do not appear to get along. Many have reported that when they upgraded to SP2, their FireWire ports stopped working entirely. At this writing, the problem has not been resolved, but we suspect that Microsoft will post patches or driver updates soon. Keep checking Microsoft's site. In the meantime, if you're a FireWire user and planning to apply SP2, hold off for awhile.

√   Be careful how you insert a FireWire plug in your PC's FireWire port. Although it's theoretically impossible to insert the plug reversed 180° from its proper orientation, a person pressing on the plug with sufficient force will cause it to bend the thin metal sides of the port and enter the port part way. The reversed plug only has to go in a fraction of an inch before the power pin will contact one of the two data pins. This will destroy the FireWire port instantly and may also damage the peripheral on the other end of the cable.

√   Do not twist or kink FireWire cables. There are two hazards in doing so: Any high-speed data cable, when kinked, will slow down the passage of data through the cable and cause errors. Worse, if a poorly manufactured cable is twisted hard enough, the conductors in one of the plugs may break or (much worse) bridge power to one of the data pins, destroying the port.

√   If you find yourself inserting a FireWire cable into your PC's FireWire port frequently, consider leaving the cable plugged into the PC and plug the FireWire peripheral (external disk drive, Web cam, camcorder, whatever) into the other end of the cable when needed. The physical portion of a FireWire port, unfortunately, is relatively fragile, and it's much easier to replace a worn cable than a worn port on the front or back panel of your PC!

√   If you discover that a FireWire device isn't recognized by Windows when you plug it into your PC's FireWire port, *do not plug another device into the port* without having the PC port looked at by an experienced technician. If the port has been damaged by physical force (say, by someone attempting to insert a FireWire plug backwards), the damaged port may in turn damage a device subsequently plugged into it. The Web abounds with reports of people plugging a $1000 digital camcorder into a damaged FireWire port only to find that the shorted-out port damaged the port electronics in the camcorder, causing a large (several hundred dollar) repair bill.

# Summing Up

More and more peripherals are being shipped with either USB or FireWire interfaces rather than those cranky old PC serial or parallel ports. There are two versions of both FireWire and USB, but the two versions of FireWire use different connectors and may be considered separate connection technologies. Be mindful of the differences between USB 1.1 and 2.0 because compatibility, while good, has its limits. USB 2.0 peripherals generally require a USB 2.0 port to work well, and such ports have only become common on PCs since about 2003. Although a single USB port may be divided and thus shared through a USB hub, some peripherals refuse to work through hubs, and hubs should be used sparingly, and with caution. If you need lots of ports, it's always better to install an add-in USB port board to your PC's PCI bus. Don't kink FireWire or USB cables, and store them in loose circular rolls rather than tight, back-and-forth bundles.

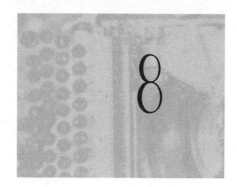

# Setting Up a Basic Network for Sharing Dial-Up Internet Connections

## Degunking Checklist:

√ Learn what hardware you need to set up a basic network with the PCs in your home.

√ Properly connect your hardware and physically create a network.

√ Use the Network Setup Wizard to share a single dial-up connection to the Internet.

√ Determine how fast the data you send travels from one PC to another.

√ Apply some basic tricks for securing your network from both outsiders and the people who access your network in the home.

√ Understand why high-speed Internet or DSL connections can't be used with Internet Connection Sharing.

This is the first chapter of four that are designed to help you better set up and degunk how your PC communicates directly with other PCs, with PC peripherals, and with the Internet. As every PC user now knows, networking—whether with your printer beside the PC or with a server in Singapore—is extremely important, and when it is set up properly and working well, you can really do a lot with your PC. Unfortunately, networking can get complicated very quickly, especially with all of the technologies and standards that are available today, and it's very easy to get into a situation in which your PC communications get really gunked up. When this happens, you won't be able to access the Internet efficiently and you won't be able to easily transfer data to other PCs or peripherals. Gunked-up communications systems can really waste a lot of your time.

In this chapter we'll show you how to set up and degunk a basic network so you can share a single Internet dial-up connection with more than one PC. If you have a dial-up connection to the Internet and more than one PC in your home, you could (and should) be sharing that Internet connection among all your PCs. If you have a PC running Windows XP, it's very simple to set up. You'll need a few pieces of hardware, though, since you'll need to physically connect the PCs so they can share information.

To set up a shared Internet connection, you'll need to be familiar with basic networking hardware and the steps involved in getting everything connected and everyone online. Of course, once the network is configured, you can do much more, including sharing files and media, playing games, and sharing hardware such as printers and scanners. In Chapter 9 we'll show you how to improve your Internet connections by getting rid of slow dial-up technology and moving to a DSL or cable broadband connection. In Chapter 10, we'll concentrate more on showing you how to degunk a complete network, and finally in Chapter 11, you'll learn how to set up and degunk a simple wireless network. As you work through these chapters, we'll show you how to degunk your communications capabilities at different levels. Since this chapter is our starting point, we'll focus on making sure your basic network is configured so that Internet Connection Sharing works as it should.

# Understand the Basic Ethernet Hardware Requirements

To share a dial-up Internet connection, your PCs must be networked. *Networked* means that the computers are physically connected and can pass data between them via appropriate hardware and software. There are several ways to create a network, many of which are covered in Chapter 10 when we show you how to degunk a full PC-wired network. For now, we'll look at the simplest way to network computers, which includes using network interface cards, a switch (or other device), and Ethernet cables. If you want to create a network and share a dial-up Internet connection with the PCs in your home, you'll need to purchase and set up this equipment.

# Network Interface Cards and Ethernet Cables

You'll need three things to share an Internet connection and set up a basic wired network:

√   A length of Ethernet cable for each computer

√   A network interface card for each computer

√   A single hub, switch, or router to connect everything together

*Ethernet cable* is needed to transfer data in a wired network. The Ethernet cable connects to each computer through the computer's *network interface card*. The network interface card is the device that communicates what comes through the Ethernet cable to the computer and vice versa. The other end of the Ethernet cable connects to a device such as a *switch* or *hub* (detailed later), and all of these things connected correctly and working together allow the data to be transferred between computers.

---

**TIP:** *If all of your equipment is new (especially if your PC is a laptop), you may have wireless capabilities and not even know it. If that's the case and you plan to only use a wireless network, skip to Chapter 11 where we show you how to set up and degunk a wireless network. There's no need to be wired first if you intend to go wireless!*

---

You'll first want to make sure each PC has a network interface card, and if any PC lacks a network card, you'll have to install one. To check, look at the back of each PC for a jack that looks like it could accept a telephone cord, only a little larger. (The jack that accepts the phone cord is the modem; you're looking for a jack slightly bigger, with eight bright copper wires visible inside it.) Almost all newer PCs have one. A sample Ethernet card is shown in Figure 8-1.

If you don't yet have a network interface card, you have three options:

√   You can purchase one and install it yourself.

√   You can take your PC to a computer store or repair shop and have one installed there.

√   You can ask a friend or colleague to install one for you.

If those are not viable options—perhaps you need to connect a laptop that can't be upgraded, or you don't have any available slots in your motherboard—you'll have to take a different approach.

**Figure 8-1**
Network interface cards are installed (or come preinstalled) inside the
PC's tower and allow the computer to communicate via Ethernet.

If you have an available USB port, you can purchase a USB-to-Ethernet adapter.
A sample adapter is shown in Figure 8-2. This type of adapter allows you to
convert an unused USB port to Ethernet. Figure 8-2 also shows how the adapter
connects to the Ethernet cable.

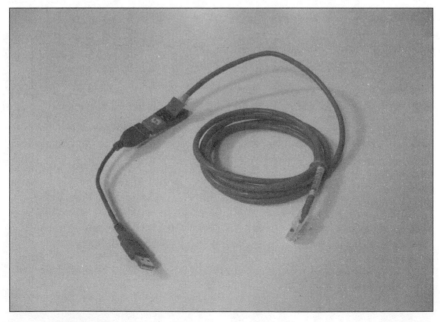

**Figure 8-2**
If adding a network interface card is not an option, a USB-to-Ethernet adapter
will do in a pinch.

If you have a laptop that lacks an Ethernet port but has an open PC card (PCMCIA) slot, you can buy an Ethernet PC card that provides an Ethernet port very inexpensively, often for less than $20 on sale. Higher-end cards often combine an Ethernet port with a 56K dial-up modem, like the Linksys PCMLM56, shown in Figure 8-3.

**Figure 8-3**

The Linksys PCMLM56 Ethernet/FAX Modem card. (Photo courtesy of Linksys.)

# Hubs, Switches, and Routers

Once you have verified that each PC has some way to connect to the Ethernet cable, you'll be ready to move forward. You'll now need to purchase a hub, switch, or router. These devices help transfer the data to the other computers on the network. Hubs are the cheapest, switches are next, and routers are the most expensive. Any of these devices accepts the other end of the Ethernet cable from each computer and allows them to communicate and share data. Figure 8-4 shows an example of a router.

If you only have a few dollars to spend, you'll have to settle for a hub. Hubs operate on shared bandwidth, though, and don't offer the network performance that switches or routers do. As you'd probably guess, you get what you pay for. If you want better performance, consider the next option—a switch.

Switches are a good choice for most dial-up users. Switches create momentary, dedicated, point-to-point connections between two PCs on a network and don't use the shared bandwidth technology that hubs do. Therefore, you'll get better throughput (performance) with a switch than you would with a hub.

**Figure 8-4**
This router is used to connect the PCs together via their Ethernet cables.

Finally, and if money isn't an issue, go ahead and splurge for a router. This is especially important if you're thinking that you may upgrade eventually to a high-speed broadband Internet connection like DSL or cable, as we'll discuss in Chapter 9. You'll need a router if you upgrade and plan to share that connection.

Routers offer much more than hubs or switches, too. A router connects networks; for example, your (tiny) network and the global Internet. The router knows what your network consists of and knows exactly where to send information that it receives from the Internet. When connected to a broadband Internet connection, it routes data from the Internet to the computers that requested it and handles data transfers among your networked PCs as well. It can also act as a firewall and provide relatively strong protection from crackers and automated network attacks from worms and scripts. Routers are a good choice for anyone, even someone with only a single computer connected to the Internet via broadband. If you can afford it—and especially if you intend to upgrade to a broadband connection at some point—we suggest going with a router.

---

*TIP: To learn more information about hubs, switches, and routers, check out Chapter 10.*

# Make the Physical Connections

With your network interface cards working properly, connect all cards to the hub, switch, or router via Ethernet cables. You'll only need one Ethernet cable per computer. There will typically be four or five Ethernet cable jacks on the back panel of the hub or switch. (Make sure you buy a hub or switch with enough ports to connect all your PCs!) Any PC can be plugged into any jack. See Figure 8-5.

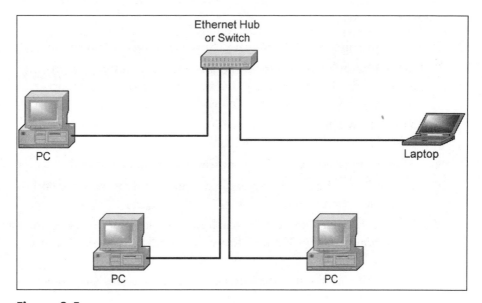

**Figure 8-5**
This is an eight-port switch. If possible, purchase a switch over a hub.

Once all the PCs are connected, turn on the hub, switch, or router.

Finally, make sure all the PCs are turned on and check the lights on the network interface cards and on the hub, switch, or router. These lights are green when everything is working properly. If they aren't, double-check your cables, cards, and hardware. If you don't see green, something isn't right. If you're having problems, refer to Chapter 10 for help, or visit the Help and Support Center on the Windows XP computer. There are several troubleshooting wizards to help you figure out what's gone wrong.

# Set Up Internet Connection Sharing

Internet Connection Sharing (ICS) lets you share a single dial-up connection with the PCs on your network. And now that you have a physical network, you can begin setting up both the network and Internet Connection Sharing. Keep in mind too that even though you'll be sharing a single connection with several computers, each PC can be configured with different e-mail accounts and settings, with different Internet favorites, and with different address books. There's no limit to what you can do, and it's important to understand that each computer stands alone, almost as though it has its own private connection to the Internet. It's a great way to get everyone in the family online without having to spend a lot more on DSL or high-speed Internet.

Before setting up Internet Connection Sharing though, let's verify a few things:

√  Every PC you want to share the connection with must have a network interface card installed and working properly, or have the appropriate adapter. Check for a green light on each card.

√  The hub, switch, or router must be installed, plugged in, and working properly.

√  All software drivers for all network hardware must be installed.

√  Each PC must have an Ethernet cable running from its network port to the hub, switch, or router.

√  You must choose one PC to be the host computer, and that computer must be running Windows XP. We'll focus on using XP's Network Connection Wizard to enable ICS. More on this in the next section.

√  A dial-up connection to the Internet must be established and connected from the host PCs.

√  The network cannot be set up as a domain but rather must be set up as a workgroup. You should not attempt to configure Internet Connection Sharing on a network that contains servers or domain controllers, DHCP or DNS servers, or static IP addressing. If this means nothing to you, you're probably fine—domains are an advanced topic and are generally used only in business environments.

## Setting Up Internet Connection Sharing

If you've met all of the criteria we just introduced, you're almost there. To complete the procedure, you have to choose a host computer and work through the Internet Connection Sharing installation wizard on it. The host computer must connect directly to the Internet via dial-up, and it must be running Windows XP. We'll use Windows XP's Network Setup Wizard to configure it. It also helps if this PC is your most powerful computer, and it must be connected to the Internet at the time the wizard is run.

After choosing a host computer, turn on all of the other PCs. Then, you'll need to perform the following tasks on the host computer:

1.  Click Start, point to All Programs, point to Accessories, point to Communications, and select Network Setup Wizard. Click Next to start the wizard.

2.  Select "This Computer Connects Directly to the Internet. The Other Computers on My Network Connect to the Internet through This Computer." Click Next.

3.  From the choices offered, select your dial-up Internet connection. Click Next. Figure 8-6 shows this wizard page.

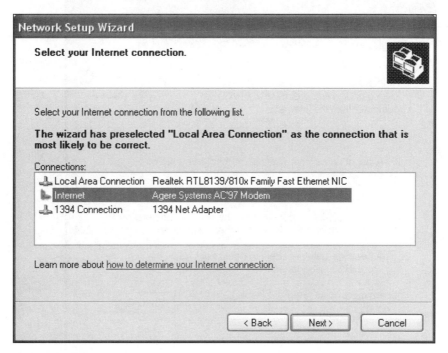

**Figure 8-6**

Select your dial-up connection when prompted.

4.  When prompted to choose what private connection to use to connect this PC to the networked PCs, select your local area connection. Click Next.

5.  Type a computer description if desired. Leave the computer name as it is. Click Next.

6.  In the Name Your Network page, type the name of your workgroup. Click Next.

7.  Choose to turn on or turn off file and printer sharing. We suggest turning it on. Click Next. Click Next again to apply the settings.

Once the wizard has completed, you need to verify that Internet Connection Sharing is enabled. To do so follow these steps:

1.  Click Start, and open Control Panel. Open the Network Connections applet.

2. Right–click your Internet connection and select Properties.

3. From the Advanced tab, verify that the options under Internet Connection Sharing are enabled, as shown in Figure 8-7. If they aren't, check them. Click OK.

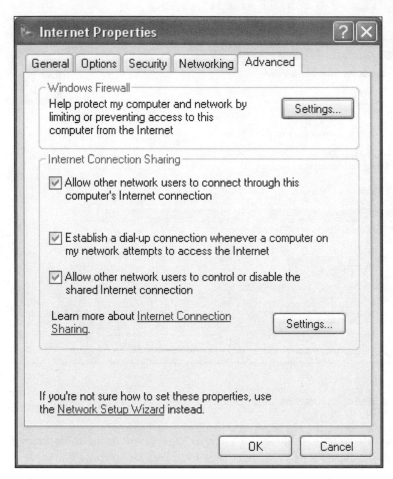

**Figure 8-7**
Verify that Internet Connection Sharing is enabled before continuing.

---

*TIP: On an existing network, you can configure Internet Connection Sharing by checking the appropriate boxes in the Internet Properties page Advanced tab (Figure 8-7) and then configuring the networked computers. You don't need to work through the Network Setup Wizard if your network already exists.*

---

## GunkBuster's Notebook: Staying in Control with Internet Connection Sharing

If you're worried that others have too much control over your Internet connection, you can degunk it. You can tighten it up a little by configuring the settings differently than we suggested in step 3 earlier. While we suggested checking all available boxes, as shown in Figure 8-7, you certainly don't have too.

The three options are as follows:

√ Allow other network users to connect through this computer's Internet connection.

√ Establish a dial-up connection whenever a computer on my network attempts to access the Internet.

√ Allow other network users to control or disable the shared Internet connection.

You'll have to check the first option to allow network users to connect to the Internet through your dial-up connection. That's how Internet Connection Sharing works. However, you *don't* have to check the other two. If you have a teenager you don't want accessing the Internet from their room at night, check this box. If you don't want another network user to have the ability to disconnect the connection, check that box. You do have some control, and if you need it, it's there.

Now, at each of the other networked PCs in the home, follow these steps to make sure all of the other computers can access the shared Internet connection:

1. Run the Network Setup Wizard. In the page that asks you to describe this computer, instead of choosing "This Computer Connects Directly through the Internet….," choose "This Computer Connects to the Internet through a Residential Gateway or through Another Computer on My Network."

2. Continue working through the wizard as detailed earlier. Make sure you correctly type the name of the workgroup when you get to that page.

3. Continue through the wizard until it ends.

4. Open Internet Explorer.

5. From the Tools menu, choose Internet Options.

6. Choose Connections.

7. Under Dial-Up and Virtual Private Network Settings, select Never Dial a Connection. Choose Set Default.

8. Click LAN Settings on that same page.

9. Clear Automatically Detect Settings. Clear Use a Proxy Server for Your LAN. Click OK.

10. Click OK, which closes the Internet Options dialog box.

11. Once all of the PCs have been configured in this manner, restart all of the PCs. Reconnect the host to the Internet.

You should now have all computers sharing that one connection!

# Security Issues to Consider

With everyone in the family on the Internet, you'll need to take steps to secure your network and your computers. There are tons of programs you can purchase to help you with this, including Norton AntiVirus or McAfee Internet Security Suite, Spy Catcher, Zone Alarm, and others, but there are also programs you can download for free from the Internet. We suggest, before going any further, that you *purchase* and install antivirus software on every computer on the network.

## Antivirus Software

Computer viruses are like head colds; if you get one, chances are everyone in your family and all of your closest friends will get it too. You have to get protected and stay protected. Of course, with a cold you can wash your hands obsessively and stay away from others who are sick. With computer viruses, it's a little more complex.

There are several antivirus software programs available for purchase that can protect you from all the latest viruses. The most popular programs offered are from Norton and McAfee. Norton AntiVirus currently offers a three-user license that allows you to install the program on up to three computers in the home. McAfee offers a comparable application at a comparable price. It doesn't matter which you choose though, as long as you get something, install it, and keep it up-to-date and running in the background at all times.

Antivirus applications from either company can be purchased from a store or purchased online and either shipped or downloaded. If you purchase it from a store or order it online and choose to have it shipped, you'll get it on a CD. Ordering a physical CD may be a good option for you if you think you'll need to reinstall it often or if you plan to purchase a new PC in the next couple of years. You'll need the CD to reinstall easily. Additionally, you may not need to purchase a new version of the software for a few years; most companies offer an online upgrade, making it unnecessary to return to the store for a new CD or new software. So, having the software on a CD makes good sense for most people.

In contrast to purchasing the software from a store or having it shipped on a CD, almost all companies also offer download delivery for their products. Downloading the software can save you upward of $20, which is certainly an incentive! If you have a CD burner, simply burn the downloaded files to a CD the moment you get it, just in case you ever need it. Make sure, no matter what route you take, that you use a permanent marker and write the installation code on the CD or on the CD case!

---

**TIP:** *If you do download the software and never burn it to a CD, you can almost always go back to the site and download it again, by way of reinstallation. However, you'll need to spend time creating a username and password and verifying that you really did purchase the product. Sometimes, this can be a gunked-up, time-consuming mess.*

---

Both companies also offer additional software you may think you need, including virus scan software, firewall software, spam killer software, anti-spyware, and anti-adware or pop-up blocking software. Let's take a look now at some of those, and then you can decide if that's money well spent or not.

---

**TIP:** *Every few months, visit the Web site of the antivirus software you purchased and look for new "builds." Builds are newer editions of the application you purchased and contain service packs and other items you'll want. These updates aren't always obtained through the online updates you schedule.*

---

## GunkBuster's Notebook: Staying Up-To-Date

There's absolutely no point in purchasing and installing antivirus software if you don't take the extra time to configure it to work as it should. Sure, after installation you're prompted to get the latest virus definitions, and we're sure you will, but you also have to make sure the software is configured to get additional definitions daily or weekly. Those definitions are what protect your PC because they spot and repair the newest viruses on the Internet, those that might not have even existed when you bought and installed the antivirus software.

You should also configure any other bundled applications to run on a schedule. This can include scanning your PC for viruses, spyware, or adware daily or weekly, scanning incoming and outgoing e-mail, and blocking scripts that can contain viruses. Some also offer options to check for problems with the operating system or optimize performance. Whatever is offered you should use regularly. Figure 8-8 shows the status page for a healthy and up-to-date system. This is the way your antivirus software status page should look all the time.

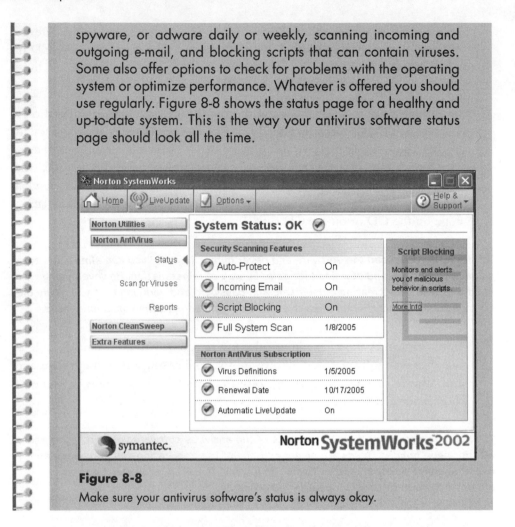

**Figure 8-8**
Make sure your antivirus software's status is always okay.

# Spyware and Adware

There are harmful things on the Internet you can catch besides viruses. Spyware and adware are two of them. Neither is a virus; instead they're more like someone going through your trash after you take it out to the curb. If they target you, they'll find out what you eat, what you buy, where you shop, and who you are. In a worst-case scenario, they'll steal your identity or find out your best-kept secrets. In this same manner, someone may be watching what you're doing on the Internet; they may be following through your movements, finding what Web sites you visit, and sometimes following your keystrokes. And, they're personalizing malicious applications just for you.

To avoid this, and to remove any spyware or adware already on your PC, you'll need third-party software for protection. It's just as important as having antivirus software. McAfee claims that 91 percent of all home PCs are infected with spyware, and we believe it. However, with spyware and adware, you don't necessarily have to purchase the software from a store or online; there are many places that offer free software just for this purpose.

Lavasoft, at **www.lavasoftusa.com**, offers a free program called Ad-Aware Personal. It's simple to download and install, and each time you run it, you're prompted to get new definitions. Ad-Aware is then run to find and delete adware and spyware on your PC. We like this program and recommend it. Figure 8-9 shows the program in action.

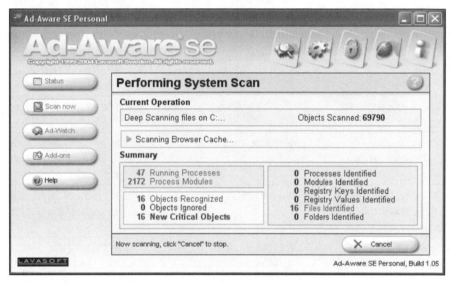

**Figure 8-9**
Ad-Aware is a comprehensive, free, adware detection and removal program.

# Schedule for Securing Your PC with Third-Party Software

If you're wondering how often you should run all of the programs, tests, and scheduled applications mentioned in the previous two sections, wonder no more. Table 8-1 details it all for you. Follow these guidelines, and you should be safe while surfing the Internet.

**Table 8-1   Schedule for Securing Your PC with Third-Party Software**

| Application | Schedule This Task | When to Run Manually |
|---|---|---|
| Antivirus: Get new definitions | At least once a week; those with sensitive systems and data, once each day. | Whenever there is a new virus alert, or if you think your PC may have a virus. |
| Antivirus: Full system scan and/or security checks | Once a week, and when the computer is idle. | Whenever you think your PC may have a virus. |
| Antivirus: Protect incoming and outgoing e-mail | Should be on all the time. | Should be on all the time. |
| Antivirus: Automatic updates | Should be enabled all the time. If you do not have an "always on" connection to the Internet, log on at least every other day to retrieve these updates. | Should be enabled at all times. However, if you have a dial-up connection and log on infrequently, perform this task each time you log on. |
| Anti-spyware | Should be enabled at all times. | Run manual scans and removal programs at least weekly. |
| Anti-adware | Should be enabled at all times. | Run manual scans and removal programs at least weekly. |
| Firewall, if your application offers it | Should be enabled at all times. | Should be enabled at all times. |
| Additional utilities: Optimize performance | Two to four times a year. | Anytime the computer is reacting slowly or unidentifiable problems are occurring. |
| Additional utilities: Find and fix problems with the operating system. | Once a month. | Anytime the computer is reacting slowly or unidentifiable problems are occurring. |
| Additional utilities: System maintenance | Only when you need maintenance information or need to run tests to uncover problems. | Anytime the computer is reacting slowly or unidentifiable problems are occurring. |
| Visit the manufacturer's Web site for new builds | If on a schedule, once a month. | Two to four times a year. |

# Degunk Your Own Surfing Habits to Stay Safe

No matter how well you protect your PC with software, you won't be able to keep your personal information and identity safe while on the Internet if you don't surf safely yourself. (Say that 10 times fast!) We're always amazed when people express surprise that their e-mail is covered up in spam or their identity or credit card numbers are stolen. They got into trouble on the Internet, they'll admit that, but they often say they have all the latest software and definitions, have adware and spyware checkers, and run virus checks on their computer weekly, so they place the blame on the software! It's hard to explain that *it isn't that trouble finds them*; it's that *they find trouble*!

To stay safe on the Internet and protect yourself, your credit card numbers, your social security number, and similar data, you have to degunk your own surfing habits. Here are some guidelines:

√   Never respond to e-mails from banks or credit card companies who ask you to log on to a specific site or reply to an e-mail with a credit card number or social security number. Real banks and credit card companies would never use e-mail to ask for this information.

√   Only give your name, address, phone number, e-mail, or credit card numbers to valid sites you know, such as large department stores, online book stores, and online software businesses. Make sure, when inputting this information, the site is secure. The Web address should start with https://. (Note the extra *s* on the end.)

√   Don't share photos of yourself with strangers. People are not always who they say they are.

√   Do not give your address or phone number to anyone in a chat room or on the Internet. Use a nickname too; never use your real name.

√   When logging on to your PC, don't log on as an administrator unless you have to. To surf the Internet, log on as a limited user. Malicious code can't get quite as far through a limited user account as it can through an administrator's.

√   If you have children that surf the Internet, put the PC in a family room and install a program like CYBERsitter, Cyber Patrol, or Net Nanny.

√   Don't use the same username and password for all sites you visit. If a hacker finds the username and password for one site, they'll know them for all the others.

√   Never respond to spam e-mail. That will only tell them they've reached a valid e-mail address.

√   Don't fall for e-mail scams. Most people asking for money or help via e-mail are not honest people.

# The Tech Side of Internet Connection Sharing, Dial-Up, Routers, and Broadband Connections

Not all connections are created equal. There are dial-up connections, cable Internet connections, Digital Subscriber Line (DSL) connections, satellite connections, and point-to-point wireless connections. At the time this book was written, the most common Internet connection was dial-up, with cable Internet or DSL (collectively known as *broadband*) coming in more than a few paces behind at second. Broadband is the current "must have" technology, though, and millions of people either are, or will soon be, upgrading to it. Broadband Internet connections are at least 3 times—and sometimes 10 times—as fast as the fastest dial-up connection.

In this chapter, we focused on ICS with dial-up, but in the next chapter, we'll talk about moving to broadband and ways to share that connection. Before moving on, though, we want to focus on a few technical aspects of both, so you'll have an idea what you're doing if and when you do decide to make the move to broadband.

## ICS and Dial-Up

When you use Internet Connection Sharing with a dial-up Internet connection, you must have two pieces of hardware on the host computer: a dial-up modem and a network interface card. The modem connects to the ISP's customer network and obtains access to the Internet through it. The modem usually obtains an Internet Protocol (IP) address automatically from the ISP, through a protocol called Dynamic Host Configuration Protocol (DHCP). An IP address is necessary to connect to the Internet.

After ICS is enabled on a network, it performs a similar task for all of your networked PCs. ICS assigns each PC on your local area network an IP address in a block of IP addresses reserved as "local." These local IP addresses always begin with 192.168. A typical local IP address would be 192.168.0.1, and the other computers on the network are given addresses that are compatible with it. Local IP addresses can be used *only* on your local home network. They cannot be accessed directly from the Internet. This is a good thing because it prevents shadowy characters elsewhere in the world from having easy access to your home.

The ICS host computer acts as both a router and a firewall. The networked computers can then obtain access to the Internet through the host computer while remaining on the same network with one another, sharing files and printers. One caution: Because all PCs share the same connection to the Internet, dial-up Internet sharing can be quite slow, especially if several users are accessing the Internet simultaneously.

## Routers and Broadband

Once you upgrade to a broadband Internet connection (cable, DSL, satellite, or point-to-point wireless), the general principles are the same. Your networked PCs all access the Internet over the network. Because there's so much more bandwidth in a broadband connection, each individual user has more bandwidth to use, and shared broadband connections "feel" much faster than dial-up connections.

The big difference is that ICS is no longer in the picture, and thus you have to buy a hardware router appliance to parcel out local IP addresses and intermediate between local addresses and the global Internet. Such routers are now quite inexpensive; at this writing, good ones may be had for less than $50 new or under $70 with built-in wireless connectivity. With a wireless router, you can add a wireless card to your laptop and check your e-mail from a deck chair out on the patio!

Virtually all routers contain a built-in network switch, with between four or six network ports, depending on the make and model. This built-in switch makes a separate switch or hub unnecessary. You create your local network by connecting all your PCs to the network switch ports on the back of the router. This allows your PCs to communicate with one another and share files and printers, even when the broadband connection is unavailable. The cable or DSL modem installed at your house by your broadband provider connects to the "WAN" or "Internet" port on the back of the router.

All the machinery inside ICS is also present inside the router. The router passes out local IP addresses to all your networked PCs and manages the traffic between your PCs and the global Internet. It acts as a strong hardware firewall between the Internet and your local network, just as ICS does.

It sounds complex, but in truth it's actually a little easier than setting up ICS. In Chapter 9, we'll explain how to assemble a broadband-based network and get it functioning efficiently.

# Summing Up

In this chapter you learned how to set up a basic network using a network hub or switch and how to share a single dial-up Internet connection among the networked computers. Internet Connection Sharing, a part of Windows operating systems since Windows 98, makes it easy. Combined with Windows XP's Network Setup Wizard, it's almost effortless.

Once online, it's up to you to secure your connections. Your router provides a good deal of protection against network hackers, worms, and "script kiddies (malicious scripts)," but it does nothing to protect you against viruses, spyware, and adware. You'll need antivirus software and spyware, as well as adware detection and repair programs. While we suggest purchasing antivirus software from well-known third-party software makers, many adware and spyware checking programs can be obtained for free. Either way, it's important to run those checks often and on a schedule for the best protection possible.

In the next chapter, we'll talk about how to move from dial-up to broadband Internet. Although it'll cost more, you'll enjoy the freedom a high-speed connection brings. Just remember to keep that antivirus software up-to-date!

# Moving to DSL or Cable Internet

## Degunking Checklist:

√ Know the difference between high-speed cable Internet and DSL and how to make the best choice when upgrading.

√ Explore other options for high-speed connections, including satellite, wireless, ISDN, and T1.

√ Select a high-speed provider in your area.

√ Understand the differences between cable and DSL modems and how to choose a router. Learn about other items you'll need to set up your connection.

√ Set up a DSL or cable Internet connection.

√ Configure your setup to get the best performance possible.

If you're tired of your old dial-up connection and ready to upgrade to something faster, you're in the right place. Getting rid of your trusty (or not-so-trusty) dial-up connection can be unnerving, especially if you don't know the difference between cable, DSL, or satellite, and how broadband figures into any of them. It's worse if you watch the commercials on television and you have more than one choice of technology or more than a few providers. How do you decide what's best and who's going to install it? These can be tough choices.

Additionally, we know you've heard horror stories from those who've upgraded before you. Your friends and family didn't know they needed this cable or that cable, or they couldn't figure out how to install the router or the modem. Maybe they didn't even know the difference between a router and a modem. It can be trying.

Not to worry, help is here. In this chapter, we'll show you how to select a type of connection, select a provider, buy or lease the proper equipment, and even install it yourself. Work your way through this chapter, perform our Internet connection degunking steps, and you'll become a member of the twenty-first century—broadband and all!

# Understand How Broadband Works

Broadband is high-speed Internet. It is generally considered high-speed cable Internet or DSL, but it is really a generic term for any type of high-speed access to the Internet. There are technologies that provide broadband connections from a satellite, or from an antenna farm on a mountaintop, though these are much less common. Cable and DSL are currently the most popular, and thus, the ones we'll focus on in this chapter. Since there are other options for broadband, to make the best choice possible, you need to know the difference between all of them and understand how each technology works. We'll start with high-speed cable Internet.

## High-Speed Cable Internet

High-speed cable Internet is an option in most residential areas in or near reasonably sized cities. Cable Internet comes through existing digital cable lines, the same lines that bring cable TV into your home. Cable is a shared network, meaning that there is only so much bandwidth available in a single segment of the cable network and all subscribers within that segment share the bandwidth. You may experience slower service if everyone in your neighborhood is online at the same time—and you may see much higher speeds in the middle of the night, when you've mostly got the local cable segment to yourself. This is rarely a problem with modern cable systems though.

Cable Internet is an "always on" connection, and stated speeds vary by carrier and by plan. Many cable Internet providers claim that their connection is two times faster than 1.5 Mbps DSL and 50 times faster than dial-up. Most never guarantee a particular speed, though, because speeds can and do vary over time as the load on the local cable segment changes. However, fast is fast, and cable is certainly that. Plus, it's always "there," and you lose no time bringing up a dialer window and waiting for all the funny noises to run their course. Cable Internet is available for a flat, monthly rate from several providers.

## DSL

DSL, or Digital Subscriber Line, uses your ordinary copper telephone line to carry data between your home and the Internet. You won't need to get off the phone to use it, though; the technology is more complex than that, and it's not simply a "super dial-up" system. Data is carried on a high-frequency RF (radio frequency) signal that can travel over the phone line at the same time as your voice audio signals. Neither interferes with the other. Most DSL providers claim speeds of 1.5 Mbps. DSL is also an "always on" service, but unlike cable, offers a dedicated line to the customer. Your data path between your home and the central office of the phone carrier is not shared by other people, and thus theoretically you shouldn't have bottlenecks with DSL as you occasionally do with cable at peak times.

However, there *can* still be bottlenecks, or slowdowns in service, even if the provider doesn't always admit it. That's because even though DSL subscribers do not share the line in their neighborhood, they do share the link between a central office and its network backbone; that means there can still be occasional problems when too many people are using the service at the same time; typically in the evening between 7:00 and 10:00 P.M. DSL, like cable Internet, is available at a flat, monthly rate. It is our experience that a high-speed cable Internet connection is faster than DSL.

---

*TIP: Setup costs for cable and DSL are about the same. You'll need a DSL modem, and if you have a home network or want extra protection, a router as well. You can rent both for an additional fee per month, or you can purchase your own. The details vary from carrier to carrier. We'll provide more information on this later in the chapter.*

---

# Explore Other High-Speed Internet Options

Currently, high-speed cable Internet and DSL are the most popular options. But other options are available that you may prefer. They include satellite, point-to-point wireless, T1, and ISDN, to name a few. Generally speaking, though, these are either more expensive or slower than cable and DSL, offering an explanation as to why they are less popular. They are most common in areas where DSL and cable are not yet available, and they may be your only choice.

## Satellite

Satellite service is a good option if no other options exist or if you already have a satellite dish. If you live way out in the woods and there's no cable or DSL service available, this could be your *only* option. Like cable and DSL, satellite service is available at a flat, monthly fee, but service plans almost always cost more than cable and DSL do.

Many satellite providers claim speeds of up to 1,024 Kbps for downloads and up to 100 Kbps for uploads if you purchase the best equipment offered. (Notice these rates are in Kbps, not Mbps as cable and DSL are.)

---

**TIP: Kbps stands for kilobits per second, or, thousands of bits per second. Mbps stands for megabits per second, or millions of bits per second.**

---

You can expect slower speeds with lower-end equipment and higher speeds with higher-end equipment. Satellite offers a connection up to 10 times faster than dial-up—but most of the time, your speed will (at best) be two or three times that of dial-up. Getting connected with satellite can be quite expensive too. For satellite, you'll need the following equipment:

√ A terminal for transmitting data through the system's antenna and outdoor electronics up to the satellite and back down to the satellite's network operations center, as well as a satellite dish. This equipment starts at around $400.

√ A router if you have a hub or switch and the terminal does not offer additional Ethernet ports that perform routing services. This equipment ranges from $30 to $300

√ Installation of the satellite dish and equipment. This usually runs between $200 and $500.

If you already have a satellite dish, you may be tempted to choose a satellite service. However, remember that it will be slower than previous options, and it also costs a little more. Look into other options if there are any.

## Point-To-Point Wireless

"Fixed wireless broadband Internet Access starting at $199 a month" reads one Web ad we recently ran across. If that's enough to scare you off, go ahead and skip to the next section! Wireless broadband access is often expensive, that's for sure—but everything depends on the local carrier. Some areas are served by wireless broadband for as little as $40 per month, with the typical price being $70 to $100. Wireless broadband Internet is offered on a sliding pricing scale too, depending on speed. Basic service is for a pretty slow connection, around 500 kilobits per second. For more money, you can connect at up to 2.5 Mbps. Make sure you get all the details on available plans when shopping.

To set up a wireless connection, you'll need a wireless network box, antenna and mount, some coax cable, and some Category 5 cable. You will also need line-of-sight to the antenna tower from which the wireless signal is broadcast. Don't even *think* about installing the equipment yourself! Simply aiming the rooftop antenna takes skill and specialized equipment. Many providers offer all necessary equipment as part of their installation plan, or they may offer it free, especially in areas where cable and DSL compete with wireless.

## Other Options

There are a few other options, including T1 and ISDN. T1 is a popular digital transmission service that moves data at a rate of 1.544 Mbps. It is used mostly by Internet service providers (ISPs) and large businesses and is quite expensive. We'd guess that it's far beyond the range of most people's dedicated Internet budget. T1 is useful for businesses because the connection isn't shared in any way and the data rate is constant, but T1's speed is often no more than a good cable connection, especially at off-peak times. During the workday and late at night, cable Internet speeds approach and sometimes exceed T1 speeds.

ISDN, integrated services digital network, is an older option but one worth investigating if you have no other broadband options in your area. Data is transferred through ordinary telephone copper wire. Users can expect transmissions speeds of 128 Mbps, twice that of dial-up. Prices are quite high, typically $75 to $120 per month. ISDN is not a popular option anymore because the technology is truly archaic, and cable and DSL have overtaken it and left ISDN in their dust. However, if cable or DSL isn't available and ISDN and dial-up are the only options, it just may work for you if you're willing to pay the higher price.

## Choose a Broadband Provider

Now that you know a little about speed and cost, it's time for you to make a choice of providers and connection types. Before you can decide what service is right for you, though, you'll have to find out what's available in your area and what it costs. If your only option is DSL and you don't have access to high-speed cable Internet, the choice is simple. If you have several choices, you'll need to compare.

## What's Available in Your Area Could Be a Limitation

As hinted earlier, those who live in larger, metropolitan areas will likely have more options than those living deep in the woods or out in the country. If you can't get digital cable TV in your home, it's a sure bet you can't get cable Internet either. If you have a phone though, you probably have other options.

One way to find out what options you do have is to watch TV, focusing on the local channels, and see what commercials are shown. If you see a commercial for satellite Internet, this may be your only choice. If you see commercials for cable or DSL, you'll probably be able to go that route.

The best way to find out what your connection options are, though, is to ask your friends and neighbors or people at local computer clubs or user groups. Not only will you find out what's available, but you'll also get everyone's take on how fast or slow the service is, and if and when there are bottlenecks. You can also find out how much it (really) costs. By the time you add taxes and pay for leased equipment and hidden fees, the final tally may be quite a bit more than you budgeted for. Keep in mind that things are never quite as cheap as the ads suggest.

---

**TIP:** *If you currently have dial-up, you can always surf the Web for options. Just go to any high-speed Internet or DSL provider's site and type in your phone number, and they'll let you know if their service is available in your area.*

---

## How Much Do You Want to Pay?

If you have more than one choice for broadband, you can compare the advertised cost and speed of each, along with anything you've heard from friends and neighbors, to help you make the best choice possible. In Dallas, Texas, for example, it appears that high-speed cable Internet, currently at about $40 a month, is cheaper than DSL by about $10.

Additionally, from what the neighbors say, the cable option provides faster service than the most popular DSL provider here does, and the technical support team is fantastic. All of these things can shape your decision.

---

**NOTE:** *We've refrained from adding a table comparing the speed and exact price for each option outlined in this chapter because these things change often. The table would likely be outdated before the book ever hit the bookshelves. Create your own list of plans and prices, and gather information by calling local providers or surfing the Web.*

---

# Popular and Trusted Providers

There are several heavy hitters in the high-speed Internet and DSL market. All are popular and trusted by tens of thousands (if not more) customers. Here is a list of some of the more popular and well-known providers:

√   Comcast: Offers high-speed Internet cable at competitive prices. (**www.comcast.net**)

√   Verizon: Offers DSL services. However, DSL is not available to everyone. You must be within a certain distance of a DSL-equipped provider office. You "qualify" by address. (**www.verizononline.com**)

√   EarthLink: Offers dial-up, high-speed cable, DSL, and satellite. (**www.earthlink.com**)

√   Speakeasy: Offers business services including T1 starting at $299 per month. (**www.speakeasy.net**)

There are hundreds of other providers though, and word of mouth is the best way to find a good one. Look around and talk to friends and family. Find out what they have, how much they pay, and how they like it. You can make an informed decision with that information.

## GunkBuster's Notebook: Keep Your Dial-Up for Another Few Days

You know gunk accumulates because you keep things *too long*, but did you know gunk also accumulates because you get rid of stuff *too soon*? It's true. If you get rid of your dial-up connection before you get cable or DSL enabled, hooked up, and working properly, you won't be able to get online to access the provider's online support pages if you need help! Having to manually find the phone number (in the phone book—egads!), call the provider, wait on hold, and work your way through two or three levels of tech support is gunk you wouldn't have to deal with if you had a connection and could just visit the FAQ page.

In addition, if you get rid of your dial-up connection too soon, you may also lose your old e-mail address before you're ready to give it up. When you choose a new provider, you may opt for a new e-mail address with the account. When you cancel your dial-up service, you will likely lose your old one. Before you switch e-mail addresses, you have to think about all of the people you have to tell. These can include online companies, Web sites, doctors' and dentists' offices, billing offices, banks, online bill paying services, family and friends, and newsletters, just to name a few.

Because of this, it's best to keep your old e-mail address (and your dial-up connection) for a few weeks or a month to make sure you know who e-mails you and let them know of your new address. Better yet, ask the dial-up company how much it would cost to continue to use the old address for a month or more without the dial-up service. Some ISPs allow you to keep an old e-mail address for a full year for about $20. If you do this, you can ensure that you never lose any important e-mail and that you get everyone switched over.

Finally, your Internet service provider will probably put icons on your desktop that contain quick links to technical support pages and online help. Don't be too quick to delete those; you may need them! The point we're making is this: Don't create your own gunk because there's enough of that going around already!

# Set Up a Broadband Modem

You'll need a modem if you sign up for cable or DSL (which are the two technologies we'll be focusing on in the rest of this chapter). This modem is not the modem you already have installed in your PC for dial-up, though. This modem is a separate piece of equipment, designed for broadband connections. The one shown in Figures 9-1 and 9-2 is typical. The modem connects to the PC and to the incoming signal. In the case of DSL, it's a phone jack; in the case of high-speed cable Internet, it's a coax jack. The modem shown here is a cable modem and connects to the wall outlet created originally for the cable TV hookup.

## Rent or Purchase

The cable modem shown in Figure 9-1 came with the self-installation kit from the high-speed Internet service provider. The fee for renting this modem is an additional $3 per month. However, it is possible to purchase the modem from the provider, which, initially and in the long run, could save you some money.

There are always things to watch out for, though. For example, you can almost always purchase a compatible modem from a computer store for less than you could from the provider. Don't get sucked in, especially when first placing your order. Go ahead and rent a modem for a few months to make sure you like the service and want to continue using it, and to allow yourself time to compare available modems. Then after a few months, replace the rented modem with one you buy yourself and return the rented one to your broadband provider.

**Figure 9-1**
The front of a cable modem.

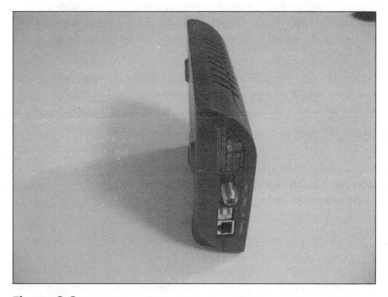

**Figure 9-2**
The back of a cable modem.

---

*Tip: Before purchasing a modem, call the ISP and ask what type to purchase. There are specific DOCSIS (Data Over Cable System Interface Specification) requirements for cable modems, and you need the modem to be compatible with your cable system. There are similar requirements for DSL modems, including compliance with ADSL2, ASDL2+, and RE-ADSL. (ADSL stands for Asymmetric Digital Subscriber Line.)*

---

## Don't Spend Too Much

There are lots of options out there for cable and DSL modems, and many can connect to both technologies. If you only need a cable modem, don't spend extra for one that also connects to DSL. If you only need a DSL modem, don't pay extra for one that also connects to cable. Either way, get one that has both Ethernet and USB connections; this way, you'll have some flexibility with how you'll connect it.

A simple DSL modem should provide a 10BaseT (Ethernet) LAN interface to connect to the local network's router and a single DSL interface to connect to the public phone network. It should also have a USB port for connecting directly to the PC if no router or network exists.

---

*TIP: More and more cable/DSL modems provide both Ethernet and USB connectivity. However, using the USB connection prevents you from using a router, which provides switch ports for your other PCs (if you have them) and strong hardware firewall connection against network intruders. Use the Ethernet port if you possibly can!*

---

A simple cable modem should also provide a 10BaseT (Ethernet) LAN interface to connect to the local network's router and a single cable interface to connect to the digital cable wall outlet. It should also have a USB port for connecting directly to the PC if no router exists.

---

*TIP: When comparing prices, note that you can purchase a working, fully functional, and compatible cable or DSL modem for under $50.*

---

## Set Up Your Hardware

Now that you've decided on a provider and a connection type, it's time to start setting up the hardware. In this section, we'll discuss your options, as well as the steps to take to perform the installation yourself.

# Self-Installation vs. Professional Installation

With just about any provider, you have the option to pay a professional installer to connect you to the Internet, or you can choose to install the system yourself. Hiring a professional takes all the fun out of it though, so we'll just gloss over that option lightly and move on.

Hiring a professional (approved by the broadband provider) to come to your home and install the cable or DSL modem will probably cost around $70. If you want them to set up the network too, you'll have to purchase a router ahead of time, and you can expect that installation to cost another $100 to $200. If you aren't sure if you can or want to perform the installation yourself, this is a good way to go. It's also a good choice if you have multiple PCs to connect but have not previously set up a network and aren't sure how—and don't have time to learn.

With self-installation, you get a self-installation kit, complete with a modem, the required cables, a splitter if cable is involved, a filter or similar device if DSL is involved, and various other hardware odds and ends. Figure 9-3 shows what comes with a generic high-speed cable self-installation kit.

**Figure 9-3**
Parts is parts is parts, and there are a lot of them!

Although it looks like a lot of parts, you'd be surprised just how many of these items you *won't* need. If you are only connecting one PC and that PC has a USB port, you won't necessarily have to install the Ethernet card. However, we recommend installing the Ethernet card if you don't already have an Ethernet port on your PC. (Nearly all PCs sold since 1997 or so have one.) Without an Ethernet port, you can't make use of an external router, either immediately or in the future. Every router contains a strong hardware firewall that needs no configuration and is enabled by default. Still, check the back panel of your PC to see if you have an Ethernet port already. It looks like a large phone jack, with eight copper wires visible if you look closely. Additionally, you won't have to install the cable splitter if you are using a cable outlet that isn't already in use or if you're installing DSL. Instructions are included with the self-installation kit too, so you won't have to worry about getting lost if you choose to do it yourself. Everything connects only one way; it's nearly impossible to connect the wrong cable to the wrong port.

If we've convinced you to do it yourself, continue with the next section. If you've called an installer, feel free to skip forward a few sections.

## Setting Up a Single Computer with Broadband

Self-installation kit in hand, let's start the installation. First, unpack everything in the kit and set it on a large counter or desk. If items are packaged together, keep them together. Read all of the material that accompanies the hardware before continuing, too. With that done, follow these steps:

1.  Check the back of your PC for both Ethernet and USB ports. If you have an Ethernet port, use it. There is an Ethernet add-in board in the kit, but if you don't want to open your PC to install the board, you can connect the modem via the included USB cable. USB is definitely a last resort, however, for both performance and security reasons.

2.  Connect the modem to the cable outlet or phone jack, depending on the technology that you selected (cable or DSL). Connect splitters, filters, or other hardware as required.

3.  Once everything is connected, go back to the PC. Open Control Panel and then the Network Connections applet. Locate your dial-up connection and select Disconnect and then Disable. You should tweak the properties of this connection so it does not continually dial out. It may also be easier to delete the connection completely. You can re-create it later if you need it.

4.  Attach the power cable to the modem and plug it into a reliable surge protector. Plug the surge protector into the wall outlet and turn it on. Turn the modem on if it does not come on automatically.

5.  Insert the CD that came with the modem and perform any procedures required of your broadband provider to complete the installation. This may include several tasks:

    √   Checking the PC to verify it meets minimum requirements

    √   Installing the modem's drivers, if required

    √   Verifying the registration and account codes

    √   Creating an e-mail account and password

    √   Connecting to technical support sites or online help pages

    √   Reset the modem, and reboot the PC.

You should now be connected to the Internet via your new broadband connection. The modem's lights should all be green, and there should be no more configuration tasks.

## Common Problems

Of course, not everything always goes as smoothly as it should. Common problems that occur when setting up broadband include improperly installed Ethernet cards or driver software; a failure (and need) to reboot the PC or reset the modem; a failure to meet minimum computer requirements; improper configuration of the modem's software or settings; poorly connected cables; slow or on-again, off-again connectivity; or a PC that insists on using its old dial-up connection and won't use the new one. If you run into trouble, do this:

1.  Check your work again. Make sure you did everything that had to be done to make your connection happen.

2.  Make sure that all cable plugs are fully inserted in their jacks.

3.  Shut everything down: both PC and modem. Then power up the modem, followed by the PC.

If things still don't work, write down the specific error messages or problem and then contact the provider by phone, or use your old dial-up connection to reach the provider's support pages on the Web.

### GunkBuster's Notebook: Don't Cause Your Own Gunk

There are several ways to ensure that you don't gunk up the new connection on your own. *You* certainly don't want to be the cause of poor connectivity, slow service, or on-again, off-again connectivity. Not only are these types of problems hard to diagnose, but when you find out your connectivity problems stem from a well-intentioned decision to staple the Ethernet cable to the baseboards with the closest available office stapler, well, it can also be downright embarrassing.

With that in mind (and really just not wanting to be embarrassed), let's look at some things that will cause gunk, all things you should certainly steer clear of:

√ Treat cables with care; don't crimp them or put them anywhere they'll be stepped on.

√ When working cables around corners, don't bend them at sharp or 90-degree angles; just angle them slightly.

√ Make tight and secure connections, but do not overtighten. You don't want loose connections, but you don't want to strip anything either.

√ Always verify that Ethernet cables are firmly secured.

√ Don't use long cables; only use cables that are long enough. (Never use cables longer than those provided in your self-installation kit.)

√ Do not staple cables to the wall or to baseboards.

√ Do not use Ethernet cable extenders.

√ Make sure the modem and any other powered equipment is plugged into a surge protector.

*TIP: Learn other ways to get better performance by visiting your provider's Web site, and by reading the last section in this chapter.*

## How to Get More Information

Your broadband provider will have a Web site that has various support pages. Usually, the Web site contains options for contacting the company via phone, e-mail, regular mail, or live chat. If you can find a provider that offers the live chat option, that's certainly a great perk. Here are some other options on most broadband providers' Web sites:

√ FAQ Pages: These pages list frequently asked questions and their answers. Chances are good that you're not the first person to encounter whatever problem you're having and you'll find your answer here.

√ Simple Fixes: These pages list one-stop or one-click fixes for common problems such as setting your home page, clearing your browser's History list, clearing the cache, creating a new account, configuring e-mail settings, clearing temp files, and more.

√ Help Forums: A forum where customers can post questions and get answers from experts and other customers.

√ Personal Settings: A place to create your own Web site, configure preferences, or get e-mail.

√ Additional Perks: Pages that include options like downloading support agents, antivirus software, free applications for sending video mail, and software to build a home page. They may even offer a place to share and print photos.

# Share Your Broadband Connection with a Router

In Chapter 8, we introduced the network equipment you'd need to set up a shared Internet connection for your home computers. In that chapter, you learned how to share a dial-up connection with Internet Connection Sharing (ICS) and using a hub or a switch. We also briefly discussed how sharing a broadband connection works. You learned why sharing a broadband connection via ICS isn't a good choice and why you need a router instead of a switch or hub when sharing broadband. In this section, we'll take it a step further. We'll first look a little more closely at what a router doe,s and then discuss how to obtain the router and how to install it.

---

**NOTE:** We're assuming you had a working network prior to upgrading to broadband. If you didn't, you'll need to create one before continuing. Details on how to create a network are included in Chapter 8 and in Chapter 10.

---

## GunkBuster's Notebook: Trust Us on the Router Thing!

Some people will tell you that it's possible to use Internet Connection Sharing (ICS) and a hub or switch to share a broadband connection. It is. Barely. Although you can technically share a cable or broadband connection with ICS, it isn't the best choice. In fact, it's downright silly and a waste of resources. In addition, there are the security issues of surfing without a firewall (the firewall that is provided by a router). If you still want to know more, read on; if not, skip ahead.

Setting up ICS is time-consuming and riddled with hardware and software requirements not required for a router setup. Just for starters, you'll need to select a host computer, and that computer will need *two* network cards. One card will connect to the cable or DSL modem, and the other will connect to the hub or switch. If you do happen to get ICS working on the network, you'll need to install a software firewall on the host computer. A firewall keeps out the bad guys. That's another purchase. Finally, because ICS runs all the time, the host computer will take a small performance hit, and that doesn't include the additional PCI slot you've taken up with the additional network card. None of this will be an issue if you install a hardware router.

If you are planning on trying ICS anyway, either because you think you can't afford a router or because you already have two network cards installed on your host computer, consider this: you can purchase a used router for as little as $15 on eBay, maybe less. And you'll get better PC performance and more security against Internet intruders.

## The Router: All You Need to Know

A router is an external device (it doesn't have to be installed inside your PC) that allows you to share a broadband connection, as well as network connectivity, among several PCs. Routers provide strong firewall protection too, protection you'll need with an "always on" Internet connection. And, because routers are not a part of the Windows operating system, they are external and independent hardware. This means that almost any computer can be connected to a router and will work properly, even pokey old Windows 95 PCs. A router connects to PC network cards via Ethernet cables.

A router basically intermediates between your (small) home network and the (immense) global Internet. It distributes local IP addresses to all your networked computers, which prevents you from having to purchase additional IP addresses from your provider. This distribution of addresses is handled by the router using a technology called Dynamic Host Configuration Protocol (DHCP), which assigns private IP addresses to all the computers on your network. This not only makes set up simple, but it also provides protection for all of the computers on the network via the router's firewall. Although there's more to it, this is really *All You Need to Know.*

## Rent or Lease? Self-Install or Not?

Your provider may offer you the choice to rent or purchase a router from them. You may also be offered the option of a professional installation. We suggest that you purchase your own router from a computer store or online, and that you opt for installing it yourself as well—unless you're hopelessly technophobic. The savings from a self-installation versus a professional one will probably cover the full cost of the router.

When shopping for a router, first visit your broadband provider's Web site and see if it has a list of compatible routers that you can purchase. For the most part, any router will do, though if the provider has a favorite, buying that model may make it easier for the provider to help you later if you have problems. If you're setting up a simple wired home network, we see no reason to spend more than $50 unless you want to go with a wireless router. Wireless routers will cost from $60 to $90.

---

**TIP: For more information on wireless networks and wireless routers, refer to Chapter 11.**

---

As for self-installation versus professional installation, well, installing a router really isn't that difficult. It is only one piece of hardware, a power cord, and a few Ethernet cables. You just have to connect them correctly. The router usually just plugs in and runs—especially newer models. (This is why we recommend getting a list of suggested or approved router models from your provider. They probably know what works easiest on their system.) If you aren't sure though, read through the next section; you'll find everything you need to know to make your decision.

## Installing the Router

Make sure you read all of the instructions that come with the router and then shut down all PCs, the cable/DSL modem, and other devices before beginning the installation. The steps beyond this point are generic to most routers. Follow the directions that came with the router if they differ from the general steps that we provide here. Figure 9-4 shows how the connections look on a typical and very popular router, the Linksys BEFSR41. For clarity's sake, the figure shows the connection to only one PC, but all PCs are connected to the router the same way, via short patch cable to an available port on the router's back panel.

---

**NOTE:** Do not connect PCs to both Port #4 and the Uplink port at the same time. Uplink is for advanced uses that we won't cover in this book. As a general rule, leave it alone.

---

To connect your router-based network, do this:

1.  If you currently have the cable/DSL modem connected directly to a PC via USB, disconnect it.

2.  Connect one end of an Ethernet cable to the Ethernet port on the cable/DSL modem and connect the other end of the Ethernet cable to the port marked "WAN" or "Internet" on the back panel of the router. This port should be labeled or somehow set apart from the other Ethernet ports, which are generally placed all in a row. Look for the port that's labeled differently or set apart somehow.

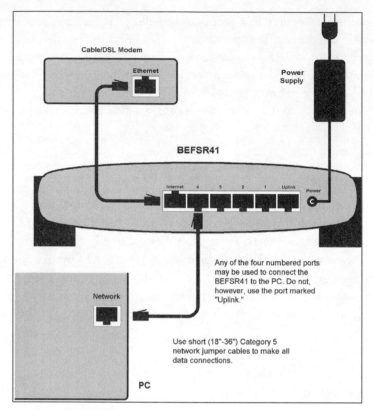

**Figure 9-4**

Connecting a router to a PC and broadband modem.

3. Connect each PC on the network to one of the router's available LAN switch ports. These are typically numbered; for example, from 1 to 4 on a router with a four-port switch. Which port you use isn't important. Make this connection with short Ethernet Category 5 "patch" cables. Make sure the cable is only long enough to reach comfortably, not too long to be a gunk magnet or become kinked and reduce performance.

4. Turn on the modem and give it time to initialize. When the lights settle in, continue.

5. Plug in the router and apply power.

6. Power up each of the PCs and any other network devices that are connected to the router's switch ports. (This might include a networked printer or Wi-Fi wireless access point.)

If the networked computers cannot access the Internet via the router as expected and you are sure that you've made the proper connections and that all cables are securely inserted into their jacks, the problematic PCs may not be configured to obtain a DHCP address automatically. To check and to change this setting, do this for each PC as required:

1. Open Control Panel and open Network Connections.

2. Right-click the local area connection the PC uses to connect to the network. Choose Properties.

3. On the General tab, select Internet Protocol (TCP/IP). Click Properties.

4. On the General tab in the Internet Protocol (TCP/IP) Properties dialog box, verify or select Obtain an IP Address Automatically and Obtain DNS Server Address Automatically. Figure 9-5 shows the choices.

5. Click OK twice to close all dialog boxes. It may be necessary to reboot the computer, and anytime you change networking settings, it's a good idea.

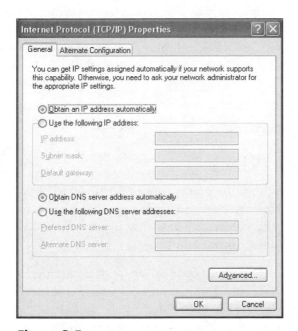

**Figure 9-5**
PCs must be configured to obtain a DHCP address automatically.

## Should You Use a Single LAN Port Cable/DSL Router with an Existing Hub or Switch?

If you already have a home network set up with a hub or switch, you may have heard somewhere that you can purchase a single LAN port cable/DSL router to connect to an existing hub or switch on your network via the existing hardware's uplink port. Although this *is* an option, a single-port router is only a little cheaper than a four-port router and doesn't offer the best option for connecting multiple computers. For example, the Linksys BEFSR11 single-port router is only $5 cheaper than the Linksys BEFSR41 four-port router.

With a four-port router (vs. a single port router), you eliminate the shared bandwidth model of the hub, which is good. When you install a four-port router, you must remove the hub completely from the network. Anytime you can remove something and replace it with something better, you've degunked.

It's easier to defend the single LAN port cable/DSL router option when your existing home network uses a switch as its center point because switches do not force all PCs on the network to share the same bandwidth, as hubs do. However, you'd still have a switch *and* a router *and* an additional cable. Gunk! Simplicity is not only tidy, it's also more reliable and less subject to loose cables and other failure modes. It is our opinion that a single device containing a router with an appropriate number of ports is the best option for setting up a shared broadband connection. The BEFSR41 from Linksys is an excellent unit, with a street price new of about $50 and wide availability at retailers like Fry's and CompUSA.

# Get Better Performance from Your Broadband Connection

There are lots of ways to improve the performance of your Internet connection. Your provider's Web site may outline several ways that pertain to your specific connection, speed, and hardware. These may involve optimizing settings or making configuration optimization tweaks.

You can get better performance on your own by way of degunking your own PC, though, including but not limited to making sure your PC is running in tip-top shape and performing Internet-related degunking tasks often. (See our book *Degunking Windows* for the full Windows anti-gunk treatment.)

Here are just a few of the things you can do to enhance Internet performance (as well as PC performance):

√ If you don't turn your PC off every night, restart it at least three times a week. This gives the computer a chance to regroup, as it were, and refresh. System memory becomes fragmented over time with use, and restarting is the best and easiest way to defragment it.

√ Make sure you have extra hard drive space, at least 20 percent free. A computer running with less than 20 percent free disk space is gunked up anyway and should be seriously looked into.

√ Use hard-drive optimization tools, such as a Registry checker or Norton Utilities, and run Disk Defragmenter and Disk Cleanup regularly. These tools help you maintain a healthy system. A healthy system is a faster system.

√ Keep anti-adware, anti-spyware, and antivirus programs up-to-date and run them on a schedule. Adware, spyware, and viruses can all slow down computer and Internet performance.

√ Clear temporary files, cookies, and history files regularly. These files can collect, and collect, and collect, and collect, and eventually become gunk.

√ Turn your modem off and on once a month, or whenever it seems to be functioning poorly. This gives the modem a chance to refresh.

√ Fully degunk your PC as outlined in the book *Degunking Windows* (Paraglyph Press) at least twice a year.

Most of these tasks are straightforward. We're sure you can reboot your PC a few times a week and cycle power your modem once or twice a month. However, other tasks may require a bit of instruction. Let's look for a moment at temporary Internet files, history files, and cookies and how and when to use Disk Defragmenter and Disk Cleanup. Performing these tasks regularly will ensure that you are getting good and reliable performance from your broadband connection, as well as your PC.

## Cleaning Up Internet Explorer

Because this book is about Windows operating systems, we're going to assume you're using Internet Explorer. If you're using something else though, the idea behind it is the same. You'll just have to understand the steps involved and why it needs to be done. In this section, we'll discuss ways to keep Internet Explorer clean, starting with cleaning out temporary Internet files.

### *Getting Rid of Temporary Internet Files*

Temporary Internet files are just that—they are temporary and obtained from the Internet. Temporary Internet files work like this: Each time you visit a Web page, some of the information on that page is stored temporarily on your hard drive. Because a computer can retrieve information from your hard drive faster than it can retrieve information from the Internet, saving temporary files to your PC makes surfing the Web faster. The next time you visit a previously viewed page, you already have some of the information on your hard drive, so you don't have to load everything from scratch.

Temporary Internet files can be Web pages, graphics, and so forth and are rarely harmful. However, failing to remove these files at least occasionally can result in not always getting the most recent version of a page, and these files can take up valuable hard drive space. Therefore, it is our suggestion that you clean out the Temporary Files folder once a month:

1. Open Internet Explorer, and from the Tools menu, select Internet Options.

   On the General tab, under Temporary Internet Files, choose Settings. Figure 9-6 shows the General tab and options.

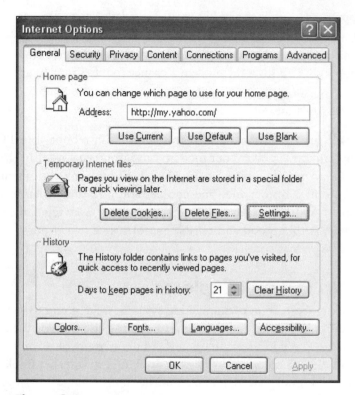

**Figure 9-6**

The General tab of the Internet Options dialog box offers a place to control and delete temporary Internet files.

2. From the Settings dialog box you can view the files, change the location of the Temporary Internet Files folder, and increase or decrease the amount of space to use for the files. The more space you provide, the more data Internet Explorer can save. If you are low on disk space, you should not increase the amount used from its default.

3. In the Settings dialog box you can also choose to check for newer versions of stored pages every visit to the page, every time you start Internet Explorer, automatically, or never. Click OK.

4. To delete existing files, under Temporary Internet Files on the General tab of the Internet Options dialog box, choose Delete Files. Click OK in the Delete Files dialog box.

5. Click OK to close Internet Options.

### Tossing Your Cookies

Cookies are small text files that Web sites place on your PC without your knowledge. They are not viruses and do not contain harmful code. Cookies do contain information the Web sites you visit want to know about you, such as what you last purchased or what you enjoy looking at when visiting their site. In addition, cookies are responsible for making online shopping and surfing easier by remembering previously input information such as e-mail addresses, phone numbers, and shipping addresses. Having cookies on your machine allows you to enter information for an e-commerce site, for example, and never have to enter the information for that site again. That is at least until you delete the cookies from your PC!

There are two kinds of cookies, persistent cookies and session cookies. A session cookie is used only for a single session and is erased once you leave the Web site and close your browser. Persistent cookies stay around until you delete them, or they may have an expiration date created by the Web site and be deleted automatically.

Since some Web sites won't work properly if you delete cookies, and since cookies contain so much valuable information, we suggest minimizing how often you delete them. You'll want to leave cookies for banking sites, online retailers, stock sites, and similar pages on your system that you refer to regularly. Cookies from the *New York Times* (and sites of its caliber) are never a threat and should be retained.

However, there may be cookies you do want to erase, either because you don't trust the site or because you don't want the information made available to the site if you visit it again. Rule of thumb: If you don't immediately recognize the name of the site the cookie came from, delete it! You might also need to delete cookies if you're degunking a PC with barely enough hard drive space to save a Word document. However, deleting all cookies in one fell swoop can make your life a nightmare. Just think about all of the information you'll have to retype!

So, let's focus on how to delete cookies manually, one at a time:

1. Open Internet Explorer, and from the Tools menu, select Internet Options.

2. On the General tab, under Temporary Internet Files, choose Settings.

3. In the Settings dialog box, click View Files.

4. From the View menu, select List.

5. From the View menu, point to Arrange Icons By, and select Type. You can also choose to arrange icons by Last Accessed. Ordering cookies in this manner lets you see which cookies you use often and which you don't.

6. Locate the cookies in the list. You can delete any cookie manually from here by right-clicking it and choosing Delete. You can select noncontiguous cookies by holding down the Ctrl key while selecting, or contiguous ones by holding down the Shift key as you select the first and last ones. Close this window when finished.

7. To delete all cookies, click OK in the Settings dialog box, and in the Internet Options dialog box, click Delete Cookies. Click Yes to verify.

8. Click OK to close the Internet Options dialog box.

## History Files

History files are used in Internet Explorer to display the list of previously visited Web sites. You can view the history files on your PC by opening IE, selecting View, Explorer Bar, and then History on a Windows XP PC. History files are kept for three weeks by default (although this can be changed) and then written over. Figure 9-7 shows an example of the History window.

**Figure 9-7**
History lists all previously visited Web sites over the past three weeks.

If you want to clear the list, for whatever reason, it's simple. Just open Internet Options as noted earlier and choose Clear History.

# Keeping Hard Drives Clean and Organized

As you are well aware, a degunked Windows system is a faster system. While we won't go into the myriad of Windows-related degunking tasks here (you'll have to purchase our earlier book, *Degunking Windows,* for that), we will discuss a few of the most important ones. Important and required tasks include checking for missing system files using System File Checker, using Disk Cleanup, and using Disk Defragmenter. For best results, you should get into a habit of running them all on a schedule.

### SFC /Scannow

You'd certainly run a computer diagnostic on your car if errors appeared on the dash, especially the dreaded (and vague) Check Engine warning. The same should be true of your PC. Unfortunately, many people simply click away their PC errors and continue about their way. If you did that with a car, you'd cause irreparable damage in a flash. Take care of your PC as you would your car; if you see an error on startup, run some tests to see if you can find and solve the problem.

One of the most powerful file system checking application is rarely used. Most people don't even know it exists. It's the System File Checker, a utility provided with Windows to search out and replace missing Windows operating system files. Missing system files are almost always the reason for mysterious startup errors, and the reason why Windows applications like Internet Explorer and Outlook Express hang up or close unexpectedly. You should run this check once a month.

To use System File Checker, do this:

1.  Click Start and click Run.
2.  In the Run dialog box, type **sfc /scannow**. Click OK.
3.  Wait while the check is performed. This could take quite a bit of time. Have your Windows XP CD ready. You'll need to insert it if the utility needs to copy missing files.

### Disk Cleanup

If we were to continue with our car analogy, running Disk Cleanup would be akin to cleaning out the car and taking it in for an oil change. You have to clean up the trash every now and then, and you have to perform some preventative maintenance so gunk won't pile up and cause problems. Disk Cleanup does that to your PC. Disk Cleanup can clean up the following:

√   Downloaded program files

√   Temporary Internet files

√   Offline Web pages

√   Microsoft error reporting files

√   Recycle Bin

√   Temporary files

√   Other files, depending on what's installed

Here's how to run Disk Cleanup:

1.   Click Start, point to All Programs, point to Accessories, point to System Tools, and select Disk Cleanup.

2.   In the Select Drive dialog box, if it appears, select the drive to clean up. Click OK.

3.   Disk Cleanup will scan the disk for files; then the Disk Cleanup dialog box will appear.

4.   Select the files to delete. You can delete all of them if you'd like, although we generally keep any setup files if they're listed.

5.   Click OK and then Yes to perform the actions.

You should run Disk Cleanup once a month.

### Disk Defragmenter

The last degunking task you'll need to perform on a schedule is disk defragmenting. Files are considered fragmented if they are not stored contiguously on the disk. Fragmentation occurs like this: A file, program, or other data is written to the hard disk in the first available space on the disk. When that data is deleted from the disk, that space becomes available for new data. If new data is written to the disk but is not written sequentially (perhaps a large file is stored in four or five places on the disk) in the first four of five available parts of the hard drive, it is fragmented. When the PC has to look for and piece together data before it can be shown on the screen, it takes much longer than if the data were stored all together.

When a disk is defragmented, the files that should be stored contiguously are put together on the disk. Other files are moved around to accommodate this.

Thus, defragmenting a disk improves performance by placing files together so the hard drive doesn't have to look in four or five places to piece them together. Better performance, more speed, and a happier computer and PC user are the immediate results!

Follow these steps to use Disk Defragmenter:

1. Click Start, point to All Programs, point to Accessories, point to System Tools, and select Disk Defragmenter.

2. In the Disk Defragmenter window, select the drive to defragment.

3. Click Analyze.

4. A dialog box will appear stating either that you should defragment the volume or that you shouldn't. Figure 9-8 shows the former.

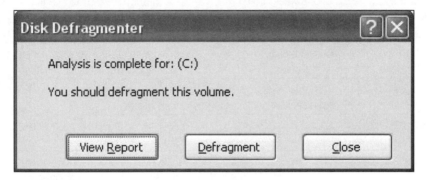

**Figure 9-8**
Check monthly to see if you need to defragment any drives.

5. Click Defragment if the analyzer suggests it. Otherwise, click Close.

6. Perform this check monthly.

# Degunking on a Schedule

It's difficult remembering to take your car in for an oil change every three months or to get a haircut every two. It's hard to remember to call your mom on the weekends. We know it's also difficult to remember to perform the required and suggested PC degunking tasks regularly. To that end, Table 9-1 outlines how often you should perform the tasks outlined in this section.

**Table 9-1   Degunking on a Schedule**

| Task | When to Schedule | When to Manually Perform |
| --- | --- | --- |
| Restart the PC. | Three to four times a week. | Whenever the PC is performing poorly, reacting slowly, hanging up applications, or producing errors. |
| Delete unnecessary files and programs to free up disk space. | Once a month. | Whenever a "Low Disk Space" error is received. |
| Optimize the Registry and the Windows operating system files and check those files for errors. | Once a month. | Whenever the PC is performing poorly, reacting slowly, hanging up applications, or producing errors. |
| Run Disk Cleanup. | Once a month. | Whenever the PC is performing poorly. |
| Update anti-adware, anti-spyware, and antivirus software. | Once a week or more. | Whenever you are suspicious that adware, spyware, or a virus may be on your computer. |
| Delete temporary Internet files. | Once a month. | If you want to erase your surfing tracks or if Internet Explorer is responding slowly. |
| Delete cookies | This varies. We suggest deleting older cookies four times a year. | Anytime you want to remove cookies from your system. |
| Reset the cable/DSL modem. | Once a month. | Anytime the modem is not performing or as properly you'd expect. |
| Run Disk Defragmenter. | Check monthly using the Analyze button. Defragment four times a year no matter the outcome. | After deleting a large amount of programs or files, or if the Disk Defragmenter analyzer suggests it. |

# Summing Up

In this chapter, you learned how to upgrade from dial-up to high-speed cable Internet or DSL. Upgrading isn't as simple as making a phone call, plugging your PC's dial-up modem into a phone outlet, and configuring a few settings. It's quite a bit more complicated.

In this chapter, you learned the steps. First you choose a connection type and then a provider. You decide to rent or lease a modem and how you'll install it. Once the modem is installed, you share that connection with others on your network via a router. All of this takes time and thought, but it's certainly possible for anyone to achieve. In the next chapter, we'll move forward and talk at length about other ways to connect a network, and then we'll move on to wireless setups.

# 10

# Creating Gunk-Free Wired Networks

## Degunking Checklist:

√ Don't kink or bend network cables sharply.

√ Don't lay network cables on the floor where they can be stepped on, and keep them away from motors and fluorescent lights.

√ Use Ethernet crossover cables because they are the cheapest and easiest way to create a point-to-point connection between two PCs.

√ Create a superfast point-to-point connection between two PCs with FireWire, keeping in mind that only Windows XP has good support for that feature.

√ Hubs cut your network throughput in half. Use a switch instead to build your home network.

√ Use a router rather than a switch or a hub if you intend to connect your network to a broadband Internet connection.

√ Even if you have only one PC, connect it to your broadband Internet connection through a router for the sake of the router's hardware firewall.

√ Don't attempt to run network cables between two homes. Use Wi-Fi instead. (See Chapter 11.)

T here was a time (not so long ago) when connecting two or more PCs to share files was so difficult that most people didn't bother and just did "the floppy shuffle," even when this involved shuffling 15 or 20 floppies. One of the great marvels of the late 1990s was cheap networking, which is now so cheap that virtually all PCs—even the super-bargain bottom-feeder PCs—contain a 100–Mbps Ethernet port. The recent versions of Windows are masters at hooking up with one another and can do it in a number of different ways.

That's the blessing, and that's the curse, as well. There are so many options in networking PCs that a lot of people stumble on the wealth of choices and create networks that don't work as well as they should. We've touched upon networking a little in previous chapters, but in this chapter we'll tie it all together, with the background that it takes to look at your network and be sure that it's as gunk-free as a network can get.

# Understand IP-Based Networking

It always helps a lot to know what's going on inside your PC so that you can fix it if—or when—it stops working properly. This usually doesn't happen because parts break, assuming you don't trip over a network cable and yank its port out by the roots. Mostly, things stop working when you buy a new PC or a wireless router (more on this in Chapter 11), or try to hook your laptop or a new PC into an existing network. So in the following sections, we're going to present a quick overview of PC networking as it is most commonly practiced today.

## Packets Carried by Services on Roads

All mainstream communications among PCs are packet-based. This means that a file (or any PC-PC conversation) is broken up into chunks called *packets,* which are usually about a thousand bytes long. Each packet is like a parcel traveling by UPS: It's wrapped up securely and has an address plastered across it so anyone who looks at the package can know exactly where it's going. A large device (say a bicycle) can be broken down into sections and the sections wrapped separately so that they're small enough to travel through UPS's system. So it is with networking. All the "boxes" are the same size, and anything too big to fit into one box is packed in as many boxes as it takes.

Once packed, UPS parcels are stamped with addresses and then loaded onto vehicles. Some of these are trucks, and some are trains. It doesn't matter to the parcels—they get where they're going regardless. Nor does it matter what type of road the vehicle travels over. It may be an asphalt road, or a railroad, or even a barge on a river or a canal. (UPS air costs extra!)

Nor does it matter (to the parcel) if the service transporting the package is UPS or Federal Express. The procedures that UPS follows are a little different from those at FedEx, but both companies get the parcels where they're going.

This metaphor is one way to think about PC networking. Pieces of bicycles are packed into parcels. The parcels are presented at a UPS office for shipping. UPS carries them to their destination on some sort of vehicle. Data goes into packets. The packets are presented to a protocol for transport. The protocol carries them over some kind of physical link. This networking system is shown in Figure 10-1.

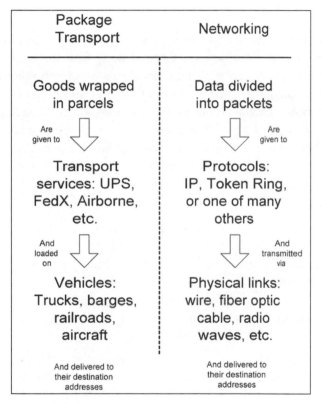

**Figure 10-1**

Networking compared to package transport.

A *protocol* is pretty much what it sounds like: a set of rules and procedures for carrying data over a network. There are many networking protocols. Only a few are commonly used, and one of them, called *Internet Protocol (IP)* is by far the one used most widely today.

A physical link is also just what it sounds like: something in the physical world that carries data. Mostly you think of cables, but there are many different kinds of cables. Some are based on electrical signals passing over wires, but others contain glass or plastic fibers that carry data as pulses of light. It sounds odd, but you can have physical links based on infrared light traveling through the air, or radio waves. These don't seem to be "physical," but they're out in the physical world and not inside the computer.

The magic in networking is that *the protocol doesn't care what physical link it's using.* A protocol works precisely the same way, whether data is moving over wires, fiber-optic cable, infrared light beams, or radio waves. Your data gets there intact, whatever road it takes.

In virtually all cases these days, the protocol your PC will use is the Internet Protocol, which we'll call IP from now on. Created along with the Internet in the late 1960s, IP has basically driven all other local area networking protocols out of the PC market. You'll often hear the term TCP/IP (Transmission Control Protocol/Internet Protocol), which is the full name of the protocol used in most home networks and also the Internet. There are actually two protocols involved (TCP and IP), but they are so rarely used apart from one another that when most people say IP they really mean TCP/IP. We'll do that in this book as well.

## IP Addresses

The single most important element in a networking scheme is addressing. To get a package where it's going, where it's going has to be clearly written on the package—and somewhere out there in the world, there must be a house, apartment, or office that corresponds to what is written on the package. In networking, every PC must have a unique address so that IP can move data from one PC to another. This address is called an *IP address,* and it looks something like this:

169.254.88.230

There are four groups of numbers from 0 to 255, separated by periods. Every PC in an IP network must have an IP address like this. Where IP addresses come from is important, and we'll return to that shortly.

## Physical Links

Something carries packets from one PC to another, and we call this the *physical link.* Most of the time it's a cable with wires in it, which in the PC realm is called a Category 5 (or more recently, 5E or 6) Ethernet cable. Category 5 is often abbreviated as CAT5. However, Windows XP can move packets across a

FireWire cable connected between PCs, and (with some special connections and a little fussing) over a USB cable as well. The Wi-Fi networking we'll talk about in Chapter 11 uses microwaves to move data from PC to PC.

You sometimes hear phrases like "IP over Ethernet" or "IP over 1394" (1394 being the standards number for FireWire), and this is one way of expressing the use of a protocol (IP) with a specific type of physical link.

## How It Works

Very briefly (and gurus should understand that we're radically simplifying things here), an IP-based network works this way:

√ Windows (or some other operating system, like Mac OS) is told (by you) to send a file to another PC on a network.

√ Windows hands the file name to its own subsystem that handles IP network communication. (We call this the "TCP/IP stack.")

√ The TCP protocol breaks the file down into packets.

√ The IP protocol looks at the address on each packet (the destination address) and then figures out where that address resides. If you have only two PCs connected by a cable, it's easy. If you have six PCs connected on a network, it's a little more difficult. If the destination is on another network somewhere (out on the Internet, which is a network of networks), IP has to work with a device called a *router* to find the destination. IP is persistent, and it will eventually figure things out.

√ IP sends the packets off to their destination and makes sure they get there.

√ The destination PC's TCP/IP stack accepts the incoming packets and reassembles them into a copy of the original file. The IP protocol software modules on both PCs are in regular communication to make sure everything happens correctly. When something breaks down, IP will tell Windows to post an error of some kind.

In a nutshell, that's all there is to IP-based networking. You need to have a grip on the process to be able to install and (more likely) troubleshoot your own network. So with all of that in mind, it's time to get down to specifics.

## Learn Where IP Addresses Come From

The core requirement of any IP-based network is that all computers on the network have a unique IP address. If a PC doesn't have an IP address, the IP protocol has no way to ship packets to that PC. There are only three ways for a PC to get an IP address:

√ You can give it one manually. This is usually unnecessary.

√ The PC can request an IP address from a configuration server somewhere on the network.

√ If there is no configuration server on the network, Windows can give itself an IP address.

One way or another, each PC *must* obtain an IP address or your network is dead in its tracks.

## Requesting an IP address from a DHCP Server

Windows can tell when there's a network cable plugged into its network port and whether other PCs are connected to that cable. When it finds a connection to other PCs (via cable or some other physical link), Windows looks for a special server called a Dynamic Host Configuration Protocol (DHCP) server. Most networks have a DHCP server somewhere. It can be on one of the PCs in the network, or it can be inside a router connected to that network. When your PC connects to the Internet, via dial-up or broadband, your Internet service provider's network has a DHCP server, and that DHCP server is what answers Windows's call.

In response to that call, the DHCP server sends back an IP address known to be available and not a duplicate of one belonging to any other PC on the network. It sends a few other things back as well, things that Windows needs to configure itself for networking, but the IP address is the most important item Windows receives from a DHCP server.

## Getting an IP Address from APIPA

If Windows calls out to the nearest DHCP server and no DHCP server responds, it waits for awhile to be sure, and then it invokes a subsystem called Automatic Private IP Addressing (APIPA). APIPA chooses an IP address from a block of IP addresses set aside for Windows to use when no DHCP server is available. An address generated by APIPA will always look like this: 169.254.*x.x,* where the *x*s represent a number from 0 to 255. (There are a couple of excluded values.) Remember that APIPA will not kick into play unless Windows detects a cable connected to its network port with at least one PC accessible through the cable. A lone PC connected to nothing will *not* trigger APIPA.

---

**TIP:** *Windows 95 does not include the APIPA subsystem! It's missing a lot of other useful things as well. If you want to network, upgrade to (at least) Windows 98!*

---

One way or another, when Windows detects that it's connected to at least one other PC via a physical link of some kind, it will obtain an IP address, and then it's ready to rock.

## Determine What Your PC's IP Address Is

It can be very useful to know what your PC's IP address is, especially for trouble-shooting. Finding out what address Windows obtained for your PC isn't difficult. For Windows NT4, 2000 and XP, do this:

1.   Click Start and then click Run.

     √  Type **cmd.exe**.

     √  When the black "console window" appears, type **ipconfig /all** and press Enter.

What you'll see will look a lot like Figure 10-2.

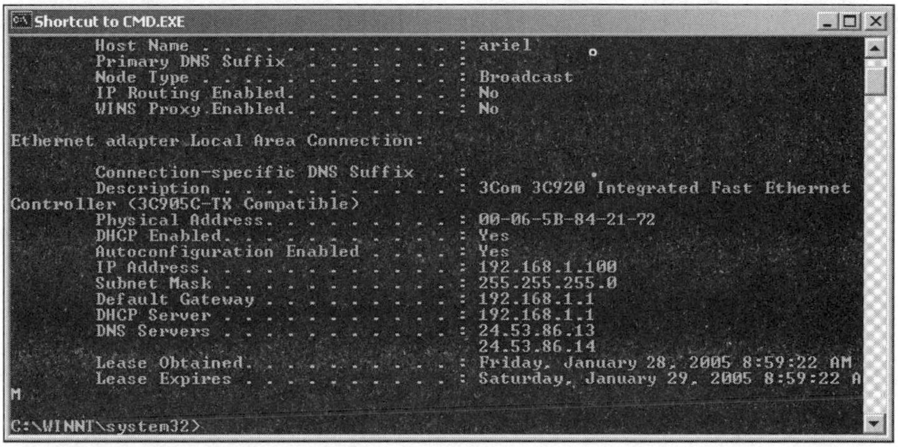

**Figure 10-2**

Displaying your IP address in Windows NT4, 2000, or XP.

Look in that jungle of text for a line that begins with "IP Address." The display will be slightly different depending on whether Windows obtained an IP ad-dress from a DHCP server or had to give itself one from APIPA. The IP address will be at the right end of the line.

---

*TIP: If you're writing the IP address down, look for and write down the PC's MAC address as well. It's called "Physical Address" for Windows 2000 and XP and "Adapter Address" for Windows 9x and Me. You may need the MAC address later on if you have problems installing a router in a cable modem system, as we'll explain later in this chapter.*

---

For Windows 9*x* and Me, the process is slightly different:

2.   Select Start | Run.

   √   Type **winipcfg.exe**.

Windows will put up a conventional dialog (not a console window) that contains a field labeled "IP Address." There it is! (See Figure 10-3.)

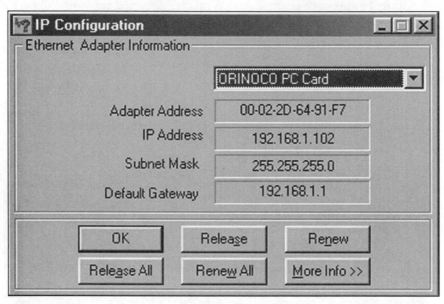

**Figure 10-3**
Displaying your IP address in Windows 9x and Me.

# Connect Two PCs via cable

The very simplest network you can create consists of two PCs with a cable between them. With PCs connected in this way, you can pass files back and forth between them. What we'll be describing here will only include connecting the two PCs. Sharing dial-up access to the Internet between two PCs connected by a single cable requires Internet Connection Sharing (ICS), which we discussed back in Chapter 8. However, once you have a broadband Internet connection installed, it's *much* better for security reasons to access the Net through an inexpensive router, as we'll discuss a little later. Even if you have only one PC to connect to your broadband modem, a router is a *really* good idea.

Most people who connect two PCs with a cable are doing it to connect their laptops to their desktop PCs. This makes it easy to move files or your e-mail mailbase onto the laptop in preparation for a trip, and to move files back to the desktop PC when you return home.

There are four reasonable ways to connect two PCs (both running Windows) by a single cable:

√ Connect an Ethernet crossover cable between the Ethernet network ports on the two PCs. (Easy.)

√ Connect a FireWire cable between the FireWire ports on the two PCs. (Easy, but only XP and—maybe—Me can do it.)

√ Connect a special USB link cable between the two PCs, along with some software. (Requires some fussing, some software, and a special cable.)

√ Connect a serial-port crossover cable (sometimes called a null modem cable) between the serial ports on the two PCs. (Requires a fair amount of fussing, works slowly, and sometimes won't work at all for reasons that never come clear.)

## Use an Ethernet Crossover Cable to Connect Two PCs

By far, the simplest, easiest, and cheapest connection between two PCs is through a Category 5 Ethernet crossover cable. If you're using either Windows 2000 or Windows XP, it's virtually automatic. In summary: You turn both PCs off, connect the crossover cable between the Ethernet port on one PC and the Ethernet port on the other, and then turn them on and boot up. In a couple of minutes, you should be connected. That's all it takes!

An Ethernet crossover cable is a special variety of the familiar Category 5 Ethernet patch cable. It can be purchased at any retailer that sells computer gear for between $8 and $12. It looks almost exactly like an ordinary Ethernet patch cable, but it will be labeled somehow so that you know it's a crossover cable. Look for the abbreviation *CRS* embossed in the plug on each end or for a label of some other kind.

---

**TIP:** *If you have a crossover cable that isn't labeled, label it right now. If you mix them up later on and try to use a crossover cable instead of a regular Ethernet patch cable (or vise versa), you will not be able to make a connection!*

---

What makes the cable a crossover cable? It doesn't look any different physically, and it's only different electrically. Old-timers may remember something called a *null modem,* which was used to connect PCs through their serial ports in ancient times. A crossover cable is a null modem for Ethernet ports rather than serial ports. It connects the output pins of one Ethernet port to the input pins of another and vice versa (see Figure 10-4). No communication can happen between two PCs on a straight-through patch cable because with a straight-through cable, the two PCs' input pins are connected together, as are the output pins. Inputs can't talk to inputs, nor outputs to outputs. The crossover cable makes sure that inputs talk to outputs and outputs to inputs.

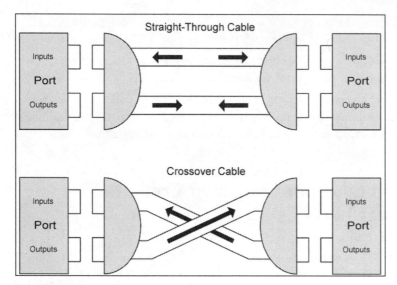

**Figure 10-4**
How a crossover cable works.

You might ask: If a straight-through cable can't connect two PCs, why is it useful at all? Good question, but one that will have to wait for the discussion of hubs and switches, later in this chapter.

Here's your step-by-step for direct connection via Ethernet crossover cable:

1.  Make sure the network ports on both PCs are enabled. To do this, click Start, then Settings, and then Network and Dial Up Connections. Look for a line labeled "Local Area Connection" and be sure that it's marked as "Enabled."

2.  Make sure the cable in your hand is indeed a crossover cable, and connect it between the two Ethernet ports.

3.  Power up or reboot both PCs. Once both PCs are past bootup, give them five minutes to self-assign an IP address with APIPA and locate one another.

4.  For both PCs, in Windows Explorer, expand My Network Places and click on Computers Near Me. Look and see if the name of the opposite PC is displayed. If so, you're there!

# If the Ethernet Crossover Connection Doesn't Work

If you run through the step-by-step and don't find a connection between the two machines, here are some things to check:

√ Is the cable *really* a crossover cable? Did you buy it in a wrapper that said "Crossover Cable" or did someone hand it to you and say, "This is a crossover cable"? If you're not techie enough to determine by inspection what kind of cable it is, get some expert advice, or buy a clearly marked crossover cable.

√ Are both ends of the cable plugged into Ethernet ports? It's possible on some PCs to plug an Ethernet cable into the telephone modem jack, and that won't work. Pull the cable out of both ports and look to see how many bright copper wires can be seen in the jack. Eight wires is an Ethernet jack. Fewer than eight wires (four or most commonly two) and it's a phone modem jack.

√ Are you running Windows 95 on either PC? Windows 95 does not support APIPA. For best results, use Windows 2000 or XP. (Even Windows 98 isn't an ace in the Ethernet department.)

√ Are both Ethernet ports enabled?

√ Is the TCP/IP protocol enabled?

If you can't make it work, you still have other options. One is using a USB port bridge cable to connect the two PCs. The other, if both PCs are running Windows XP, is to connect them with a FireWire cable.

# Use a FireWire Cable to Connect Two PCs

The two most recent versions of Windows (XP and Me) contain built-in support for networking over a FireWire cable. This support is called IP over 1394 because IEEE 1394 is the standards document defining the FireWire technology. Unfortunately, Windows support for FireWire is marginal, and neither Windows 2000 nor Windows 9*x* has the drivers for IP over 1394. Furthermore, Windows Me support for IP over 1394 is buggy and doesn't always work.

Unless you're connecting two Windows XP machines, your best bet is to use the Internet crossover cable described in the previous section or the USB bridge cable in the next. However, if you are connecting two Windows XP machines, you can proceed pretty much as described for the Ethernet crossover cable in the previous section. Windows XP support for IP over 1394 is Plug and Play, so if you plug the cable into both PCs and power up or reboot, Windows XP will recognize the connection and establish an IP-based connection between the two PCs. Some potential issues:

√ If you have one or both of the PCs already networked over Ethernet, Windows may get confused and not establish the link. IP over 1394 works best when there are no other active IP-based connections to either PC.

√ Windows Me does not always trigger APIPA when you plug the FireWire cable into the Windows Me PC. If this happens, you may have to assign a local IP address manually to the Windows Me PC. Try 192.168.2.1. Better yet, upgrade to XP!

√ FireWire cables are necessarily short. The maximum length is 4.5 meters, which is about 15 feet. Both PCs just about have to be in the same room.

√ FireWire cables tend to be stiff, and if you bend them sharply or kink them, they will not pass data as quickly as they will unbent and unkinked. Handle them carefully.

√ If you can't establish the connection, make sure that TCP/IP is enabled on both ends and that both FireWire ports are enabled. Also, make sure that any front-panel FireWire ports you're trying to use are connected to the motherboard internally. Sometimes they are connected incorrectly, or not connected at all! (FireWire support is not good in the PC world. It's really an Apple technology.)

Still, if you can get the link to work, it will be *very* fast, faster than anything else you can inexpensively and easily run between two PCs, including a 100Base-T Ethernet crossover cable.

## Direct Connections via USB and Special Cables

The third way to connect two PCs isn't precisely networking in the same way that networking over an Ethernet crossover cable or a FireWire cable is networking. When you use an Ethernet crossover cable or FireWire cable, you have a two-PC IP-based network. With a special USB cable and software (available at many retailers for about $30), you can transfer files between two PCs, and while it isn't as versatile as an IP-based connection, it's certainly better than nothing.

A special cable is needed because USB is a master-slave technology and the two ends of the cable are different. The PC end is the larger end, carrying a connector that is technically the "A" connector. The smaller "B" end is for plugging into peripherals; you will not find a "B" jack on PCs. USB requires a little persuasion to support a peer-to-peer connection between two PCs. This persuasion comes in the form of a custom cable that has an "A" connector (the PC side) on both ends and a lump in the middle containing some mediating electronics.

All such custom USB link cables that we've looked at are sold with a CD containing both drivers and a software utility (often an older version of something called PC-Linq) that allows transfer of files between the two PCs. Installation is basically a matter of installing the software on the CD and then plugging in the cables. Windows Plug and Play takes it from there. Nearly all such cable products work at USB 1.1 speeds, which will give you from 4- to 6-Mbps file transfer speeds. A few USB link cable products are now appearing for USB 2.0, and those will move files *much* more quickly. Be sure that you have USB 2.0 ports on both ends of the link, though!

---

**TIP:** *If both your PCs have USB 2.0 ports, they probably also have Ethernet network ports, and connecting two PCs with an Ethernet crossover cable is both cheaper (the cable costs only $8 to $12) and far more powerful. Use an Ethernet crossover cable if you possibly can.*

---

The downside to all USB link products that we've tested is that they allow file transfer only. You can't share an Internet connection through a USB link, nor can you share printers. All you can do is move files from one PC to another. That can be very useful—but it's not real networking.

USB link cable/software packages like this are widely available online. Search for "USB link cable" or "USB bridge cable." CompUSA carries such a product in their retail stores. The part number is 283437, and it lists for $24.99.

## Your Last Resort: Connecting through Serial Port Cables

If you have a pair of really old PCs without Ethernet ports, FireWire ports, or USB ports, you can still create a connection of sorts between them. You need a special cable called a serial crossover cable (also called a null modem cable, back in ancient times) and software to create and manage the link. The most famous product of this type is LapLink, and LapLink is still the smoothest of its genre. LapLink comes in many versions, most of which have a lot of features completely unrelated to connecting PCs. What you're looking for is LapLink Filemover. It costs about $30, including the cable (see **www.laplink.com**). This is a good deal, as the crossover cable itself will cost you $30 at most retailers, without any software at all.

LapLink's only downside is that it is no longer supported by Windows 95, and that's where a lot of the need for this sort of link actually falls. For Windows 95, your best bet is to buy a serial crossover cable (CompUSA has them for about

$30) and download the free software Kermit to manage the link. Kermit is a file transfer utility created and supported by people at Columbia University in New York City. It requires a little study, but it does work and will do the job.

The Kermit 95 Project for Windows: **www.columbia.edu/kermit/k95.html**.

# Understand Why Routers Are Better Than Hubs

Connecting two PCs with a cable is definitely bottom-feeder "networking." If you're going to connect, do it right: Set up a proper network using Ethernet cables and a hub, switch, or router. We spoke of setting up a network in Chapter 8, and at some point you should refer back to that chapter for step-by-step instructions.

Quick recap: An Ethernet network consists of a central connection device with several Ethernet ports (inexpensive devices have from 4 to 8 ports) and individual cables connecting each networked device (PC, printer, etc.) to the central connector. The cables are available at any computer retailer and are called Category 5 patch cables. You can run longer cables through the ceiling and connect to the network PCs that are as far as 300 feet from the center connector. The center connection device performs the "crossover" function among all devices connected to it. This is why you don't need Ethernet crossover cables when you build a network with a central hub, switch, or router. The device in the center makes sure that all inputs are connected to all outputs when appropriate. PCs connect to the center device with standard, straight-through CAT5 cables. Crossover cables are only necessary when you connect two PCs without a hub, switch, or router between them.

There are three types of center connection device: hubs, switches, and routers. We'll describe each separately.

## Hubs: The Choke Point in the Middle

The ancient patriarch of Ethernet networking is the *hub*. A hub is nothing more complex than a small circuit board that connects all of its several ports together, inputs to outputs, so that every PC on the network can talk to every other PC on the network at the same time. (See Figure 10-4 for this business of connecting inputs to outputs.) What this means is that when a PC places a data packet on its network port, that data packet is instantly transmitted to all the far corners of the network. Every PC on the network finds that packet on its Ethernet port.

So what good is that? The answer lies in addressing. Each packet has to be labeled with the address of the PC for which it is intended. All PCs on the network find the packet in their laps, but only the PC to which the packet is addressed will "grab" the packet and store it internally. The other PCs simply shrug and ignore it (see Figure 10-5).

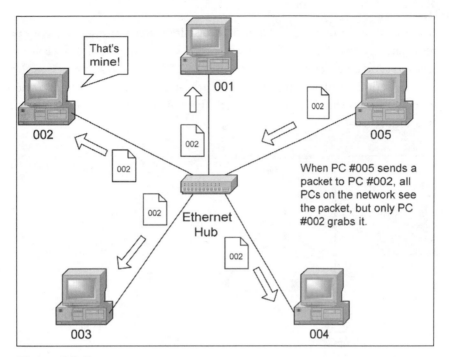

**Figure 10-5**
How hubs work.

In a sense, the entire hubbed network "lights up" with every data packet transmitted by any PC to any other PC. (Ever hear the expression "the ether vibrates"? That's where the name Ethernet came from.) Every PC gets every packet, and every PC must decode the address and determine if each packet is intended for it or some other PC. This is a lot of wasted effort for all the PCs who are not recipients of data. Worse, a hubbed system is inherently slow. Every PC has to "pay attention" to every packet sent from any PC to any other. With two PCs connected via hub, you could lose as much as half of your potential network throughput. If multiple conversations are going on between several PCs simultaneously, the performance can slow down even more than that.

The hub is a choke point at the center of your network. Hubs are cheap, but they are not a great deal cheaper than switches, which are better in a great many ways. Read on.

# Switches: Momentary Data Superhighways

Hubbed networks are *so* 1995. If you're going to build a network in the twenty-first century, it should be a switched network. A network switch can replace a network hub, cable for cable, and requires no fussing or additional configuration. Simply connect each PC via patch cable to one of the ports on the back of the switch and it's done.

A switch does something that a hub cannot: It creates a momentary connection between any two PCs on the network. The connection lasts only as long as it takes to send a packet from one of those two PCs to the other. As far as the two PCs are concerned, for that moment they are the only two PCs on the network, and the other PCs are not aware that data is moving through the switch (see Figure 10-6).

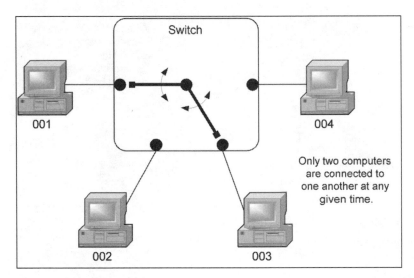

**Figure 10-6**
How network switches work.

Please understand that the figure is a metaphor; network switches are purely electrical and there are no mechanical contacts inside the box! The figure only serves to explain that the switch can connect any two PCs in the network while leaving the others blissfully unaware that anything is going on. The other PCs waste no time trying to decide if a packet that comes to their network ports is theirs or not. This makes switched networks inherently faster than hubbed networks.

Switches are inexpensive and work well. The Linksys EZXS55W switch is an excellent example, with a street price of about $25 to $30. However, don't buy it yet. Switches are excellent networkers, but in today's Internet-intensive world, they're incomplete. Read on.

## Routers: A Switch and the Internet Too!

If all you want to do is connect your several PCs together, an Ethernet switch and some patch cables are all you need. However, an Ethernet switch only connects the PCs on your network. It's helpless to connect to the Internet. To connect a network to the Internet, you need a router.

A switch is a way to connect two PCs. A router is a way to connect two *networks*—typically, your home network and the Internet. A router is always a piece of software, but it's usually purchased as something embedded in a small router appliance. Windows's Internet Connection Sharing (ICS) software acts as a router, but it runs on one of your PCs. ICS is okay for Internet dial-up accounts (see Chapter 8), but it's unnecessarily slow and crude for a broadband Internet connection.

Most routers sold as inexpensive appliances for home networks also include an Ethernet switch in the same box. That means that one inexpensive gadget (street price $40–$60) knits all your PCs together into a network and handles the interface between your network and the Internet. One of the most famous router/switch appliances is the Linksys BEFSR41, which combines a four-port switch with a router. (There's an eight-port version called the BEFSR81, if you need to connect more than four PCs in your home network.)

We discussed using a Linksys BEFSR41 router to create a network in Chapter 9. The connections are simple: Each PC is connected to the router with a CAT5 patch cord to one of the numbered ports. The broadband modem is connected to the port marked "WAN" (Wide Access Network) or "Internet." (The Internet is a WAN that spans the world. You can't get much wider than that!) You can see a diagram of how to make the connections in Figure 9-4, back in Chapter 9 on Page 194.

Assuming that you leave the router's defaults unchanged, and that your ISP has a DHCP server available to its customers, the router should work correctly as soon as you cable everything together and power everything up. Here's what happens once everything's powered up:

1.  The router requests an IP address for itself from your ISP's DHCP server.

2.  The ISP's DHCP server sends the router the requested IP address along with a few other values necessary for the router to configure itself. The router now has an IP address.

3.  Each of your PCs connected to the network requests an IP address from any available DHCP server. Without a router in the network, this would be the ISP's DHCP server. However, the router has its own DHCP server, which is the DHCP server that hears each PC's request.

4.  The router's DHCP server sends each PC on your network an IP address and whatever else each PC needs to network successfully.

    √  Windows puts the finishing touches on its networking support for each PC (now that the PC has received its own IP address) and the network is up and running.

## Why You Should Have a Router—Even With Only One PC

What's the sound of one PC networking? Basically, a sigh of relief. It may seem ridiculous to buy a router when all you have is your desktop PC, but there is a huge benefit in using a router that has little to do with connecting PCs: Virtually all routers contain a hardware firewall using the Network Address Translation (NAT) technology.

A NAT firewall is *strong* protection against all but the most determined attacks from the network "black hats" looking to compromise PCs for various illegal purposes. More specifically, NAT firewalls block all automated network attacks. Internet worms and scripts just can't get past them. (A determined human being may be able to get through a NAT firewall, but it's not easy, and it's almost never attempted.)

You don't have to do anything to set up, enable, or configure a NAT firewall. You just have to connect your PC to one of the router's ports and your broadband modem to the router's WAN or Internet port and you're protected. How a NAT firewall works is interesting, but not germane to this chapter. For more details, see *Jeff Duntemann's Wi-Fi Guide* (Paraglyph Press, 2004.)

## The MAC Address Authorization Problem

There is only one serious gotcha to be encountered when you install a router, and then only if your broadband connection is via cable rather than DSL. Not everyone runs into it, but it's common enough to warrant some explanation here. Your ISP may have a system in place to authorize a PC that tries to connect to its cable system. In a system like that, your PC must identify itself to the ISP by presenting its Media Access Control (MAC) address to the ISP network.

Every piece of PC hardware that can access an Ethernet network has its own unique MAC address. This includes the network adapter in your PC and also the network interface inside every router. A MAC address is nothing like an IP address. The MAC address is a hyphenated number expressed in base-16 (hexadecimal) notation and looks something like this:

00-40-96-49-61-BB

Letters from *A* to *F* exist in hexadecimal numbers to stand for base-16 digits from 10 to 15. If you don't understand hexadecimal notation, that's all right. Treat the MAC address as an alphabetical ID code, which is almost precisely what it is.

The problem with MAC authentication (which has nothing to do with Mac computers, by the way!) usually happens when people add a router between their PC and their cable modem after they've been using the cable modem for a while in a direct connection to their PC. If you have the router ready to go when the cable installer comes to set up your system—or when you do the increasingly popular self-install—you will probably not experience the problem at all.

It works like this (follow along on Figure 10-7): When you first have cable Internet service installed, the cable system (through the cable modem) asks your PC what its network adapter's MAC address is. The PC identifies itself with its network adapter's MAC address, and the cable system records that MAC address on its servers. From then on, anytime your PC tries to connect to the cable Internet system, the system asks your PC for its MAC address. If the MAC address returned in answer to the cable system's query is *not* the same address logged during cable modem installation, the cable system does not let your PC connect to the Internet.

The cable companies do this so that people can't "tap in" to the cable with their own cable modems and get Internet access through the cable without paying for it. The PC network adapter's MAC address identifies the PC to the cable system as a legitimate paying customer.

Now, when you insert a router in between your cable modem and your PC, the cable system can no longer ask your PC what its MAC address is. When the authentication query comes down the cable, the router is the one that responds—and the router has its own MAC address that is not the same as the

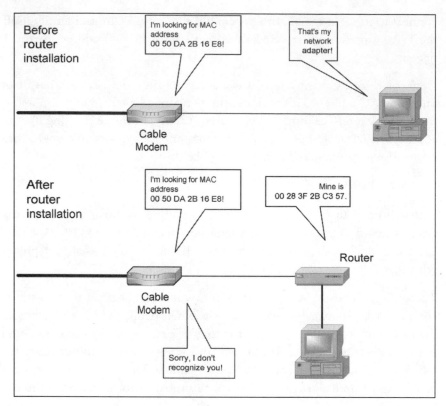

**Figure 10-7**

How MAC address authentication works.

address in your PC's network adapter. The router's MAC address has not been recorded by the cable system, and so the cable system doesn't recognize it and it won't let your PC access the Internet.

There are a three different ways to deal with this problem:

√ Some cable systems will automatically reauthenticate a residential broadband account after it's been disconnected from the cable for several hours. If you can stand to be without your Internet connection for 24 hours, disconnect the cable modem from the router, power down the cable modem, and don't attempt to reconnect the cable modem to the router for 24 hours. Then reconnect the cable and power up the cable modem. This may prompt the cable system to rerecord the MAC address that it "sees" (this time, the one belonging to your router) and make everything work together again.

√ If the first technique didn't work, call your cable company, explain that you've put a router in between the PC and the cable modem, and ask that they reauthenticate your system. They have to do this anyway every so often when people buy a new PC, which has a different MAC address than the PC for which cable Internet service was originally installed. Because people generally change PCs more often than they change routers, having a router is actually to the cable company's advantage and will help you avoid tech support calls down the road when the PC at the account changes.

√ If the cable company refuses to reauthenticate your PC (and this attitude isn't common anymore), you may have to "clone" the MAC address of your PC's network adapter and insert it into your router. This sounds scary but it's not as difficult as all that—and the newer routers help you do it. Read on.

## Cloning Your MAC Address

The ironic thing about authenticating by MAC address is that any PC can pretend to have any MAC address its owner wants it to have—which is a little like being able to change fingerprints at will. However, this does give you a way to get around the MAC address authentication problem described in the previous section. What you need to do is take the PC's MAC address—which is what the cable company's system is looking for—and apply that address to your router. This is called "cloning" your MAC address, since you're copying it into another device. At that point the router will respond to the cable system's queries with the same MAC address that your PC used to use, and everything will be in the groove.

This may be easier than it sounds if you have a recent router. Most routers manufactured since late 2003 have a built-in feature to make MAC address cloning almost effortless. And even if you have an older router, MAC address cloning isn't all that difficult. You just have to write some numbers down and type carefully.

The hardest part, in fact, may be logging into your router's control screens. These screens are accessed through a Web browser, even though all the information stays on your PC and doesn't travel over the Internet. Do this:

1. Bring up a Web browser.

2. Look in the router's documentation to find the IP address that the router responds to. This address is hardwired into the router, and while it can be changed, it rarely is. For Linksys routers, the address is almost always 192.168.1.1. Some routers from other manufacturers (especially D-Link) respond to 192.168.0.1, and others 192.168.2.1. To find out how to log into a router that doesn't respond to one of these addresses, go to the Port Forward site on the Web (**www.portforward.com/routers.htm**) and click on the make and model of your router.

3. Once you have the router's IP address, type it into the URL bar at the top of your browser and press Enter. A login dialog should appear. If it doesn't, you don't have the correct address for the router. Keep looking, or find the manufacturer's Web site and ask its tech support what the login IP address is.

4. If your router is new and you haven't changed the login ID and password, your router documentation should provide you with those two items, which you should enter into the login dialog. If you received the router used from someone else, you may not know the login and password that they used. In that case, you may have to reset the router to its default values. This is something you may have to contact the manufacturer's tech support about, or ask in a forum devoted to routers, like Port Forward.

5. Once the router accepts your login, you'll see a configuration screen. They're all different, so we can't reproduce them here. Poke through the menus and find an option called Clone MAC Address or something close to that. If you can't find it, again, you may have to ask questions in a forum or contact the manufacturer's Web site.

6. Many newer routers have a button marked "Clone." If you click this button, the router will ask the PC for its MAC address and replace its default address with your PC's address. At that point, you're done! Your router will present your PC's MAC address to the cable system, and you'll be in.

7. Older routers may require that you enter a MAC address manually. This first requires that you know what your PC's MAC address is. Fortunately, you already learned how to determine it, back on page 211 when you determined your PC's IP address. The PC's MAC address is shown in the same display. For Windows 2000 and XP, it will be after the label "Physical Address." For Windows 9x and Me, it will be after the label "Adapter Address." Either way, find it and write it down. It will be a set of six numbers separated by dashes, like 00-40-96-49-61-BB. (Letters from *A* to *F* are okay.)

8. The screen where you enter the PC's MAC address will have six entry fields and a label like "User-Defined WAN MAC Address" (Linksys) or something close. *Carefully* type the PC's MAC address into the six fields. Do not type the dashes. You may have to backspace over the existing numbers (if there are any) in the six fields. These are often 00. Backspace over them until the field is empty, and then type the two-digit number for that field. Then tab or mouse-click to the next field. When you're done, click the OK or Apply button. That's all you have to do.

It's a good idea, after cloning your MAC address, to power down your PC, cable modem, and router and then power them up in this order: cable modem, router, and then your PC. Give each a minute or two to self-test before powering up the next in line.

# Get the Scoop on Network Cables

It's easy to get in the habit of thinking of Ethernet network cables as "just wires" (especially because they look a lot like telephone cables), but in truth Ethernet cables are subtler than simply an electrical conductor running from one PC to another. Inside the cable are actually four pairs of wires, twisted together very precisely. Network cables carry data imposed on radio frequency currents. These radio frequency currents run up into the hundreds of megahertz, and at those frequencies things like how sharp a bend you make in the cable matter a *lot*.

There are seven categories of unshielded twisted-pair (UTP) cabling recognized and defined by standards bodies, running from Category 1, which is simple telephone cable, to Category 6, which is capable of comfortably carrying network data at Gigabit Ethernet rates. The only ones you'll encounter are the three highest-speed cable categories: 5, 5E, and 6. These are very much alike physically and mostly differ in the maximum data rate that they can carry:

√ Category 5 cables are very common and work well for the older 10Base-T networks as well as modern 100Base-T networks.

√ Category 5E cables can carry faster data streams, up to (barely) 1000Base-T. Category 5E patch cables are gradually replacing Category 5 cables in retail outlets.

√ Category 6 cables are fairly new and can comfortably handle 1000Base-T connections at their top speed. These are slightly stiffer and still significantly more expensive than Category 5E cables.

If all you have are conventional 100Base-T network ports, you can do just fine with Category 5. Category 5E and 6 were created to support low-cost networks using Gigabit Ethernet technology, more precisely called 1000Base-T. Network ports for Gigabit Ethernet are still expensive and generally show up only on more expensive PCs. If you do decide to create a 1000Base-T network, you'll be laying out more money for network add-in cards and switches anyway, so go the distance and buy Category 6 cabling. Category 5 cables won't hack gigabit data streams; they will bring a 1000Base-T network down to barely more than 100Base-T speeds.

We've heard numerous reports that Category 5E cabling will allow slightly higher throughput than Category 5 for a 100Base-T network, but we've not found that to be true in testing network speed. Our suspicion is that badly installed in-wall Category 5 was involved in some of these tests, with a much higher error rate than nice new lengths of Category 5E lying unstapled, unkinked, and otherwise unmolested on the test-room floor. *The quality of cable installation matters!*

# What Not to Do with Ethernet Cables

One important source of gunk in your network lies in damaged or badly installed Ethernet cabling. Cables need to be handled with reasonable care and installed with certain cautions in mind. There are certain things you just can't do with Ethernet cable and expect your network to perform at top speed:

√ Do not kink or bend network cables at sharp angles, and especially do not bend it 180 degrees; for example, to store cable in a center-tied hank. To store cables, carefully gather them into circular rolls no tighter than 8 inches in diameter.

√ Do not stretch network cables, even to remove a kink. Once it's kinked, a network cable will never carry data as quickly again. Stretching cable changes the electrical relationships of the twisted pair conductors, increasing the error rate and reducing its throughput.

√ Don't just leave Ethernet cables on the floor to be stepped on, and certainly don't put them under a carpet! Stepping on the cable will distort the twisted pairs inside and increase the error rate.

√ Do not run Ethernet cables in parallel with electrical wires. 120V power lines induce currents in network cable that radically increase the error rate.

√ *Do not pull Ethernet cable through conduit that already carries electrical service wiring!* Not only is this a safety hazard that breaks every electrical code in the world, but the close proximity of network and electrical conductors will induce noise in your network cable and render the cable almost useless.

√ Network cables must never rest on, or cross over, florescent lamp fixtures or ballast transformers. If you're running cable above a dropped ceiling, give fluorescent lights a wide berth. They are electrically very "noisy."

√ Keep network cables away from motors and things that contain motors, like fans. Motors are electrically "noisy" and can induce that noise in network cables, increasing their error rate.

√ If you must use wiring staples to hold Ethernet cable in place, don't hammer them down so tight that they pinch the cable. Leave the cable some wiggle room. Pinching the cable is akin to kinking it, and it will raise the error rate.

√ Keep cables away from hot pipes or vents carrying hot air.

Damaged or badly installed cables will cause packets to be corrupted, as will the influence of motors, fluorescent lamps, and electrical mains too near the cables. Bad packets are detected by the Ethernet system, which is then forced to re-transmit the bad packets. The more bad packets detected and re-transmitted, the slower your network will be. This is what we mean by "error rate." You won't see these errors in a Windows error dialog. Ethernet handles them transparently; what you'll notice (in a network with bad cables) is that throughput slows down considerably.

# Installing Your Own Network Cabling

The best time to wire a house for Ethernet networking is while it's being built. After that, well, it's a lot of work and requires more care than running telephone or electric power wiring through existing walls. If you're handy with tools and have an accessible attic or basement to run cables through, you can manage it. Large home improvement stores like Home Depot now have wall outlets for network ports, bulk Category 5E cable, and the other fiddly bits you'll need to install cables and outlets. We can't explain how to do this in detail in this book, but many recent books on house wiring now include sections on network and media cabling as well.

---

*TIP: The **big** rule in installing network cabling is simple: **Don't make sharp bends in the cable**. That, and reasonable care handling and stapling the cables, will allow you to install a top-speed network.*

---

## GunkBusters' Notebook: Don't Run Category 5 Cables Between Homes!

This isn't common, but it comes up regularly: People find themselves living next door to relatives or close friends and get the idea of running an Ethernet Category 5 cable from one home to the other so that the PCs in both houses can be on the same network.

In one word: *Don't!* You'll probably blow out your network cards!

The issue sounds odd but is very real: The ground conductor common to all the wiring in a single house is connected to the soil outside the house. Because the soil is apparently the same, and the houses are close together, it would be easy to assume that the ground potential in both homes would be the same. Unfortunately, there's nothing that guarantees that this has to be the case, for these three important reasons:

√ Differences in soil composition, degree of moisture, and so on can create ground potential differences between the ground tie points of adjacent homes, even if they're only a few feet apart.

√ Differences in the length of the ground conductor tied to the soil can create differences in ground potential between adjacent homes, especially if the ground conductor wire is thin or corroded.

√ Badly installed or corroded ground systems can cause ground potential differences between adjacent homes.

When two ground systems existing at different potentials are connected by an electrical conductor, current will flow from one ground system to another. If the path for this current flow passes through a pair of Ethernet network cards or motherboards, the port logic can be destroyed by these unexpected currents.

If you insist on connecting two buildings via network cable and the two buildings have separate electrical and ground systems, the only safe way to proceed is to buy Ethernet fiber-optic cable for the house-house link. This isn't cheap and it's not easy to do correctly, and if you intend to do it, we suggest that you find a professional installer with experience in Ethernet over fiber optics. Realistically, you're much better off using a Wi-Fi wireless link. See Chapter 11.

# Learn How to Measure Your Network's Throughput

You don't have to take anyone's word for how fast Ethernet networks pass data. You can test the throughput of your own network yourself, using free tools you can download from the Internet. This requires a little more tech savvy than most of the things described in this book, but it's not so arcane that you can't do it with a little study.

Our favorite throughput measurement tool is called QCheck, and it's available as a free download from software company Ixia:

**http://www.ixiacom.com/products/qcheck/index.php**

You have to answer a Web questionnaire to be allowed to do the download, but we've not heard of the company misusing the information, and the QCheck product is worth it. The QCheck utility has a simple and interesting user interface, shown in Figure 10-8.

## How QCheck Works

The QCheck tool actually comes as two parts. The main part (see Figure 10-8) is a control console, which you install on only one of your networked PCs. The secondary part is a performance testing "endpoint," which is a small program

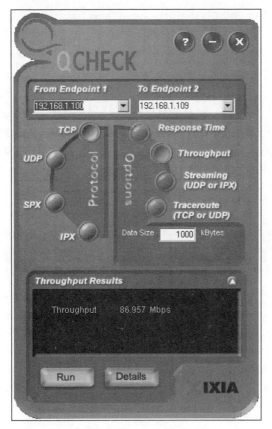

**Figure 10-8**
The QCheck user interface.

that must be installed on every one of your networked PCs. There is a different endpoint for each different operating system. You should download the one for the version of Windows that you have, again, from Ixia's Web site:

**http://www.ixiacom.com/support/endpoint_library/**

An endpoint is automatically installed on the PC where you install the main QCheck utility. The endpoints are automatically run by Windows (as Windows services) when you reboot your PCs. You don't have to do anything yourself to launch them. They have no user interface, so you will not see them running unless you bring up the task manager process list.

QCheck can run a throughput test between any two endpoints installed on your network. This allows you to test throughput over the cables running between any two of your networked PCs. The QCheck utility sends messages over your network to the two endpoints that you select, and the endpoints pass a 1 MB file between them while keeping track of elapsed time. The endpoints send their results back to the QCheck utility, which displays the throughput value in megabits per second.

## Selecting Endpoints for Throughput Tests

The only tricky part to using QCheck is telling the QCheck utility which endpoints to use. QCheck needs the IP addresses of the two PCs on which the endpoints are running. We explained how to determine any networked PC's IP address earlier in this chapter, on page 211. Go to each of the PCs on your network with a notepad, and write down its IP address.

QCheck has two entry fields, for the "From" endpoint and the "To" endpoint. Type each of the IP addresses that you wrote down into the From field. An IP address typed in either field will immediately appear in both, so you only have to enter each IP address once.

Once all your PC IP addresses have been entered, you can set the "From" endpoint and the "To" endpoint by choosing an IP address from the drop-down menus. You'll see the word *localhost* in both menus. Localhost indicates the PC on which the QCheck utility is running. If localhost is chosen as one of the endpoints for a test, the PC on which the QCheck utility is running will be one end of the test.

## Performing Throughput Tests

QCheck can perform several different tests. The one you want is labeled "Throughput." The other tests are interesting but not pertinent to this book. We encourage you to read the online help (click the ? button on the top of the window) and try them out.

To run a throughput test, do this:

1.  Click the Throughput button.
2.  Type **1000** in the Data Size field below the buttons. This indicates the size of the data block passed back and forth during the throughput test itself. You can enter smaller values than 1000, but 1000 gives you the greatest accuracy.
3.  Make sure that the TCP button is selected (it's the default.) This selects the TCP network protocol as the one to be used for testing.
4.  Pull down the From menu and select the PC to be one end of the test.
5.  Pull down the To menu and select the PC to be the other end of the test.
6.  Click Run.

The test will take only seconds. When the test is complete, QCheck will display the measured throughput in the black window, in megabits per second.

## Interpreting Your Test Results

The throughput readings you get with QCheck will depend on a number of things, most of which are beyond your control:

√   The type of cable between the PCs: CAT5, CAT5E, or CAT6

√   The type of Ethernet adapters installed in your PCs: 10Base-T, 100Base-T, or 1000Base-T

√   Whether your network is connected at the center with a hub or a switch

√   Whether the cable is of high quality, low quality, or damaged somehow

√   (Very rarely) How the network adapter is configured to communicate with other network adapters

A healthy, well-installed network using CAT5 cables between PCs containing 100Base-T network adapters will give you throughput readings from 50 to 80 Mbps. Good category 5E cables may reduce the error rate slightly and give you readings as high as 90 Mbps—and we've seen readings as high as 94 Mbps. Note that no 100Base-T network can give you readings over 100 Mbps. That's the maximum "bit rate" for the network, without any consideration for packet framing and other network overhead. In practice, it *must* be less, and it's often a *lot* less.

---

**TIP:** If you have a hub at the center of your network rather than a switch, your throughput will be roughly half what it would be with a switch. On a 100Base-T network that could potentially run at 75 or 80 Mbps with a switch, a hub may pull it down to 35 or 40 Mbps. Dump that hub and get a switch instead!

---

Nearly all PC network adapters these days use the 100Base-T Ethernet technology. If you find that a wired connection (not Wi-Fi) between two PCs comes in at less than 10 Mbps, one of the two PCs acting as endpoints in that test may be running an older 10Base-T network adapter, which cannot transfer bits faster than 10 Mbps. PCs used in large businesses before 1996 or 1997 often had 10Base-T adapters, but such machines are generally very slow (think Pentium 166!) and you will have other, worse problems with them today than slow network throughput.

Ideally, all the legs in your network (that is, all the possible paths between two PCs) should come in at about the same speed. If one leg comes in radically slower than the others, you may have bad cables, loose connectors, or an ancient PC with a 10Base-T network adapter. Do some troubleshooting. Change cables if you can and test again.

If you run a test in which both endpoints are the same PC, you may get stratospherically high readings. QCheck allows such tests, but the results are not meaningful.

## What About Gigabit Ethernet?

1000Base-T network gear is still expensive and uncommon. As the years go by, the prices on 1000Base-T network adapters will fall, 1000Base-T switches will become cheap and common, and built-in network ports on PCs will become 1000Base-T. If you have a high-end PC now, it may already have a 1000Base-T network adapter in it. You may dream of throwing MP3s or movie files up and down your cables in a fraction of a second, but a few things may be in your way:

√ A switch containing 100Base-T technology will not pass data at 1000Base-T speeds. You will need to buy a 1000Base-T switch. The good news is that these are now under $100 (the Linksys EG005W has a street price of about $85) and will get cheaper over time.

√ Ordinary CAT5 cables can carry 1000Base-T data at rates faster than 100Base-T rates, but not a *lot* faster. Once you have a gigabit switch, older CAT5 cables will be your main choke point. To get the full throughput 1000Base-T can offer, you'll need good-quality CAT5E or CAT6 cables installed correctly, without kinks or sharp bends.

√ The throughput between two PCs is as slow as the slower of the two network adapters. Any leg containing a 100Base-T network adapter will move data at only 100Base-T rates.

One caution: Don't try to drop a 1000Base-T network card into a slow PC. Managing a 1000Base-T connection is a lot of work for the CPU. For best results, 1000Base-T should be installed in PCs having a minimum clock rate of 1.7 GHz.

The throughput between two 1000Base-T adapters will be higher than between 100Base-T adapters, but not necessarily 10 times higher. We haven't yet been able to do a lot of testing of gigabit networks, but you shouldn't expect much more than 300–400 Mbps, especially with older, non–CAT6 cables. Still, that's a *very* fast network!

## Is Your Network Adapter Autonegotiating?

If you have a PC with a network adapter that only gives throughput in the 5 to 8 Mbps range, it probably contains an ancient 10Base-T adapter. If that's the case, you can buy a 100Base-T add-in card very cheaply (under $20 now) and install it in the PC. If the 10Base-T adapter is itself a drop-in card, remove it from the PC. If the 10Base-T adapter is on the motherboard and can't be pulled, go into the Network and Dial-Up Connections applet and disable the older 10Base-T adapter.

In very rare circumstances, the slowpoke adapter may be a 100Base-T adapter set to run at 10Base-T speeds. This was done in older times when new PCs had to be added to existing 10Base-T networks. The new PCs had to be "slowed down" to avoid various network problems. (Networking today is way more reliable than it was even 10 years ago!) If you inherited an older PC from a business, it's worth checking to see if this was done.

Here's how:

1.  Open the System applet from Control Panel.
2.  Click the Hardware tab.
3.  Click the Device Manager button.
4.  Expand the Network Adapters line by clicking the + box.
5.  Highlight the wired Ethernet network adapter. (If you have a Wi-Fi adapter installed, it may also be displayed, but you should be able to identify the wired adapter.)
6.  Right-click the adapter name and select Properties. Click the Advanced tab.

At this point you may need to do some sleuthing. On the Advanced tab is a window labeled "Properties." These are configurable options for your particular network adapter. Unfortunately, they are not standard among network adapters, and the same property may have different names, depending on who manufactured the adapter. You're looking for the property that sets link speed and duplex mode. Here are some names for that property that we've seen:

√  Media Type

√  Connection Type

√  Network Link Selection

√  Link Speed and Duplex

As you click on a property, its current value will be shown on the right, labeled "Value." You can display all the selectable values by pulling down the list. Go down the list of properties, displaying the values for each, until you find a list of values containing the terms *100Base-T* and *10Base-T*. If both those options exist and 10Base-T has been selected, that's the reason the network card is running slow. However, don't select 100Base-T just yet. There may also be an option named "hardware default" or "autonegotiate." That's the value you want, if it's available. When the card is set to autonegotiate, it will automatically set itself up to operate in the most efficient way over the network in which it's installed. If there's no such option, select 100Base-T.

In some adapters you'll see additional options for "half duplex" and "full duplex." This may be part of the Connection Type property, or it may be broken out as a separate property. Again, if you see a "hardware default" or "autonegotiate" option, select it. Otherwise, leave it alone.

# Summing Up

Modern Ethernet networking is surprisingly foolproof. Windows XP and Windows 2000 handle networking extremely well, Windows Me and 9x less so. If networking is important to you, upgrading from Windows 98 to Windows 2000 will probably work and will make networking a lot easier to deal with. The two major gunk-reducers in Ethernet work are to use switches or switch/router appliances rather than hubs and to treat Ethernet cables with care and avoid stepping on, kinking, or sharply bending them. If you have a broadband Internet connection, install a router, even if you only have one PC—you can always add another later, and the router's hardware firewall will greatly increase your protection against Internet attacks.

# 11

# Going Wireless While Staying Gunk–Less

## Degunking Checklist:

√ Having all your wireless networking gear from the same manufacturer works best.

√ When you install a new wireless access point or router, change its default SSID *before* you allow any of your PCs to attempt to connect to it.

√ When you install a new Wi-Fi access point or router, change its configuration login and password immediately.

√ Test your new Wi-Fi network without encryption first to be sure everything else works, and then turn on encryption.

√ When you detect interference to your wireless network, take note of what (if any) other wireless devices are being used in the house at that time.

√ Avoid using older analog 2.4 GHz cordless phones in the same house as a Wi-Fi network.

√ Don't buy handheld devices with both Bluetooth and Wi-Fi built-in.

√ Use a Wi-Fi field auditing utility like NetStumbler to spot weak spots and dead spots around your house.

√ If a single access point won't serve a large house, try a HomePlug system to carry data to a second Wi-Fi access point elsewhere in the house.

People who have created networks in the past by laying Ethernet cables on the floor, sometimes running them down the hall to the kids' rooms, probably thought of the coming of wireless networking as pure salvation. And it's certainly true that wireless networking makes it less necessary to drill holes in the wall or drag cables over the top of a suspended ceiling—much less battle black widow spiders while dropping wires through interior walls from the attic. And while you're certainly cutting loose from a tangle of cables, in reality you're trading one set of problems for another. Nothing comes without a price, and no computer technology is ever immune from gunk.

Wireless gunk comes about in different ways than wired gunk, primarily through interference with other wireless devices. Data in wired networks stays nice and tidy inside its cables. Data in wireless networks is everywhere around you—along with signals from things like your cordless phone and your Bluetooth PDA sync system, as well as radio noise leaking from your microwave oven, not to mention your neighbor's wireless network next door. Add to this various incompatibilities among different manufacturers' products, problems with encryption, and distortions and shielding effects from metal objects and even water-filled things like your big salt aquarium in the den, and you've got plenty to degunk and untangle, wires or no wires.

# Understand How Wireless Systems Work

As with wired networks, it's very useful to know how wireless systems work before you try to degunk them. Wireless is *subtle;* we're not talking about kinked cables anymore. Nonetheless, there's a lot in wireless networking that relates closely to wired networking, so if you haven't read Chapter 10 yet, please go back and read it now because we won't repeat everything in this short introduction.

Nearly all wireless networking these days is a technology called Wireless Fidelity, or Wi-Fi. Wi-Fi was designed to be "wireless Ethernet." If you recall from early in Chapter 10, we explained that Ethernet networking doesn't care what the physical link is, just as UPS doesn't care what type of vehicle gets the packages to their destinations, as long as they get there. Cables work. Infrared light beams work. And radio waves work. Wi-Fi is Ethernet over microwaves, which are radio waves of extremely short wavelength.

## Wireless-A vs. Wireless-B vs. Wireless-G

Alas, it's never as simple as it looks. Wi-Fi comes in three different versions: Wireless-A, Wireless-B, and Wireless-G. They're all wireless Ethernet, but they implement Ethernet in different ways, sometimes on different microwave frequencies. You need to understand a little about them, especially if you intend to mix them:

√  Wireless-A is fast (54 Mbps) but relatively short range. It works on the 5 GHz microwave band. It's not very popular, and it costs more than Wireless-B or Wireless-G. Wireless-A devices will connect only to other Wireless-A devices.

√  Wireless-B runs at 11 Mbps and thus is not as fast as A or G. It's very reliable, has a longer range, and is extremely inexpensive, especially on the used market. Wireless-B operates on the 2.4 GHz band. Wireless-B devices do not talk to Wireless-A devices, but they will talk to Wireless-G devices.

√  Wireless-G runs at 54 Mbps, and thus is as fast as Wireless-A, with greater range. Like Wireless-B, it operates on the 2.4 GHz band, and will talk to Wireless-B devices—but only at Wireless-B speeds. Wireless-G will not talk to Wireless-A devices. Wireless-G gear is less expensive than Wireless-A, but it's still somewhat more expensive than Wireless-B.

Wireless-A is a sort of odd man out in wireless technologies. It was difficult to manufacture and thus expensive, and it never really caught on. It has one significant use: as a networking technology when unavoidable interference makes Wireless-B and Wireless-G unusable. We'll have more to say on this topic later in this chapter.

At this writing, Wireless-G is in the saddle and is slowly driving Wireless-B off the market. Wireless-B is thus a great bargain, and if you're not interested in throwing huge files around your home network, it will work beautifully for you. Because Wireless-B is still much faster than any broadband connection we've ever heard of, it will allow you to share a broadband Internet connection among several PCs without slowing down the connection in any way.

Nevertheless, Wireless-G is considered state of the art, and unless we say otherwise, in this chapter *Wi-Fi* refers to Wireless-G.

Wireless-A is increasingly uncommon as a separate product line. However, it is still present in new lines called Wireless A+G, which combines the functionality of both Wireless-A and Wireless-G in the same unit. Wireless A+G gear is about twice as expensive as Wireless-G gear and thus about as expensive as Wireless-A gear in its heyday.

## Wireless Hubs and Wireless Routers

The best way to understand wireless networking is to think of it as Ethernet networking through a hub (see Chapter 10 for more about hubs); computers, printers, and other devices connect to the hub without wires. In the Wi-Fi world, a wireless hub is called a *wireless access point.* It works pretty much the same way as a wired hub works—and that includes all the disadvantages of using a hub. All devices connecting to the network through a wireless access point share a single block of bandwidth available through the access point. If only one device connects, it gets all the bandwidth the access point can offer. If two devices connect, each gets half the bandwidth. If three devices connect, each gets a third of the bandwidth, and so on. Especially with Wireless-B, connecting more than four devices through a single wireless access point will perceptibly slow your network, especially at those times when all four devices are active and moving data.

In the wired world, a single device can combine the function of a hub or a switch with that of a router. A router allows your home network to communicate safely and efficiently with the Internet. Wired routers have been with us for some years now, and in the last four years or so, wireless routers have also appeared. A wireless router typically combines three different technologies into a single small box:

√ A router for Internet access, including the all-important NAT firewall. (See Chapter 10 for why NAT firewalls are crucial.)

√ A wired Ethernet switch, with (typically) four wired ports on the back, for connecting PCs and other devices via Ethernet cables.

√ A wireless access point, which allows multiple wireless-equipped devices to connect to your home network and also the Internet.

Perhaps the single most popular wireless router these days is the Linksys WRT54G, shown in Figure 11-1. It looks a great deal like a wired router with antennas because that's precisely what it is. The WRT54G has a street price of between $55 and $65. It's extremely reliable and it's the wireless router we have recommended for some time.

## Wireless Client Adapters

The wireless access point or (more commonly) the wireless router is the center connecting point of your wireless home network. Each device that wants to connect to the wireless network must in turn have a wireless adapter installed in it. This adapter is called a *wireless client adapter.* When installed in a PC, a wireless client adapter listens for a wireless access point or router, and if it hears one, it will attempt to connect. If you configure it correctly, the wireless client adapter will connect to your network only, and not to your neighbors'.

**Figure 11-1**
The Linksys WRT54G wireless router. (Photo courtesy of Linksys.)

There are several different kinds of wireless client adapters. For your laptop, they're in the form of PC cards that plug into a laptop's PCMCIA or CardBus slot. You can buy add-in cards for your PC's PCI bus, though we don't recommend those for various reasons, not the least of which is the fact that you have to open up your PC to install one. Perhaps the easiest wireless client adapters to install and use are those that connect to your PC through a USB cable. For your printer to join a wireless network, you'll need to connect it to a wireless print server, which has additional intelligence to compensate for the fact that a printer is not a PC.

Most wireless client adapters can be purchased these days for $50 or less. Wireless print servers cost between $80 and $140.

### GunkBuster's Notebook: Avoid PCI Wireless Adapters

Our testing of Wi-Fi wireless gear (which goes back to the dawn of Wi-Fi time in 2000) has shown an interesting trend: internal Wi-Fi client adapters implemented as PCI cards don't have the range that external adapters of any kind do. The reasons are simple and mechanical: A PCI card has a small rubber antenna that sticks out the back of your PC. There is almost always a drooping mess of cables connected to the back of the PC, and in addition to being right next to a large shielding body of metal (your PC's case), the PCI card antenna is usually smack in the middle of this web of cables, which also shield the antenna from incoming signals.

PCI card adapters have one additional disadvantage: They are fixed in place in your PC and can't be moved. Sometimes if the signal is weak at your PC, moving an external Wi-Fi client adapter on its cable even a few feet (especially if you can put it higher up, as on the top of a bookshelf) can bring the signal up significantly.

The most common type of external Wi-Fi client adapter is based on USB technology and generally comes with a 6- to 10-foot USB cable. These are very reliable and, because they can be moved away from your PC, do not suffer from the same problems that PCI client adapters do.

## The Two Uses of Wi-Fi

There are two major uses of Wi-Fi, and while both focus on doing away with cables, each has its own set of problems and considerations:

√   Infrastructure: Erecting a network of fixed-location PCs and printers without having to run wires in walls or above ceilings

√   Mobility: Being able to carry around a laptop or other Wi-Fi-equipped portable device and connect to the network from wherever (within the wireless network's range) you happen to be

The majority of people create a wireless network so that they don't have to run cables through walls to connect all the PCs in their homes. Mobility with a laptop is usually an afterthought, something that they don't discover until all the desktop PCs in the home are connected. Then, *Wow! I can surf the Web from out on the patio!* Planning for infrastructure means that you only have to take into account where all the fixed PCs and printers are located. Planning for mobility means you have to take into account all the possible places you'd like to be able to connect to the network with a laptop, and that's a whole different challenge.

# Wireless Range and Dead Spots

Wireless access points and routers are deliberately short-range devices. Ideally, you'd like the range of a wireless network to include all the areas inside your house, but nothing outside—except maybe the patio or the garage. Microwaves are not great respecters of walls, so if your range is too great, the kids next door may be able to connect to your network in the middle of the night and start uploading and downloading MP3s and pirated movies, which may not seem like a serious problem until the copyright enforcers knock on your door with a lawsuit. *Your network has your name on it.* You must keep that in mind as you plan and configure your wireless network.

The useful range of Wireless-B and Wireless-G networks is roughly the same, and within a typical residential building it's about 100 to 150 feet. Beyond that, the connection slows down radically and may become intermittent. A well-positioned access point or wireless router will just about fill a 2,500-square-foot house. Beyond that, things get thin at the fringes.

The range issue is complicated by the fact that signal strength does not decline smoothly with distance from the access point or router. Microwaves can go right through wooden walls, but they are severely distorted by large blocks of metal like refrigerators, range hoods, and pantries full of pots, pans, and canned goods. In the real world, you will have "dead spots" here and there within your house where your wireless signal will be weak and it will be difficult to connect. Dead spots can be finessed by moving the access point, or by adding gain antennas, as we'll explain later in this chapter.

## GunkBuster's Notebook: Buy All Your Wireless Gear from the Same Vendor!

We catch a certain amount of flack for this advice, but we give it for important reasons: Don't mix gear from different vendors in a single home network. In other words, choose a vendor with a full product line (Linksys, D-Link, Netgear, and so on) and outfit your network *only* with gear from your chosen vendor. Don't mix D-Link and Linksys (or any other vendors) in the same network, even if you can get a great deal by shopping hard and buying what's cheap. There are two important reasons for this:

√ The Wi-Fi standard is a strong standard but a *limited* one. Vendors are building more and more goodies into their Wi-Fi products, but these goodies are not standardized and often don't work with similar goodies designed by other manufacturers. Beyond that, simple things like different configuration

IP addresses can make it infuriatingly difficult to get a wired router from one vendor to talk to a wireless access point from another. Most important of all, the enhanced encryption options (128-bit, 256-bit, and so on) often do not work between gear from different manufacturers. Encryption is crucial. If your gear is from different vendors, you may have to fall back to the standard—but weak—64-bit encryption.

√ Wi-Fi vendors have a tendency to blame gear from other manufacturers when they take tech support calls about a mixed-vendor network. Often you'll see in the fine print of Wi-Fi vendors' documentation and Web sites that

"We do not support our products when used with products of other vendors." Their logic runs like this: They can guarantee that their own stuff works with their own stuff. Trying to troubleshoot mixed-vendor networks assembled by nontechnical people can take a huge amount of time and may not be possible at all. (Some options just don't play nice; see the first point.)

The $5 you might save buying a wireless router from one vendor and a wireless client adapter from another will seem like nothing after you've spent five fruitless hours trying to get encryption to work between them. Choose one vendor—they're all good— and stick with it.

## Don't Mix Wireless-B and Wireless-G in the Same Network!

Industry vendors have made much of the fact that Wireless-G is backward compatible with Wireless-B. In other words, if you buy a Wireless-G router or access point, your Wireless-B-equipped computers can still connect to it.

True enough. There is, however, a worm in it: Even *one* Wireless-B device connecting to a Wireless-G access point or router slows the whole network down to Wireless-B speeds or very close to them. Not much has ever been said about this, but our tests show that it's absolutely true, no matter whose Wi-Fi gear you use.

The advice here is simple: If you're just starting out in wireless networking, buy Wireless-G gear only. If you already have a Wireless-B wireless network, be aware that replacing the wireless access point or router with a Wireless-G equivalent won't buy you much in terms of data throughput. Only when you replace the *whole* network with Wireless-G gear, including all Wireless-B client adapters, will the network operate at true Wireless-G speeds.

# Choose the Best Wireless Networking Setup

There are many ways to skin a cable, and with Wi-Fi, you have a wealth of choices. In fact, most of your choices will be limited not by the Wi-Fi technology itself, but by your physical environment: the structure of your home, where your broadband Internet modem is placed, and whether you can run cables into the attic or through the basement. (Some choices, alas, do involve a little cabling.) In the following sections, we'll explain how to choose the best wireless setup for your home given what you require your wireless network to accomplish.

## Wireless Access Point or Wireless Router?

You can add a wireless access point to an existing wired network just by running an Ethernet CAT5 patch cable from one of the switch ports on your wired router to the wireless access point. This allows you to keep your wired router and has another, unappreciated advantage: You can move the wireless access point around on its cable. This may help you finesse dead spots (more on those later).

On the other hand, if you're just building your first home network and want wireless capability, a wireless router bundles everything up in one neat package, which is almost always sufficient for a typical 2,500-square-foot suburban home or anything smaller. For larger homes, the location of the wireless connection point (access or router) becomes important. If your broadband modem and wireless router are in one corner of a large home, your wireless signal may not make it out to the opposite corners. Being able to run an Ethernet cable into the attic and centrally locate the access point in the attic is useful for filling large homes. *Really* large homes may require more than one wireless access point, and that's a much more complex topic for a much larger book. (See the section on HomePlug networking at the end of this chapter for a novel way to finesse this problem.)

## The "85% Network"

But for most home networks—we suspect at least 85 percent of them—a wireless router installed where the broadband modem is located will be more than sufficient. The wireless router provides both cable-free network connections to PCs and laptops throughout most or all of the house and strong worm/script protection because of its hardware-based NAT firewall.

The cabling for this kind of network is simple and is shown in Figure 11-2. Your PC connects via CAT5 patch cable to one of the switch ports on the back of the wireless router, and the wireless router connects via patch cable from the port marked "WAN" or "Internet" on the back of the router to the single network port on the broadband modem. And that's all there is to it! Cabling is easy. Most of the work in creating a simple network like this lies in configuring the wireless router and the wireless client adapters installed in your PCs.

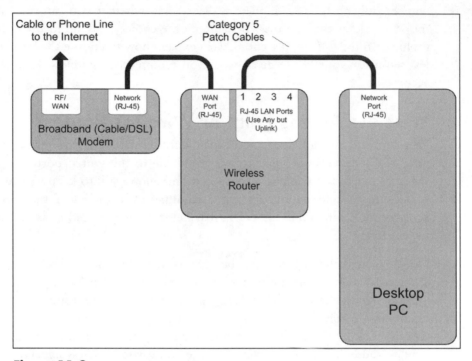

**Figure 11-2**

A wireless network for 85 percent of all users.

## Adding a Wireless Access Point to an Existing Wired Network

If you already have a wired network based on a wired router (see Chapters 9 and 10 for more on creating this kind of network), you can add a separate wireless access point to the network very simply. The cabling is shown in Figure 11-3. Just connect the access point to one of the switch ports on the back of the wired router. Use any except the one marked "uplink."

It's *very* important that the wired router and the wireless access point be from the same vendor. Gear from different vendors can use different subnets, which will prevent you from reaching your access point's configuration screens. Untangling a subnet conflict is a pretty technical matter, best avoided if you can; it's

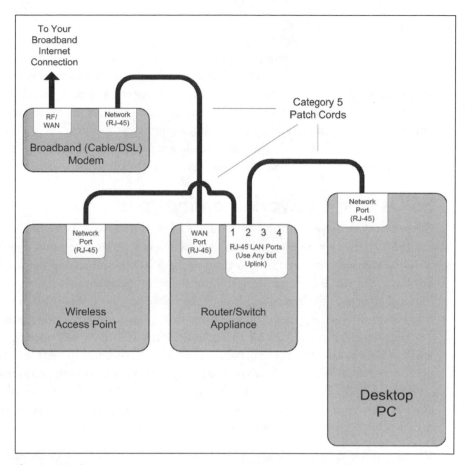

**Figure 11-3**

Adding an access point to a wired network.

completely avoidable by purchasing an access point made by the same company that made your wired router. If you encounter such a conflict, solving it is covered in detail in Chapter 9 of *Jeff Duntemann's Wi-Fi Guide.*

---

**TIP:** *Using a separate wireless access point with a wired router allows you to place the access point up high on the wall or atop a bookshelf, where it's above a lot of obstructions and may have greater range.*

---

The real work in creating a wireless network is not in connecting cables but in configuring the system correctly after everything has been connected. Even if you connect all the cables and things somehow fall into place and seem to work "automagically," resist the temptation to leave it at that. The security of your network depends on proper configuration. Keep reading.

# Change Your SSID

There are a host of configuration options available within all the modern Wi-Fi wireless access points and wireless routers, but only two of them are really crucial: setting your SSID and turning on the encryption system. Failing to handle these two things correctly puts you at risk of having your wireless network confused with that of a neighbor's and (much worse) allowing casual intruders to connect to your network and either browse your shared directories or do illegal things over your network, which are then traceable back to you.

## SSIDs and Network Identity

Every wireless network must have a name. This name is its Service Set Identifier (SSID). Every wireless access point or wireless router comes with a default SSID so that whether or not you change the SSID to something unique, the network will still have a name. Many nontechnical people cable up a wireless network, discover to their astonishment that it works, and then refuse to touch it for fear of "messing it up." This means that there are many *many* networks out there with the same default name. In the early days of Wi-Fi wireless networks, this was less of a problem. Today, however, it's common to be able to pick up the signals of three or four (or more) wireless networks from inside your house, especially if you live in an urban area where the houses are small and close-set or in an apartment or condo complex where your neighbors may be only a few feet away from you.

When you boot up a desktop PC or laptop with a wireless client adapter installed in it, the adapter will "listen" for available wireless networks. Unless you configure it otherwise, when it hears one or more networks, it will automatically connect to the strongest signal it can hear. These days, that may not be *your* network!

A simple example: Suppose you live in a condo or townhouse in which you have neighbors on the other side of an interior wall. You have installed a wireless router in one bedroom, and you take your laptop to work at the desk in the den, on the opposite side of the condo or townhouse. Now suppose that your neighbor has installed a wireless access point or router *right on the other side of the wall from your den*. Your neighbor's wireless router will have a stronger signal in your den than your own wireless router will. Your laptop will thus, in the absence of any other guidance, connect to your neighbor's wireless router. Worse, if both your network and your neighbor's networks are named linksys (the default SSID for Linksys wireless products), you won't necessarily know *which* network your laptop has connected to! This is important, because no matter how saintly your own ethics are, it works both ways: If your neighbors can connect to *your* network, they might be able to read your files and misuse your Internet connection.

The way to avoid this is to tell your laptop's client adapter to look for a network with a particular unique name. Of course, to do this you must first give your network a unique name and then configure all your wireless client adapters to connect to a network with that name and that name only.

Changing the SSID of a network is done in slightly different ways, depending on the manufacturer of the access point or wireless router that you're using. One very important caution: Change the SSID of a brand new wireless access point or router *immediately* upon installing it, and change it *before* any of the wireless-equipped PCs in your home "see" the access point or router for the first time. In other words, when you get a new wireless router or access point, install it according to this general plan:

1. Power down all PCs, wireless and wired, as well as your broadband modem.

2. Take the new wireless access point or router out of its box and cable up the network as required for the sort of network you've chosen.

3. Power up the broadband modem, followed by the wireless access point or router.

4. Power up the PC that is connected to the access point or router through a cable. This is the PC that you use to configure the access point or router. Leave all other PCs powered down.

5. Change the default SSID of the new router or access point to an SSID of your choice.

6. Change the default login and password to something of your choice. (Don't forget to do this!)

7. One by one, power up the PCs that connect via wireless clients, and configure them to connect to the new wireless access point or router.

The key issue is *not* to configure a new access point or router while wireless PCs are attempting to connect to it. We've seen wireless client adapters get "fixated" on the default SSID of a new access point or router and then fail to connect after the SSID has been changed. (This appears to be a problem specifically with Windows XP Service Pack 2.) So always change a router's default SSID *before* any of your wireless PCs connect to it for the first time.

---

**TIP:** It should be obvious if you think about it, but nonetheless, do not try to configure a wireless access point or router through a wireless connection! Always configure it from the PC attached to it via cable.

---

As for the process of changing the SSID itself, here are the broad strokes:

1. Bring up a browser on the PC connected to the router by cable and type the access point or router's configuration address into the address field. This address is given in the device's documentation and probably looks like 192.168.1.1. If you don't have the documentation, you can look for the IP address on the Port Forward Web page: **www.portforward.com/routers.htm**.

2. Log in to your router or access point. If it's new, the login ID and password will consist of default values as well, and you can log in by clicking OK. However, *change the login values as soon as practical!*

3. Since the SSID is a very basic configuration item, the field it lives in should be easy to find. For Linksys devices, it's under the Wireless tab. See Figure 11-4. Check your documentation to find the field if it's not obvious where it is.

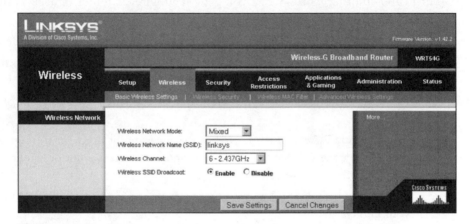

**Figure 11-4**
Where to change the SSID on Linksys routers and access points.

4. Come up with a unique name that someone else in the next condo is unlikely to think of independently. Although people do it, we recommend against using your real name or street address. Use an uncommon word, like *mastodon, dogwood, yttrium,* or *vacuole.*

5. Type the new SSID into the field and click OK, Save Settings, or whatever button your particular device shows on the screen to indicate that you're done.

That's all it takes. Your network now has a unique name. Your next task is to configure all your wireless client adapters to look for and connect to that name only. For Windows 9*x,* 2000, and Me, you'll have to launch your adapters' client manager utilities to do this. The client manager usually puts a small icon in the

Taskbar tray. Double-click it, and read your documentation or help files to see how to set your adapter to a particular SSID. Most of the time this involves editing a "client profile." Many wireless client adapters allow you to set up several different wireless profiles, each of which is configured for a different wireless access point or router. For example, you can set up a profile to connect your laptop to the wireless network at the office and a separate profile to connect your laptop to your wireless router at home. The SSID (and other things, like encryption keys) will be different in the two profiles. When you're at work, you select the work profile. When you're at home, you select the home profile.

For Windows XP, the process is done through Windows itself and (when it works) is very easy. Setting the SSID on a client adapter is not an operation done separately. Instead, Windows presents you with a list of all the wireless networks it can "hear" and allows you to choose the one to connect to. This is why you need to change the default SSID of your access point or router right away. If you're presented with three networks, all of which have the default SSID of linksys, it may not be clear which one is yours! (This is not completely hypothetical. We have seen exactly that situation!) When you select a wireless network to connect to, that network's SSID is stored in the PC's client adapter as the SSID it will connect to until you repeat the process and choose a different one.

Under Windows XP, changing the SSID and enabling encryption are generally done in one operation. For other versions of Windows, they're separate operations.

# Turn On Encryption

People who haven't had any experience with two-way radio often forget how easy it is to eavesdrop on electronic communications. Ten years or so ago, cordless phones were basically low-power two-way FM radios, rather like walkie-talkies. Any scanner radio could tune in to the cordless phone frequencies, and whole books were written on how to do this. Using directional gain antennas to scan the neighborhood for late-night cordless phone sex was a clandestine hobby all by itself.

Cordless phone technology has moved on, but those wireless lowlifes are still with us, and some of them now make use of other people's Wi-Fi wireless networks to download kiddie porn and launch attacks on their enemies, all using a third party's wireless network. They can do this for a simple reason: *Two thirds* of all wireless network users do not enable encryption. Their networks are "wide open," and any 15-year-old with a laptop and a wireless card can connect to the global Internet—and to your network shares—through an unencrypted wireless network.

This is a problem for a simple reason: Your wireless network receives an IP address from your ISP, and that IP address is associated with your Internet account and your name. If someone else commits a crime while connected to the Internet through your connection, the first person that law enforcement will come looking for is *you*.

Wi-Fi networks all have an encryption system that is relatively effective at keeping outsiders out. However, all wireless networks are wide open by default, and you have to explicitly enable encryption to be protected. Wi-Fi encryption requires that both the access point or router and each client adapter be configured separately with a passphrase or encryption key. In broad strokes, here's how it's done:

1. Power down all PCs that connect wirelessly to your access point or router.

2. From the PC connected to the access point or router by cable, launch a Web browser and bring up the access point's or router's configuration screen. (We explained how to do this in the previous section.)

3. Locate the configuration page that governs encryption. For Linksys products, this is the Wireless Security subtab under the Wireless tab. See Figure 11-5. Select the type of encryption you intend to use, and enter a passphrase or numeric encryption key as appropriate.

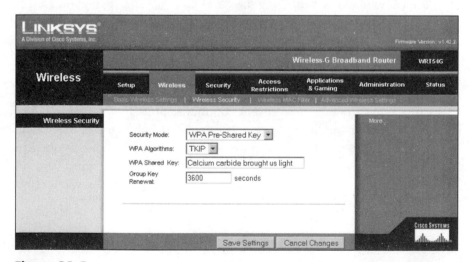

**Figure 11-5**
Enabling encryption on Linksys access points and routers.

4. Save the new settings by clicking the Save Settings button.

5. One by one, bring up each PC equipped with a wireless client. Under Windows XP, Windows will present a list of available networks, which in almost all cases will include only your own network. (If you have close-in

neighbors, you may see one or two more.) Select your network and click the Connect button. Windows will display a dialog requesting an encryption passphrase or key. (We'll explain the two encryption schemes shortly.) Enter it as appropriate and click OK.

6.  For client PCs running Windows versions prior to Windows XP, you have to run the wireless client adapter's client manager utility, usually by double-clicking its icon in the Taskbar tray. Client manager utilities are all different, and you'll have to consult your documentation to determine how to enter an encryption key or passphrase.

## Wired Equivalent Privacy (WEP) vs. Wi-Fi Protected Access (WPA)

The biggest single source of confusion in Wi-Fi work lies in the two different security schemes found in Wi-Fi gear. Our suspicion is that this confusion is the main reason why two-thirds of all wireless networks remain unprotected. (The other reason is that gear from different manufacturers doesn't always "play nice" in the encryption realm. Always buy your Wi-Fi gear from the same manufacturer!)

The older of the two encryption technologies is called Wired Equivalent Privacy (WEP). WEP is present in every piece of wireless gear certified under the Wi-Fi standard. That's the good news. The bad news is that WEP is not as strong as it should be, and there are ways to crack it, especially by people who can covertly monitor your network for a period of weeks or months without your knowledge (think: the kids across the alley).

The standard WEP technology offers a 64-bit encryption key. Most manufacturers have enhanced WEP to support at least a 128-bit encryption key, and some a 256-bit key. These larger keys are stronger and much tougher to crack. The downside is that the key extensions are nonstandard and 128-bit encryption from one manufacturer may not be compatible with 128-bit encryption from another manufacturer. It's yet another reason to buy all your gear from the same manufacturer. Still, 64-bit encryption is better than nothing, and in a "vendor-mixed" network, it may be the best that you can do.

In early 2004, a new encryption technology became generally available: Wi-Fi Protected Access, or WPA. WPA is not easily cracked—in fact, cracking it is way beyond casual malefactors. The bad news with WPA, of course, is that it's relatively new and only Wi-Fi gear of very recent manufacture is likely to support it. Gear manufactured before 2004 generally will *not* support WPA without a firmware upgrade, and possibly not at all. Worse, unless you're using Windows XP Service Pack 2, WPA requires additional software that may or may not be included either with Windows or with your client adapter. If you're using older versions of Windows, you'll have to do some additional research, and we won't cover the use of WPA on pre–XP Windows in this book. For the full technical story on WPA, see *Jeff Duntemann's Wi-Fi Guide*.

---

*TIP:* Microsoft and the major Wi-Fi vendors have handled the WPA upgrade very badly, for reasons that defy analysis. The latest copies of Windows XP Service Pack 2 contain reasonably seamless support for WPA. Older versions of XP will need to be patched, and for Windows 2000, the patching is not trivial. If you're not a technophile, it's probably better to stick with WEP on copies of Windows delivered before 2005. For home networks, WEP is more than good enough.

---

## WEP Keys and Passphrases

Good ol' WEP is better than most of its critics make it out to be, especially if you buy your gear from one manufacturer and use its 128-bit or 256-bit encryption options. Few people—even those rascally kids across the alley—will be so patient as to spend most of a year trying to crack a network with 128-bit WEP enabled.

Unlike WPA, which uses textual passphrases, WEP uses numeric keys. These keys are made of groups of two hexadecimal numbers and look something like this (the letters represent base-16 digits from 10 to 15):

00 30 4D 21 FB 47 20 00 83 01 D6 2F 09

The downside to pure WEP is that you have to invent such strings of numbers from scratch and then type them into each PC on your network. Creating a key means thinking of 5 groups of 2 digits (for 64-bit WEP) or 13 groups of 2 digits (for 128-bit WEP) and writing them down. The key must then be typed manually into both the access point or router and each client adapter in your network.

Some manufacturers make things easier. Perhaps the easiest system comes from Buffalo Technology. Its One Touch Secure System will select the strongest encryption system supported by all Wi-Fi devices on your network and implement it without your having to think up keys and type them everywhere. One Touch Secure System only works, of course, if all Wi-Fi devices are from Buffalo Technology.

A close second is Linksys, which builds a passphrase key generator into all its Wi-Fi products. You type a textual passphrase (up to 16 characters long) like *superannuation* and the Linksys software will generate a WEP key from the phrase.

All Linksys products generate the same WEP key from the same word, so you don't need to remember a numeric key. You only need to remember the passphrase.

In an all-Linksys network, you can use the same textual pass phrase on every PC in the network. If your network isn't so blessed, there are still some partial solutions. You can generate keys from pass phrases using an online generator: **www.kiddspc.com/wep.html**. If you access this site from the PC on which you're in the process of entering the WEP key, the site will load the generated key into the clipboard, from which you can paste it into the WEP key field.

With other manufacturers, you'll have to do some research. Some provide key generators, and some don't. Some provide them on certain products but not all products. Make sure you know precisely what you're getting before you lay your money down!

## Advice from the Trenches

Turning on encryption, unfortunately, isn't as easy as it should be, especially if you're nontechnical and not inclined to tinker. Here are some tips to help you along:

√ If you're mixing Wi-Fi products from several manufacturers in your network, always make sure your various PCs can connect to the access point or router *before* you turn on encryption. Fix any non-encryption-related connection problems before you dive into encryption.

√ Contrary to certain things you may read in the press, configuring WPA is *difficult,* especially if you have no stomach for patching Windows, searching for accessory software, or updating firmware on your Wi-Fi devices. It might make sense to implement WEP first to make sure that you can get at least a minimal encryption system to work. If you can get WEP to work, try WPA. If you can't make WPA work, fall back to WEP.

√ Once you've successfully gotten all PCs to connect, turn on 64-bit WEP at the access point or router and bring all client adapters into the network using the common WEP key. If you can get all PCs to network using 64-bit WEP, try using 128-bit WEP. If you can't get the mixed network to connect using 128-bit WEP, fall back to 64-bit WEP.

√ If you're using a brand-new version of Windows (XP Service Pack 2 with all patches up to February 1, 2005) and all your Wi-Fi devices except for one can handle WPA, replace the straggler with a new WPA-certified device. WPA works reasonably well using up-to-date copies of Windows, so if all that stands between you and WPA security is a $40 client adapter, well, peace of mind is worth at least that.

√ Using either WEP or WPA is enough on the security side. (Of course, change your default SSID and router login and password on new equipment before you begin to confront encryption.) Other advice you may read in the press, like using MAC address filtering or turning off the access point's or router's broadcast beacon, buys you little or nothing in terms of security and may cause your network to malfunction in weird ways.

√ If you're using WPA, the software changes encryption keys on a regular basis and passes them out to all PCs connected to the network. If you're using WEP, you don't get that automatic key update feature, and it's a good idea to change your WEP keys manually every so often, ideally once a month. Because it can take intruders as much as three months to crack a lightly used network, changing keys once a month makes WEP *much* stronger protection.

There's one more point on encryption that's a little odd but it's worth noting: the "low-hanging fruit" effect. Even though 64-bit WEP is a little weak in theory, in practice it's strong enough because other people are lazy or stupid. Two-thirds of all wireless networks are not protected in any way. Someone wanting to swipe Internet access is unlikely to break a sweat trying to crack into your WEP-protected network when four or five other networks on the same block are wide open. This may not always be the case, but for the near term the low-hanging fruit effect makes even 64-bit WEP strong enough to put you at ease.

## GunkBuster's Notebook: Is Windows XP's Integrated Wireless Support a Good Idea?

When Windows XP was released in 2002, it was hailed as finally making wireless networking easy and foolproof. Our experience has been different: XP's wireless support is by no means foolproof, and it's only easy when it works—which is far from all the time. Windows XP Service Pack 2, in particular, seems prone to peculiar and inexplicable lapses in wireless network behavior. Figure 11-6 shows a little bit of this peculiarity. A single pane of a dialog shows "Not connected" at the top and in the middle contradicts itself when it says, "You are currently connected to this network." A nontechnical person might not be blamed for running away screaming.

We have a theory about why Windows XP's wireless network support is so flaky: Microsoft tried to treat the multitude of wireless networking adapters as though they were all alike in every respect. This is foolish; the 802.11 (Wi-Fi) standard does not cover a great many things, and the various equipment manufacturers

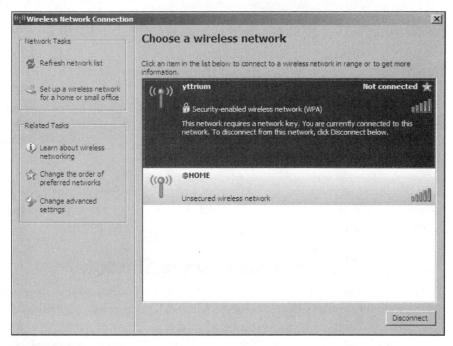

**Figure 11-6**

A Windows XP SP2 dialog that can't make up its mind.

have implemented a lot of the details of wireless networking in their own ways. The *only* reliable way to handle wireless networking is to let each manufacturer provide a client management utility written specifically for that manufacturer's own products. This is how it was done prior to Windows XP: Each manufacturer provided a CD that installed drivers and a client manager. The client manager parked an icon in the Taskbar tray, and you double-clicked the icon to configure the client manager. The wireless client adapter and its manager utility were literally created for one another and can work together in ways that Windows simply can't, not reliably and not all the time.

Unfortunately, if you're using Windows XP, you don't have any choice. Windows demands to have total control over its wireless networking clients and won't even allow the manufacturer's client utility to be installed. If you're lucky, installing and configuring wireless networking hardware will go the way it's supposed to go. If you're not lucky, you will probably require expert assistance. And if you have a choice, don't use Windows XP. Windows 2000 will treat you way better, at least on the wireless networking side. It's not as "smooth," but at least it works.

# Audit Your Wireless Network's Field

Once you've set up a wireless access point or router in your home, you'll probably find that certain places around the house won't allow a PC or laptop to connect at the top bit rate—and sometimes, not at all. The microwave field that carries data through your house is not uniform. There will be weak spots here and there, as well as dead spots, especially if your home is large. With small homes this is usually not a problem—but because you can't see microwaves, you simply won't know until you try to connect.

In the following sections, we'll talk about why Wi-Fi fields are not uniform and how you can determine the "shape" of your wireless network's field and take action accordingly.

## Things That Cast Microwave Shadows

Microwaves go through certain things better than others. Wood, no problem. Drywall, no problem. Brick, some problem. Metal or water, *big* problem. Most people probably understand intuitively that microwaves won't pass through metal and that if there is a large piece of metal between your wireless access point or router and one of your PCs, you're going to have difficulty getting a good connection. Less obvious is the fact that water—and things that contain water—are almost opaque to microwaves and cast shadows as well.

Here are some things to look out for:

√  Kitchens cast shadows. Kitchens are full of metal: a refrigerator (sometimes two!), a stove, cabinets full of metal things like pots and pans, and a pantry full of canned goods. A modern kitchen fetish is to put stainless steel everywhere, in terms of sink backsplashes and who knows what. Try to avoid having the kitchen between your wireless access point and PCs that need to connect. If a PC is on the same floor with the kitchen, try to mount an external client adapter (like a USB adapter) up high on the wall or atop a bookshelf.

√  Waterbeds cast shadows. People have found that in narrow, multistory townhomes and row houses, a waterbed on a middle floor will reduce the strength of your field on the upper story if the access point is below it and vice versa.

√  Large aquaria and large indoor plants can cause dead spots. Plants are full of water, and dense foliage is mostly opaque to microwaves. This usually isn't a problem indoors, but if you have a hedge between your house and your garage, don't count on being able to pick up the access point or router from the garage.

√ Chicken wire like that used as a stucco base in stuccoed homes is a partial shield against microwaves, and stucco over chicken wire will reduce the strength of the field slightly (about 25 percent) outside your home. That's not always a bad thing; you don't want neighbors and drivers-by connecting. But it will reduce the range of your access point and make it more difficult to connect by the pool or in the garage.

√ Ductwork is usually metal and opaque to microwaves. Basements are a bad place to mount a wireless access point or router. Furthermore, if you mount the access point on the upper story or in the attic, you may have trouble connecting in the basement.

√ Metal grillwork will pass microwaves unless the gaps in the grill are less than about an inch in extent. As mentioned, chicken wire is on the edge and will reduce the strength of your field somewhat. Half-inch hardware cloth will block most of your field, and quarter-inch hardware cloth is essentially opaque to microwaves. Aluminum window screen is also opaque to microwaves and will cast shadows. (However, most window screen is now plastic, and microwaves will go right through.)

Over and beyond outright blockage, metal and water will distort the shape of the field in ways impossible for you to predict. A metal filing cabinet beside your desk may block your access point and put you in a dead spot—or it may act as a reflector and not be "noticed" by the field. The only way you will know is if you "go look."

## Auditing Your Wi-Fi Field with a Laptop

The way to "go look" is to use a Wi-Fi auditing utility that displays signal strength. If you run such a utility on your laptop, you can walk (slowly) around your house taking note of where the signal strength of your wireless access point or router dips sharply. If you have blueprints or even a good scale sketch of your house, it's often useful to mark points of high or low signal strength for future reference. If you find a dead spot and try to fix it by moving your access point around, an auditing utility is the fastest way to find out whether moving things around has done any good.

By far the best Wi-Fi field auditing utility is NetStumbler by Marius Milner. It's a free download without adware or spyware (we use it all the time), though a donation of at least $10 (through PayPal) is suggested. Download it here:

**www.netstumbler.com/downloads/**

There is a version for Windows and a separate version for PDAs running Microsoft's Pocket PC version of Windows. Not all Wi-Fi client adapters are supported, and you should check the list on netstumbler.com to see if yours is. NetStumbler works best with Windows XP and supports the most client adapters. For older operating systems, fewer network adapters are supported. If you install NetStumbler and it can't detect your Wi-Fi client adapter, there's not much you can do, unfortunately.

To use NetStumbler, install it on your laptop and run it. Make sure the "Scan" button is pressed. (It's the one with the green triangle.) If you're close enough to your access point or router to connect, NetStumbler will honk and it will display the SSID and physical (MAC) address of your station. If you click on the circle to the left of the MAC address, the field strength display will appear in the right pane.

With the field strength indicator displayed, walk *slowly* around your house. The green lines will go higher or lower, depending on the field strength where you happen to be standing. After a few minutes, you'll see a display something like that shown in Figure 11-7.

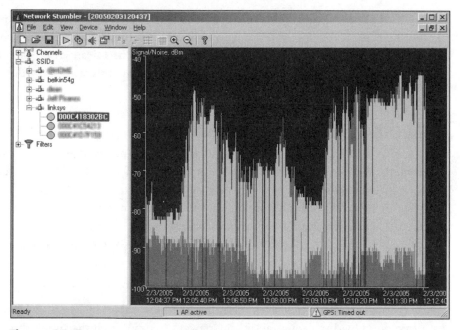

**Figure 11-7**
Auditing your Wi-Fi field with NetStumbler.

Figure 11-7 came about during an audit of a brand new wireless router placed in a largish (3,000-square-foot) home. You can see that the field strength varies widely. What you're looking for are places where the green lines get very short.

It will look like a hole on the graph, and the red line will be very close to the green line. In the figure, the left extreme shows the near dead spot as we stood just outside the front door. Once we walked in, the field increased significantly and was (surprisingly!) adequate throughout the house, though there was a weak spot in the laundry room (a little right of center on the graph) because the washer and dryer cast a microwave shadow in the middle of the room.

If your wireless client adapter in your laptop is set to look for the SSID value set in your access point or router, NetStumbler will display only the wireless access point or router having that SSID. If you temporarily change your laptop client adapter's settings so that the SSID field is blank, NetStumbler will display any networks it can "hear" from your laptop. In Figure 11-7, no fewer than *seven* neighboring networks are displayed, though two of them were sensed only when we stood outside the house on the front porch. None of the networks sensed during this field audit were strong enough to cause interference, but it indicates how popular wireless networks have become in modern suburbia.

---

*TIP: If you haven't changed your SSID to some unique value yet, do it now. Figure 11-7. shows three networks with the default SSID "linksys." The strongest was obviously the new router that we were setting up, but if you're trying to troubleshoot interference from several close-in networks (as in an apartment or condo complex), it may not always be obvious which network is yours on the NetStumbler display! Pick an odd word, perhaps the name of a plant or animal. Don't use your own name or address or other identifying information.*

---

## Finessing Dead Spots

So if you audit your field and find dead spots in bad places (like at your desk or anyplace else you'd want to put a PC), what can you do? Here are some things to try:

√ If you followed our advice and purchased external USB client adapters for your desktop PCs, try moving the adapter around on the end of its cable. Often a position change of just a couple of feet can make a difference in field strength. Definitely do *not* use PCI adapters. They are stuck immobile inside the PC and are often shielded to some extent by the PC case and the jungle of wires hanging from the back of the PC.

√ Look at the geometry of where a dead spot is with respect to the access point or router. If there's a shadow you can't do anything about (like the kitchen, or a metal garage door, or a closet full of metal things), see if moving either the access point or the desk in the room improves things any. Sometimes only a few feet can make a big difference.

√ Most of the bigger Wi-Fi equipment vendors now offer gain antennas for their access points or routers and (sometimes) their client adapters. Many of these are simply longer versions of the "rubber duck" antennas that come stock with Wi-Fi routers and access points. Also, there are client adapter gain antennas for Wi-Fi that hang on the wall like pictures. These are called "patch antennas" or "panel antennas" and can be had from several vendors. Our favorite is Fleeman, Anderson, and Bird (**www.fab-corp.com**). They cost $25 to $60.

√ If you can't move your wireless router very far because of its connection to the broadband modem, see if you can move the router *and* the broadband modem to another room. Most broadband (DSL and cable) modems can be installed at any phone or cable outlet. If you can move modem and router to a more central position in the house, it may help. If the den won't work, see if you can use one of the bedrooms or vice versa. Keep in mind that it's important to have a PC near the router (and connected via cable) to configure the router without depending on the wireless connection to do so.

√ If you can't move the broadband modem to another room, consider getting a wired router and a separate wireless access point and moving the access point around the room on the end of a 15-foot CAT5 cable. Get the access point as high as possible, perhaps on the top of a bookshelf, and as far from the router as possible, and audit your field again. You may be pleasantly surprised.

Relocating an access point to another position within the same room as the router and broadband modem is easy. If you have the ability to run a cable through an interior wall to the attic, mounting the AP in the attic can work, except in places like Arizona where the attic temps can top 150 degrees. The higher and closer to the center of the house the access point is, the more likely you'll have full coverage throughout the house—except perhaps in the basement.

If you can't run cables to a separate access point, you might also consider a HomePlug Ethernet bridge or HomePlug Wi-Fi access point. See the section at the end of this chapter for details.

# Eliminate (or Avoid) Wireless Interference

Even back when you were the first on your block to have a wireless network, your network may not have been the first wireless device in your neighborhood, or even in your own home. And when two wireless fields attempt to occupy the same space at the same time at the same frequency, things happen. These things are called interference. For all the warnings in the press, interference to Wi-Fi wireless networks is uncommon, and in most cases you can easily fix it. Some cases can be nasty, however, and you need to understand how interference happens—and with what other technologies—so that you have the best chance of getting things untangled and degunked.

# Who Shares the Band with Wi-Fi?

The microwave radio neighborhood where Wi-Fi operates is a pretty crowded and extremely busy place. There are only so many radio bands, and government authorities around the world have tried to cope with a shortage of electromagnetic spectrum by allowed shared access to certain frequencies, especially by low-power devices like wireless networking gear.

The band around 2.4 GHz is shared by several different technologies, as well as a number of services licensed by the U.S. Federal Communications Commission (FCC.) The primary technologies competing for space are these:

√   Wi-Fi (802.11 wireless networking)

√   Bluetooth (802.15 Personal Area Networking)

√   2.4 GHz cordless phones

√   Some microwave ovens

√   Certain industrial and medical equipment using microwaves for heating and imaging

There are others, but these are the most common. The FCC has licensed a number of communication-oriented services to operate on the 2.4 GHz band, and they include these:

√   Part 90 Public Safety Radio (police and fire)

√   Parts 80 and 87 Maritime and Aviation Radar

√   Part 74 Electronic News Gathering

√   Part 97 Amateur Radio

Clearly, your wireless network has lots of company. The bad news, from a legal standpoint, is this: *Almost every one of the other services and technologies using the 2.4 GHz band has a better claim on the band than Wi-Fi does.* All of the FCC-licensed services are "primary" in the band, which means that if you and one of those services conflict, the service doesn't have to do anything. Even the Part 18 industrial equipment like microwave welding gear has priority over Wi-Fi; if the welder across the street disrupts your network, well, there's nothing you can do.

The good news is that the FCC-licensed services are rarely an issue for Wi-Fi. Residential networks are rarely close enough to aviation or maritime radar systems, or microwave welding shops, for interference to be an issue. In fact, the sources of interference you're most likely to encounter are Bluetooth devices and 2.4 GHz cordless phones, as well as the #1 interference issue: other Wi-Fi users.

# How Do You Detect Interference?

Interference to a Wi-Fi network rarely causes the network to simply cease to work. You're really looking for two interference telltales:

√ Unexpected dropping of the Wi-Fi connection, followed immediately (or within a few seconds) by reconnection

√ (More commonly) a noticeable slowdown in network throughput

As we described in Chapter 10, Ethernet networks (including Wi-Fi, which is basically wireless Ethernet) pass data as a stream of many small individual packets. Ethernet's protocols keep track of whether each packet arrives where it's addressed; if it fails to arrive, the protocols shrug and try sending the packet again. Ethernet keeps trying these resends until a packet gets through. In most cases, the interference is short, and after a small fraction of a second, the resent packet arrives and the protocols move on to sending the next packet in line.

What this means is that interference most often manifests itself as slow network operation. When the interference is strong enough so that Ethernet has to send each packet several hundred times, your network will *not* be fast. Digital interference (from Bluetooth devices and other nearby Wi-Fi networks) comes in short bursts, and in a great many cases, there may not be enough packet resends for you to even notice that interference is happening. (This is why even nearby networks can coexist on the same Wi-Fi channel without completely disabling one another.)

More serious but less frequent interference may cause your Wi-Fi connection between your wireless access point or router and a PC to abruptly "hang up" and then immediately reconnect. Anytime this starts happening, take note of what else is happening in your house at the same time:

√ Is someone using the microwave oven?

√ Is someone using a cordless phone?

√ Is someone using a wireless audio system (cordless headset) or some other radio-based device?

√ Have you recently installed a Bluetooth-based device like a PDA?

This is by no means an exhaustive list of things that will interfere with a Wi-Fi network, but being in your home, they're the ones you have the most control over. Let's speak of some of them in more detail.

# Cordless Phone Interference

Rarely, but more than once, we've observed that data traffic over a Wi-Fi network simply ceases whenever a 2.4 GHz cordless (not cell) phone is in use in the same house as the network. Cordless phones, especially older ones, are generally analog devices. They're like conventional radio transmitters in that they broadcast a continuous signal on a given frequency. As long as they're transmitting, it's difficult for other devices to get anything through on that frequency. Digital devices fire off packets as if they're machine gun bullets, with plenty of space between the bullets for other bullets. Except when a packet is being sent, there's little radio activity on the channel in use. Analog devices, by contrast, are like fire hoses, spraying radio energy as if it's an uninterrupted stream of water. For that reason, they can monopolize the channel all the time that they're in use.

---

**TIP:** *If you have a cordless phone, check to see if it operates on the 2.4 GHz band. And if you ever have mysterious "outages" on your wireless network, see if the cordless phone was in use when the outage occurred. You may have to buy a new cordless phone on the 5.8 GHz band. These can now be had for as little as $50.*

---

# Microwave Oven Interference

Much has been written about microwave oven interference to Wi-Fi networks, but we've never seen it actually happen. If you suspect your microwave is leaking energy and slowing your network down, do this:

1.  Send a large file (perhaps a DVD rip of a movie or TV show) between two of your PCs over your Wi-Fi network. Time how long it takes for the transfer to take place. Then delete the file from the destination PC.

2.  Throw a packet of microwave popcorn in the oven and start it up. (It's not a good idea to run a microwave oven empty, and you might as well have something good to snack on after the test.)

3.  Immediately transfer the same large file between the same two PCs, timing it as before. Differences of more than a few seconds may well indicate interference from the microwave oven.

4.  Repeat the test, sending the file once with the oven off and again while the oven is working, to make sure that your test results are consistent and not a fluke.

Because leaking microwave ovens can indicate a malfunction that could cause various health hazards, it's a good idea to get a suspicious oven checked by a qualified repair tech.

## Bluetooth Conflicts

The name *Bluetooth* indicates a relatively recent technology for "personal area networking," that is, networking and connecting computer devices *within a single room*. Bluetooth devices are used to synchronize PDAs and send data wirelessly to printers, among other, less-common uses. They are very low power, which is good because they operate on precisely the same microwave frequencies as Wi-Fi. Here are some tips regarding Bluetooth interference:

√ Bluetooth devices generally send a small amount of information and then stop. It doesn't take long to sync a PDA or send a text file to a wireless printer. You may have to get used to intermittent "slowdowns" of your Wi-Fi network when a Bluetooth device is in use.

√ If you possibly can, arrange your work area so that your wireless access point or router is at least six feet from any Bluetooth device. If you make heavy use of Bluetooth, consider moving to a wired router and a separate wireless access point (assuming you're already using a wireless router) and hanging the access point from the wall, close to the ceiling. (The antennas work just as well pointing down as they do pointing up!) You'll need to run power and an Ethernet cable to the access point, but putting the cable high up on the wall instead of burying it somewhere on your desk will give you the benefit of better coverage for your Wi-Fi network.

√ Avoid buying portable devices that contain both Bluetooth and Wi-Fi wireless subsystems. Although in most cases either one wireless technology or the other can operate by itself, it's very likely that trying to use both at once will cause both wireless connections to fail. Two microwave radios within scant inches of one another cannot help but interfere.

## Other Wi-Fi Networks

Ironically, the #1 cause of interference to Wi-Fi networks are those belonging to your immediate neighbors. This is especially common in dense urban areas where houses are set close or apartment/condo complexes and townhomes where your neighbors are right on the other side of an interior wall. The symptoms of such interference include slow network operation and, in severe cases, the inability of your PC client adapters to connect to your wireless access point or router.

How can you know if another wireless network is causing interference? Basically, if a network is close enough to cause interference, it's close enough to be displayed in the Windows XP "site survey" window, or the site surveys in the client manager programs installed along with drivers for older versions of Windows. On the flip side, if you can't see networks other than your own on your site survey window, it's a pretty sure bet that you are *not* suffering interference from another Wi-Fi network.

## Moving to Another Channel

The Wi-Fi band is divided into 11 channels, which sounds like a lot of room for people to coexist, but that's misleading: Most of those channels overlap adjacent channels by 75 percent. In other words, if your wireless router is on Channel 3, moving to Channel 4 really only moves about 25 percent of your signal out of Channel 3. Yes, it's crazy, but it's how things are.

There are only three completely independent and non-overlapping Wi-Fi channels: 1, 6, and 11. Out of the box, most Wi-Fi gear defaults to Channel 6, which is right in the middle of the band. This means that a lot of wireless routers and access points purchased by non-technical people are operating on Channel 6. If you're on Channel 6 and the guy in the next condo is on Channel 6, there *will* be problems.

Here's how you finesse interference from close-in neighbors:

1. Bring up a wireless network auditing utility like NetStumbler. (NetStumbler was described earlier in this chapter.)

2. See what channel your router or access point is on, and see what channel or channels the other networks visible from your PC are on.

3. If you have only one visible neighbor network, it's easy: Move to the channel farthest from the one your neighbor is on.

4. If more than one other network is visible, determine which of them has the strongest signal. Nothing beats NetStumbler for doing this!

5. Change your access point or router channel to the one farthest from the strongest signal.

Changing the channel on which your access point or router operates requires getting into the configuration screens, which are accessed through a local IP address in your Web browser. Find this address in your documentation or online at Port Forward (**www.portforward.com**) and type it into the browser address field. (It will be something like 192.168.1.1.) Then log in to the router or access point and find the channel set field. For Linksys gear this will be in the Wireless tab; for other makes you'll have to look it up in the doc or sniff around. After you change the channel on the access point, you may have to reboot all your wireless-equipped PCs to get them to "follow" the access point or router to the new channel. Some client manager utilities require that you set the channel value explicitly to the new channel. See your documentation for details.

## Your Last Resort: Wireless-A

We've never heard of interference being so bad that it drove a Wi-Fi user off the 2.4 GHz band entirely, but it's certainly possible. If you live next door to a police or fire station that uses Part 90 Public Safety Radio on 2.4 GHz, you may have no choice. If you live in a large upscale condo complex full of Wi-Fi networks on 2.4 GHz, it's probably the easiest way to make things work again.

Wireless-A works on a higher frequency with fewer users, near 5 GHz. The band it uses is part of the National Information Infrastructure allocation and is generally pretty clear. Wireless-A has other advantages, especially for people living in townhomes and condos: It's inherently shorter range than Wireless-B or Wireless-G. Microwaves at 5 GHz don't go through walls as easily, especially dense walls. Wireless-A will fill a two- or three-bedroom condo nicely, but it won't fill much more than that and has particular difficulties with multistory construction.

The big downside to new-build Wireless-A is its cost, especially if you've already purchased Wireless-G or Wireless-B gear. On the other hand, a scan of eBay's completed auctions show used Wireless-A PC cards going for as little as $10 each (cards that cost upwards of $120 new). Many of the big hardware vendors no longer offer Wireless-A gear per se; now, Wireless-A is usually offered in the form of "dual-mode" Wireless-A+G gear, which includes both a Wireless-A and a Wireless-G radio. Wireless-A+G is quite a bit more expensive than Wireless-G alone, so again, it may pay to do some research and buy some older Wireless-A-only gear on the used market.

# Consider HomePlug Powerline Networking

There's another networking solution that falls into a sort of gray area between wired and wireless networks. Powerline networking is wireless because you don't have to run wires to use it—but it's wired because it sends data over the ordinary 120V power wires throughout your house. The idea has been with us for some time—it's how those notorious X10 cameras work—but only very recently has a standard been created for powerline networking. It's called HomePlug, and it can solve some gnarly problems for you, especially if you live in a large (or very long) home with your broadband Internet modem at one end of the house and PCs requiring connections at the other.

There are two general ways to use HomePlug networking:

√ As your sole "wireless" technology, distributing Internet access and sharing files among all the PCs in your house

√ As a way to position a Wi-Fi wireless access point somewhere in your house away from your router without having to run a physical cable to it

The first option basically treats your power wiring as a "backbone" for networking, carrying data around the house. You plug one HomePlug adapter into the wall near your broadband modem and router and connect the HomePlug adapter to a switch port on the back of the router with a CAT5 cable. Anyplace in the house that there's a PC, you can plug a HomePlug adapter into a wall outlet and run the included CAT5 cable between the adapter and your PC. See Figure 11-8.

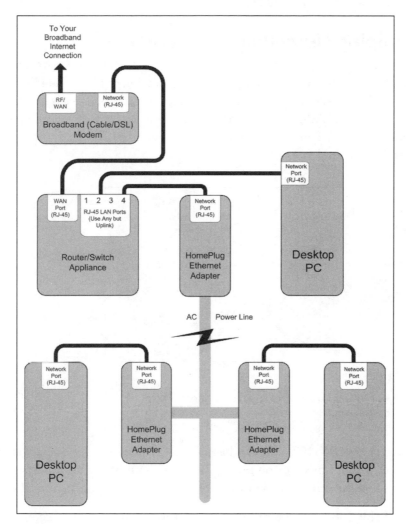

**Figure 11-8**

Using HomePlug as your home network backbone.

In this scenario, HomePlug replaces Wi-Fi entirely. The physical link is not microwaves sent through the air, but lower-frequency radio signals confined (mostly) to your power wiring.

The power lines, in a sense, act as an Ethernet hub. You can plug any (reasonable) number of PCs into the power lines around the home, but all the PCs must share the block of bandwidth (currently a maximum 14 Mbps) that the HomePlug technology offers. As with Wi-Fi, the more PCs you connect, the slower each will run when all are active at once.

## Combining HomePlug with Wi-Fi

HomePlug by itself gives you infrastructure but not mobility. However, you can have it both ways by using new products that combine a HomePlug Ethernet adapter with a Wi-Fi access point. One of the first and best-regarded in this genre is the Netgear WGXB102, which actually consists of two separate physical devices, sold as a pair for about $120. They look like large, wall wart power supplies. See Figure 11-9.

**Figure 11-9**

The Netgear WGXB102 HomePlug-Wi-Fi Bridge. (Photo courtesy of Netgear.)

By using the WGXB102, you can have a second wireless access point at the other end of your house (or on the top story) without having to run Ethernet cable through the walls or ceilings. A typical setup is shown in Figure 11-10.

One nice thing about a system like this is that you can move the access point module of the WGXB102 around the house by plugging it into various wall outlets to see which position gives you the best coverage.

Some tips and issues on the HomePlug technology:

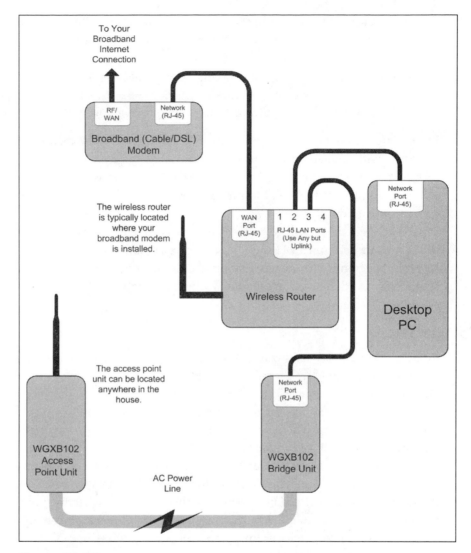

**Figure 11-10**

Using Netgear's WGXB102 to add a second wireless access point.

√ HomePlug devices are still very expensive compared to Wi-Fi. You will probably have to spend almost twice as much per PC (about $100) to equip each PC with a HomePlug adapter.

√ Depending on how the power wiring is implemented in your neighborhood, your immediate neighbors may be able to pick up your network signal if they implement a HomePlug system of their own. Although HomePlug is still pretty rare, it's a very good idea to enable encryption on your HomePlug system after you get it connected and running.

√ Don't plug a HomePlug adapter into a power strip, especially those with noise filters or surge suppressors. Noise filters may filter out the HomePlug radio signal and prevent the device from connecting.

√ As with any bleeding-edge networking products like this, it's a good idea to create your network entirely with products from one vendor, be it Netgear, Linksys, or any other company offering a full product line.

HomePlug technology is now about where Wi-Fi was in 2000: expensive, bleeding edge, with limited choices to the consumer. Very recently, a higher-speed technology called HomePlug AV was created and in fact is being built into a growing number of high-end homes as they are constructed. HomePlug AV can transmit audio and video as well as data files and Internet traffic. It's too early to tell whether it will go mainstream or remain an expensive curiosity, but in the meantime, ordinary HomePlug can solve certain wireless coverage problems in your home without you having to pull cables for a second access point. If you can afford the costs, it's well worth investigating.

# Summing Up

To have the greatest success with a Wi-Fi network, choose a manufacturer with a full product line, and buy gear made only by that manufacturer. Wi-fi is a strong but limited standard, especially in areas like encryption where manufacturers have extended standard features for good reasons. Most of the time, a single Wi-Fi router or access point will serve an entire 2,500-square-foot (or smaller) house with only a few weak or dead spots, and to find those spots you must use a field auditing utility like NetStumbler. When you detect interference, look first for other wireless technologies inside the house, then for nearby Wi-Fi networks on the same Wi-Fi channel, and finally for other licensed services nearby (police and fire radios, industrial equipment) that may cause interference on the 2.4 GHz band. Persistent interference from priority licensed services outside the home may require a move to Wireless-A on the 5 GHz band.

# 12

# Degunking Your Backup Strategy

**Degunking Checklist:**

√  Understand the choices for hardware backup devices and choose the one that's best for you.

√  Know the pros and cons of backing up by burning to CDs or DVDs, saving to an external hard drive, or using Microsoft Backup, and learn how to back up to each.

√  Work through the checklist of files that you should be backing up.

√  Make sure you back up important files that are easy to overlook, such as your Internet favorites, key e-mail data, and Internet cookies.

√  Learn the steps for creating a backup schedule with Microsoft Backup.

√  Organize your backups stored on CDs and DVDs.

√  Understand the advantages and disadvantages of the various backup strategies.

√  Test your backups.

√  Learn how to restore from backups.

√  Learn why purchasing and installing a backup UPS power device is also a good decision.

What would happen if your house caught fire? Most likely, all of your family photos and movies, your music collection, and your valuable documents (like your homeowner's insurance policy, your will, and letters from an old flame) would be damaged or lost. It would be nearly impossible to have a "backup" of all of that stuff somewhere. You wouldn't purchase two CDs or DVDs every time you acquired one and then store it in another location, *just in case* there was a fire. You wouldn't scan or copy every single photo or document either. You simply take your chances with these things.

Now, what would happen if your hard drive crashed or if your PC was stolen? What if your toddler spilled milk on the tower, or your golden retriever jumped on your desk while playfully chasing the cat? Although it's not practical to have backups of your physical things, you *can* have backups of your virtual ones. Having backups is the only way to protect yourself in case of a hard drive crash. They'll have to be good, reliable, and recent backups though; you can't be willy-nilly about these things. If you don't believe us, just imagine losing everything on your computer: personal documents, downloaded music, family movies, pictures, important e-mail, Internet favorites and cookies, and software registration codes. Believe us, it's a nightmare trying to re-create all of this stuff, and it's usually impossible.

If you're convinced you need good, reliable backups, continue on. If not, reread the previous paragraphs. Once you're convinced and ready, we'll go ahead and create (or degunk) your personal backup strategy, including choosing a backup device, performing the backup, getting on a schedule, and finally, organizing the backups you create.

# Choose a Backup Device

There are several ways to create a backup of data, and it doesn't matter which one you choose as long as you choose one. If you have a CD or DVD burner, you can drag and drop and burn your backups to physical media that you can archive easily. If you have an external hard drive, again, you can drag and drop. You can also use Microsoft Backup. If your hard drive ever fails, you can recover. Each of these options has pros and cons though, so we'll work though each and you can choose the one you feel is right for you.

## The Simplicity of CD and DVD Drives

CD and DVD burners offer a great way to back up data. You can drag and drop and use XP's built-in burning application or any third-party one to create reliable backups. This is a good option for a lot of people. However, if you decide to go this route, keep the following in mind:

√ It's going to be difficult to remember to do this, and you'll have to be disciplined to stay on a regular schedule.

√ You'll need to burn CDs of new data weekly to have up-to-date backups. The cost for this will be high.

√ Getting the right amount of data on the disk can be tricky, and you'll have to know a little math, as well as how to find out how large your files and folders are.

√ Unless you create subfolders every time you add new data to your hard drive, when backing up folders such as the My Documents, My Music, My Pictures, and My Videos, you're going to create a ton of duplicate data in your CD or DVD archives.

√ CDs don't hold much data. If you only have a CD burner, as your data grows, you may find that you'll need several CDs to create a single backup. DVDs hold a lot of data though, so if it's possible, acquire a DVD burner.

√ People tend to store their CD and DVD backups in a drawer or on a shelf next to their computer. If there's a fire or flood, they'll be destroyed along with everything else. If you create backups this way, at least move the CDs and DVDs to another room, or preferably another home or office.

Don't let any of this discourage you. CDs and DVDs make great backups: don't get us wrong. They will last for years, there are no compatibility issues if you get a new computer, and you can move them off-site to protect them.

## Opting for an External Hard Drive

External hard drives are, well, external, and they are hard drives. They store data just as the one inside your PC does. Figure 12-1 shows an example. External hard drives connect to the PC using a USB cable and are Plug and Play. Just plug it in, connect it to the PC, and you're ready to go.

As with backing up to CDs and DVDs though, there are disadvantages to this option:

√ It's going to be difficult to remember to do this, and you'll have to be disciplined to stay on a regular schedule. However, with an external drive, it's easy to drag and drop at the end of each workday. You just have to get into the habit.

√ People tend to keep their external drive on the desk or on a shelf next to their PC, or worse, on top of the PC's tower. While this will protect you in the case of a computer crash, it won't protect you if there's a fire or flood, or if the tower is tipped. If you create backups this way, the only way to truly be safe is to remove the drive from the office at night and store it somewhere else.

**Figure 12-1**
An external hard drive is small, as you can see here in comparison to the
printer on the left.

Don't let these two things discourage you though; external hard drives make
great backups. Each day you can drag and drop the new data to the hard drive
and simply write over existing data. Figure 12-2 shows the message you'll receive at each backup. (While there are various backup strategies to avoid re-
writing old data, it really isn't necessary for the home user. Just drag and drop,
and click Yes when prompted.)

---

**TIP:** *If you have an older Zip disk and don't want to invest in an external hard drive, you
can use that instead.*

---

## Using Microsoft Backup

Microsoft Backup is a utility that is available on Windows XP Professional.
However, it can be installed on previous versions of Windows quite easily. With
this utility, you can create backups of data that you choose, including entire
drives, parts of drives, specific folders, and folders you've created. You can also
back up data that would otherwise be difficult to find or create, such as the
system state. You can even run the utility on a schedule! Being able to schedule
the backup is a definite plus and takes the pressure off of you to remember to
do it on your own. Figure 12-3 shows an example of Microsoft's Backup interface, with some items selected.

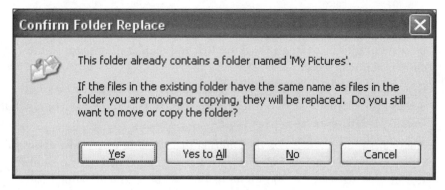

**Figure 12-2**

Write over old data.

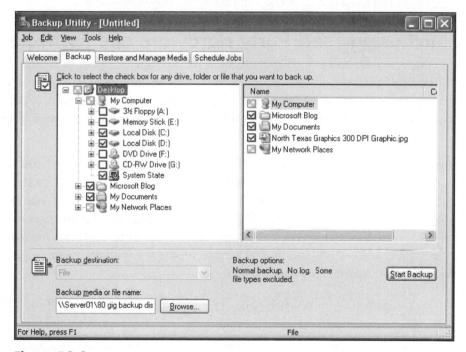

**Figure 12-3**

Windows Backup offers a myriad of choices for backing up data.

As with the other options, this backup option does have its disadvantages:

√ The files created can be read only by PCs running the same version of Windows. If you decide to move to a Mac, you won't be able to use the backups.

√ If your Windows Me hard drive crashes and you decide to purchase a new Windows XP PC, you won't be able to use the backups you've created. You must use the backups on the same operating system.

√ The backups must be saved to a network place, external hard drive, or internal hard drive. They cannot be burned directly to a CD or DVD. However, you can create the backups first and then transfer them to the chosen hardware later.

√ If you've purchased an OEM version of Windows XP Home, it may not include the files necessary to install Microsoft Backup. You'll have to install it from someone else's XP CD.

√ There are a lot of articles on the Internet that detail horror stories about this utility failing to restore a PC after a hard drive crash. There are no similar stories (that we're aware of) of CDs or DVDs failing to work after a hard drive crash. Keep this in mind when deciding on a strategy.

√ Most of the backups created by Microsoft Backup will be too large to fit on a CD. You'll really need a DVD burner if you choose this option.

# Purchasing Third-Party Hardware and Software

Finally, you can choose third-party options such as tape drives, optical disks, or online storage. Tapes drives and optical disks can be quite expensive and difficult to use properly. You have to know quite a bit about backups and backup types, and you really need to run a backup every day. For the home user, both are likely going a little overboard.

Another option is online storage. If you travel a lot, share data with others across the globe, or really want to protect your data from fire, flood, or theft, online storage is a great choice. With online storage, you upload your data to a storage site, where it is protected 24 hours a day by professionals who get paid to take care of it. Storage owners create daily backups to protect your data. That's their job. You can also share your data on the site with others or access it from a laptop when you're out of town.

## GunkBuster's Notebook: Using a Memory Stick for Backup and Travel

One of the challenges with backing up and restoring data involves traveling and using multiple computers. Many people who work while they travel have a desktop PC at home and a laptop they use on the road. With a setup like this, it's difficult to ensure that you are backing up properly and that you have the data you need when you travel. From all of the issues we encounter, we could probably write an entire book on this topic of syncing up and backing up data.

One suggestion we have is to invest in a memory stick (flash drive). These devices can store quite a bit of data and you can plug them into the USB port of your computer. Recently, we found a memory stick that costs $49.99 and stores as much as 512 MB. Before you go on a trip, you can back up all of the important files that you might need from your desktop PC on the memory stick. You can even encrypt the data so that it is secure in case you accidentally lose the memory stick. As you are working while on the road, you can access the data you need from the memory stick. If you edit documents, you can just replace them on the memory stick. When you get home from a trip, you can copy the files stored on the memory stick back to your desktop PC to restore them. It's amazing how easy this is!

Another advantage of the memory stick is that you can bring it with you on a trip and get some work done even if you don't have a laptop with you. For example, if you are traveling, you can visit a friend or relative and access your data. Or if you have access to an Internet café that has computers, you can plug in your memory stick and away you go. Just make sure that you have access to a PC that has a USB port.

# Select What to Back Up

Hopefully you've selected a backup option you feel will work for you. Now you just have to know what to back up. We'll show you how to do the backups later in this chapter, but in the following sections, we'll just talk about what you should back up, and we'll separate the things you should back up into three categories to keep you on the right track. After you've learned what you should back up regularly, feel free to skip to the section that details how to perform the backup for your selected strategy.

## Know What to Back Up and How to Back It Up

Backing up your PC might seem like a daunting task, especially if you don't do it very often. Many people we talk to forget to do regular backups and then they panic when their PC starts acting up. They then rush and try to back up their files, and in the process, they forget to back up important information. It can also be confusing because it might seem to you that there are a million files on your PC and that you have no idea what they actually are! You might be asking yourself if you really need to back up all of those files and what files you can skip.

There are items you absolutely *have* to back up. Some of them you are likely familiar with, such as the documents you have been creating with Word or Excel or your home videos and music. Other files might not be as obvious. There are things you may not think to back up, including e-mail messages, your address book, your PC's system information, your Internet Favorites list, programs you've downloaded, and cookies. In addition, you may not know *how* to back them up, even if you *wanted* to. This is especially true of fonts, drivers, and downloaded updates. We'll introduce some things you need to remember to back up, and then we'll give you a quick lesson on how to find what you need to back up.

The categories of files that are critical for any type of backup you do are as follows:

√   Personal data files: These files include all of the documents that you create or documents you receive from others. Often, these are the documents that are stored on your D: drive or in your My Documents folder. Don't forget to consider all of the files that you receive as e-mail attachments.

√   System-level or program-level personal data: There are likely applications that you use on a regular basis that store data in special files in specific folders on your hard drive, such as Outlook or Outlook Express. These applications store data such as your e-mails in uniquely formatted files that are often hidden away on your PC. A program such as Quicken is another example of an application that uses special files to store your personal data. We recommend that you make a list of the different applications that you use on a regular basis and consider the data files that each of these applications use to store their data. It's easy to overlook this important data, but think about what the impact would be if you forget to back it up and you ever have a system crash.

√   System-level data: This data consist of files that Windows requires so that it can keep your particular PC configuration running the way that you have it set up, and keep it running smoothly. This category includes device drivers, downloaded service packs and upgrades, fonts, and so on.

Much of the data described in the first bullet above, your personal data files, can be backed up by dragging and dropping them to CDs, DVDs, Zip disks, or external hard drives. Dragging to external hard drives is as simple as right-clicking, dragging and dropping, and then choosing Copy from the choices. When you're dragging and dropping your personal data though, don't forget about all of the personal files you have. You keep more than just documents, music, movies, and photos (which are covered in the first bullet here):

√   All data folders, including My Documents, My Pictures, My Videos, My Music, and any folders you've created. These are almost always located on the root drive, C:, or the data drive, D:. You can use My Computer or Windows Explorer to browse to these files.

√  Folders that contain downloaded applications or the ZIP files for the applications, shown in Figure 12-4. These files will probably by on the C: drive. Hopefully, you've created a special folder for this type of data.

√  Client files or work files. Again, these are personal folders you've created or documents in the My Documents folder.

√  Data including tax information, wills, personal letters, personal projects, diaries, and so on. Check your personal folders on the C: or D: drive.

Figure 12-4 shows a folder with setup files for downloaded applications, which include a program for Registry compaction, Microsoft's Live Meeting, a system file checker, Media Player and Movie Maker fun packs, an anti-spyware program, and more. If these files aren't backed up, you'll have to download them all again if your computer crashes.

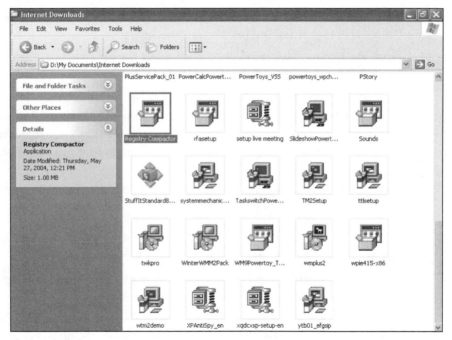

**Figure 12-4**
Don't forget to back up downloaded program files.

*TIP: Some of the software in Figure 12-4 is total gunk, by the way. Some of the applications were downloaded, used once, and never used again; some don't work; and some were shareware never purchased. Some work great though, like the Registry Compactor (selected). Only back up what you want to keep. Delete the rest.*
*We'll now focus on showing you how to locate and back up some of the important*

*system-level data. This includes data created with or by Internet Explorer and Outlook Express. Both contain information you'll need if you ever have to recover from a hard drive crash or if you purchase a new PC.*

### Back Up Key Internet Explorer Information

Open Internet Explorer. Do you have a home page configured? When you go to Amazon.com, do they know what you like to read? Are you automatically logged in when you visit your favorite sites? Do you maintain a list of favorite Web sites? If so, you need to do some backing up in Internet Explorer. Specifically, you need to back up your Internet favorites and cookies. Favorites are the list of Web sites you've marked that you like to visit; cookies let these sites know who you are and what you like to look at or purchase when you visit.

To locate, and thus back up, Internet favorites, follow these steps:

1. Open Internet Explorer, and from the File menu, select Import and Export. Click Next to start the Import/Export Wizard.

2. From the Import/Export Selection page, select Export Favorites. Click Next. (You'd select Import Favorites if you needed to restore the file.)

3. In the Export Favorites Source Folder page, select the Favorites folder. Click Next.

4. In the Export Favorites Destination page, click Browse. Select a folder to save the data to. You may want to create a new folder. (Once the folder is created, you can back it up by dragging and dropping or using Microsoft Backup.)

5. In the Select Bookmark File window, name the file Favorites, and type the month and year. Click Save.

6. Click Next and Finish to complete.

Do this to locate and back up cookies:

1. Open Internet Explorer, and from the File menu, select Import and Export. Click Next to start the Import/Export Wizard.

2. From the Import/Export Selection page, select Export Cookies. Click Next. (You'd select Import Favorites if you needed to restore the file.)

3. In the Export Cookies Destination page, click Browse. Select a folder to save the data to. You may want to create a new folder. (Once the folder is created, you can back it up by dragging and dropping or using Microsoft Backup.)

4. In the Select Cookie File window, name the file Cookies and type the month and year. Click Save.

5. Click Next and Finish to complete.

You'll now have a folder that looks like what's shown in Figure 12-5. This folder can be backed up easily.

**Figure 12-5**

A folder that is created to store favorites and cookies can be easily backed up.

## Back Up Your Outlook Express Information

Occasionally, you need to back up the information in Outlook Express. Losing archived e-mail messages along with every contact's e-mail address can bring a home business to a halt and can create a virtual nightmare for everyone else. The information you can back up includes your address book, Internet account settings, and mail messages. While Microsoft has made backing up an address book and Internet account settings quite simple, it's made backing up e-mail messages a chore. You don't need to be a rocket scientist, but it certainly doesn't hurt. In this section, we'll start with the easiest of these three tasks and move to the most difficult. First, we'll back up the address book, then the Internet account settings, and finally, mail messages.

Here's how to locate and back up your address book:

1. Open Outlook Express.

2. Choose File, point to Export, and select Address Book.

3. In the Address Book Export Tool dialog box, select Text File (Comma Separated Values) and click Export.

4. In the CSV Export dialog box, click Browse.

5. Browse to a location to save the file. You may want to create a new folder entitled OE Settings and Mail, with the month and year. (You can then add the other backups to this folder.)

6. Name the file Address Book. Click Save and click Next.

7. In the next CSVExport dialog box, select all of the items. This is shown in Figure 12-6. Click Finish, OK, and then Close when prompted.

To back up your Internet account settings, do this:

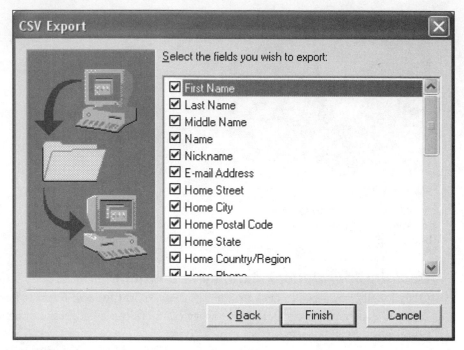

**Figure 12-6**
Export all data in your address book.

1. Open Outlook Express.

2. From the Tools menu, select Accounts.

3. From the Mail tab, choose the account you want to back up and click Export. Figure 12-7 shows an example.

4. In the Export Internet Account window, browse to the folder created earlier for storing Outlook Express backups. Verify the file name and click Save.

5. Repeat steps 3 and 4 for additional accounts.

6. When finished, click Close.

With those two tasks out of the way, let's move on to mail messages. You might have noticed that from the File menu, in the Export choices, there was a choice to export messages. If you've tried that, you probably got a rude awakening. Figure 12-8 shows what happens when we try to choose that option.

If you try to back up messages by exporting, you'll quickly find that exporting only moves the messages from one program, in this case Outlook Express, to another one, such as Microsoft Outlook or Microsoft Exchange. That isn't what you want to do. You want to back up your messages, so you'll have to find

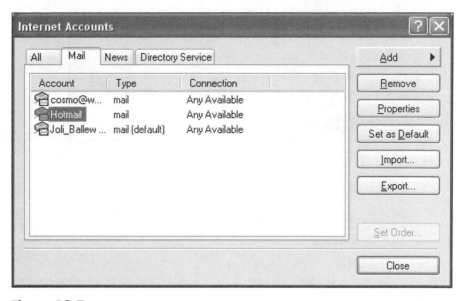

**Figure 12-7**
Choose an account whose settings you wish to back up (export).

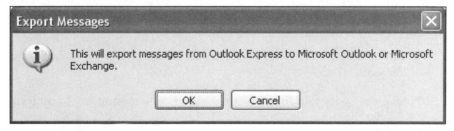

**Figure 12-8**
Exporting mail messages doesn't work like exporting the address book or Internet account settings.

another way. We do believe that most of you have thought about backing up your Outlook Express messages but simply don't know how. E-mail messages can be backed up. Don't panic; you just have to know how to do it.

To locate and back up your mail messages, follow these steps:

1. Open Outlook Express.
2. From the Tools menu, select Options.
3. In the Options dialog box, choose the Maintenance tab.
4. Click Store Folder.
5. Use your cursor to highlight the store folder; then right-click and choose Copy. Figure 12-9 shows what you'll see.

**Figure 12-9**

Select and copy the folder in which mail messages are saved.

6. Click Cancel twice to close both boxes.

7. Exit Outlook Express.

8. Click Start, and then Run.

9. In the Run dialog box, right-click and choose Paste. Click OK.

10. In the Outlook Express window, which shows the folders in which all of your mail messages are stored, click Edit and then Select All.

11. Choose Edit and Copy. Close this window.

12. Open the folder where you want to store the information. (You may want to create a subfolder called Mail Messages.)

13. In that folder, right-click and choose Paste. Wait while the messages are copied.

You can now copy that folder to any backup device, using any backup strategy.

### Back Up Work Created in Other Applications

Some applications store their data in folders that are not easily accessible. One application we use, Arts and Letters, has a special folder on the hard drive created by the program for storing data. Another program we use, Microsoft Outlook, also has folders stored in difficult-to-find places and the backup options are not the same as they are in Outlook Express. As mentioned earlier, you'll have to figure out where that data is stored and how to back it up.

In Arts and Letters, the folder where all files created with the program are saved on the C: drive in My Graphics, which is a subfolder in another subfolder named ExpressOffice. We know this because when we choose File and then Save As, that's the folder that appears in the Save In text box. To find out where any program you use creates saved files by default (we'll talk about Microsoft Outlook separately), you can do the same:

1.  Open any program you use: Quicken, Photoshop, Excel, MSN Messenger, Web camera software, or anything similar.

2.  Create a document, picture, image, or file using that program. It can be one word or one number; just create something.

3.  From the File menu, select Save As. If you don't see one of these options, check for others that may be appropriate, such as Open or Save.

4.  All programs will open some sort of dialog box that allows you to see where the file will be saved. Make a note of that location. You may have to click the down arrow in the Save In option or something similar to see the entire path.

5.  Close the program.

6.  Right-click the Start button and choose Explore.

7.  Browse to the location of the folder. This folder can now be backed up by dragging and dropping to the appropriate media.

If you use Microsoft Outlook, you can back up your data using the tools provided with the program. To back up your address book, open the address book, choose Select All, and then File and Save As. To back up mail messages, select the mail pane, and from the File menu, choose Import and Export, Outlook, and Export to a File. From there, you can work through the wizard to back up personal file folders in a variety of ways. When you get to the Save Exported File As choices, browse to a location to save the backup and then drag and drop the backup to your backup media.

The point is, all programs differ. However, you can always use File and Save As or use the program's export options to back up the data you create.

### Back Up Your System Information

Creating a backup of the list of system information is just as important as backing up personal information. Using a tool called System Information, you can list and save vital information about your computer. You can use this information if you ever want to replace hardware such as a nonworking network interface card or CD-ROM drive with the exact same model and type, if you need to replace a corrupt driver but don't know its version or name, or if you need to view problem devices.

You open the System Information window by typing **Msinfo32** in the Run box. (Click Start, choose Run.) Here are some of the items you can access and save information about:

√    Hardware, including name, model, manufacturer, and type

√    Display settings, including color planes, drivers, IRQ channels, and resolution

√    Input devices, such as their type, driver, and manufacturer

√    Network connections, adapter types, and protocols used

√    Available ports, including serial, parallel, USB, and FireWire

√    Printers and print jobs

√    Storage devices, including drivers, disks, SCSI, and IDE

√    Signed drivers

√    Running services

√    Microsoft applications

This is just a smattering of what is included in the report. If you have a full report saved though, you can save a technician time when they need to replace a part or find a driver. The technician can also view the running services, problem devices, and other information when troubleshooting a problematic computer.

While the information from System Information is only a list of components, drivers, and internal parts and workings, you can also physically back up important system files such as the Registry, fonts, drivers, and downloaded updates and service packs. You should do this occasionally, perhaps two or three times a year.

Backing up the Registry can be achieved using Microsoft Backup and backing up the system state. Backing up fonts, drivers, and downloaded updates can be done using Windows Explorer:

1.  Right-click the Start button and choose Explore.

2.  Expand Local Disk, expand the Windows folder, and locate Drivers. Right-click the Drivers folder, drag to a backup location, and choose Copy Here. Be careful not to choose Move Here; your data will be moved and a nightmare will result!

3.  Below the Drivers folder, locate Fonts. Back up this folder in the same manner.

4.  If there are other folders you'd like to back up, locate them and perform the same tasks. You may want to back up the folders ServicePackFiles, Offline Web Pages, or others.

---

*TIP: Don't forget about System Restore! System Restore creates a backup of the system state daily, including the Registry, and you can use it to revert to a previous state anytime you need to. Verify that System Restore is enabled by right-clicking My Computer, choosing Properties, choosing the System Restore tab, and making sure Turn Off System Restore on All Drives is not checked.*

---

# Perform the Backup

Now that you now how to isolate the data that you'll need to be backing up, we'll show you how to perform the important steps to actually save your data on a backup device. We'll talk about each of the options we've introduced in this chapter, so if you already know what back up device or strategy you're going to use, go ahead and skip to that section.

## Burning CDs and DVDs

If you have a CD or DVD burner, you can use that hardware to easily create a backup of data stored on your hard disk. Creating a backup is as simple as dragging and dropping the files to an application that allows it. As mentioned earlier though, if you're burning to a CD, you have to remember that you can't copy more than 700 MB of data. This makes creating a CD a little more complicated than creating a DVD because you have to keep track of the amount of data you're planning to copy. This usually isn't such a huge issue with DVDs though, because DVDs hold over 4 GB of data. Figure 12-10 shows what might appear on a Windows XP PC when a writable CD is inserted in a CD burner.

**Figure 12-10**

With a Windows XP PC, you have the option to burn the CD in various ways.

As you can see from Figure 12-10, we have four options:

√   Open writable CD folder using Windows Explorer

√   Burn a CD (using Windows Media Player)

√   Create a CD (using iTunes)

√   Take no action

You may have more options, or less, depending on what programs you have on your computer. You may have choices for MusicMatch, Nero, or InCD, for instance. And, if you've never used iTunes, you won't have that option as we do. You may not be prompted with any choices, though, because you either have an older operating system, you chose at some point to always open a specific program when you insert a blank CD, or your system is buggy. If that's the case, you'll need to select the program from the Programs menu choices or browse to your CD burner's drive in My Computer.

Because there are so many options, the actual process of burning a CD will differ depending on what program you choose. If you choose a third-party program like Nero or InCD, you'll have to work through the program's inter-face to add data to burn. However, it is our experience that most programs use a drag-and-drop procedure. With third-party software, most keep track of the data you're adding too, which will help you know when you've collected enough data for the CD. Once you've collected the data, simply use the interface op-tions to burn the CD.

---

**TIP:** *Refrain from checking Always Do the Selected Action when prompted about what to do. You will want the options to appear each time you place a CD in the CD burner. Some days you may want to burn a music CD, others a data CD.*

---

## GunkBuster's Notebook: Choose a Third-Party CD Burning Program

If you want to burn CDs to create backups, you shouldn't think that you can count on Windows XP's CD writing utility for the task; it's better to opt for third-party software instead. The CD writing utility that comes with Windows XP has one major flaw. It does not keep a running total of the data you've added. Figure 12-11 shows an example.

Although three files have been added, the Details pane still shows 702 MB of free space. Unless you manually count the MBs of data you've added (by hovering your mouse over each icon),

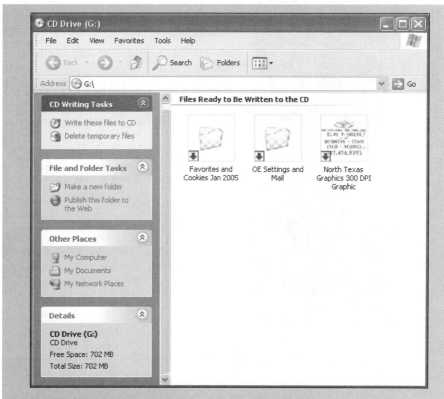

**Figure 12-11**
Windows XP's CD writing utility has its downside.

you won't know until you start the burn process if you've added too much or too little. Figure 12-12 shows the error you'll receive if you choose more than 700 MB of data to burn.

Working through the process by guessing or using a calculator to manually add up what you've added is gunk you shouldn't have to deal with. It wastes time, and you often have to remove files, break up files, and burn multiple CDs. With third-party software, almost all keep a running tally so you never have to deal with this.

On the upside though, the Windows XP CD writing utility is extremely easy to use. Other than the annoying error that too much data is selected or that you've created a CD with hardly any data on it, well, we can say that it *always* works. We cannot say that of any other third-party CD burning program (and especially DVD burning programs)!

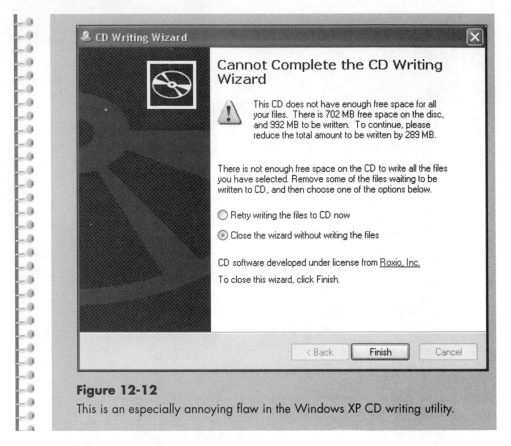

**Figure 12-12**
This is an especially annoying flaw in the Windows XP CD writing utility.

# Dragging and Dropping to an External Drive

External hard drives are even easier to use than CD burning software. You simply drag and drop the data. In fact, it's so easy you can do it at the end of each workday. It's unlikely you'll burn a CD or DVD every day, or even take the time to add to an existing CD+RW or DVD+RW. However, dragging and dropping and clicking Yes to proceed makes for a pretty easy backup! Figure 12-13 shows a backup in progress.

Before you can use the drag and drop method to effectively back up your system daily though, you need to create a shortcut to the device on your desktop. You'll use that shortcut to drag and drop to. Here, we'll outline two procedures for doing that: the first, to create a desktop shortcut for an external drive that is connected directly to your PC, and the second, to create a desktop shortcut for an external drive that is connected to another PC. (Note that another PC can serve as a backup device too.)

To create a shortcut to an external hard drive that is connected directly to your computer, follow these steps:

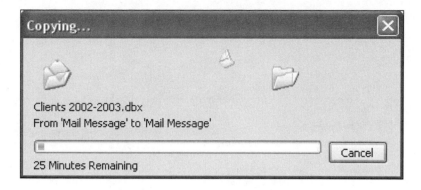

**Figure 12-13**
Dragging and dropping to an external drive is the simplest way to back up data

1. Open My Computer, right-click the icon for the external drive, and select Create Shortcut.

2. When prompted to create a shortcut on the Desktop, click Yes.

To create a shortcut to an external hard drive that is connected to another, networked, computer, do this:

1. Open My Computer.

2. From the Tools menu, select Map Network Drive.

3. Click Browse.

4. Locate the backup device, select it, and click OK. See Figure 12-14.

5. Click Finish. The drive will open automatically.

6. In My Computer, right-click the new network drive and select Create Shortcut.

7. Click Yes when prompted to place that shortcut on the Desktop.

Now, all you have to do is drag any folder you want to back up over the new desktop icon and drop it. A copy of your important data will be stored on that drive. If there is duplicate data, it will simply be written over. (Now the trick is how to keep that drive organized…stay tuned for more on that!)

# Using (and Scheduling) the Windows Backup Utility

You know you should back up your important files regularly, and that includes your pictures, music, and videos, as well as your data. Many people prefer to drag and drop the folders to an external drive or use CD burning software to

**Figure 12-14**
If the external hard drive is on another PC, you should map a
network drive before creating a shortcut.

burn their data to CDs because it's straightforward and simple. Unfortunately,
this way of backing up leaves you wide open for procrastinating, and many
times, the job simply doesn't get done.

Windows XP Professional contains a backup utility that can help you in your
quest for regular backups. The backup utility, called Microsoft Backup, helps
you back up automatically and on a schedule. And, although it doesn't let you
burn your backups directly to CDs or DVDs, there are ways around that. The
backup utility and our workarounds make using it a good option for those who
need a little reminder every week.

The backup utility also lets you back up things that would otherwise be difficult, or things you'd forget to back up, like the following:

√  System state (the Registry files, system boot files, and other data)

√  Files and folders in My Network Places

√  Fonts

√  Drivers

√   Offline Web pages

√   Downloaded programs

√   Unzipped files

√   Service pack files

### Installing Microsoft Backup in XP Home Edition

Unfortunately, the backup utility that is native to Windows XP Professional isn't included by default in the Window XP Home Edition. If you have the Home edition, you'll have to take some steps to install it manually.

Here's how to install Microsoft Backup for Windows XP Home:

1.  Place the Windows XP Home Edition CD into the CD-ROM drive.
2.  If it starts automatically, click Exit.
3.  Open My Computer, right-click the CD drive's icon, and choose Explore.
4.  Locate the folder \VALUEADD\MSFT\NTBACKUP.
5.  Double-click the Ntbackup.msi file and work through the wizard. When complete, click Finish.

### Creating a Backup

To create a backup, you must first open Microsoft Backup:

1.  Click Start, point to All Programs, point to Accessories, and point to System Tools. Click Backup.
2.  By default, it opens in Wizard mode. Although you can work in Wizard mode, it's best to choose Advanced mode. To access Advanced mode, click the Advanced Mode link shown in Figure 12-15. Once in Advanced mode, you can begin to create and configure the backup that's right for you.
3.  Choose the Backup tab.
4.  Work through the folders and drives listed. Click the plus sign by any folder to see its subfolders. Check any items you want to back up. You can back up folders that contain mail messages or personal data, entire drives or parts of drives, the system state, data stored in My Network Places, and more. You can even browse to the Windows files on your root drive and select the Drivers folder or Fonts folder, the ServicePackFiles folder, and more.
5.  After all data has been selected, click Browse. Browse to a location to store the backup. Hopefully, you have a network drive or an external hard drive to store it in. Click Save.
6.  Click Start Backup.

**Figure 12-15**
Don't use the Wizard mode when creating a backup; choose the Advanced option.

7.  In the Backup Job Information dialog box, make the selection to append this backup to an existing backup or to replace all data on the media with this backup. Click Start Backup. (Notice the option Schedule here. We'll come back to that later.)

8.  Click Close when the process is complete.

If anything ever happens to your PC and you have to use your backup, simply open the backup utility again and choose the Restore tab. There will be options there for restoring saved data. The process will be detailed in the last section of this chapter.

### Storing the Backup and Moving It to a CD or DVD

Once you've created the backup, you can burn it to a CD or DVD if you desire. This is a good option if you don't have or don't trust your external hard drive. (Having a backup stored on the same computer that you're backing up just doesn't make good sense. If that one crashes, you'll lose your backup too.) Copying the data to a CD or DVD was detailed earlier in this chapter; the process here is the same.

---

**TIP:** *You'll find that almost all of the backups you'll create with Microsoft Backup will be quite a bit larger than 700 MB, which is what will fit on a single CD. You can't break up these backups either, so your best bet is to copy them to DVDs instead of CDs.*

---

### Creating a Schedule

If you want to run your backups on a schedule, you'll need to click the Scheduled Jobs tab in Microsoft Backup, configure a job and save it, and then create a schedule for the job. When you save a scheduled job, you won't have to reselect the items you want to back up the next time you run the utility and you can create a schedule for it to run automatically. Creating a schedule can help you remember to create backups, and you'll never have to worry that you didn't. To create a schedule for a previously configured backup, follow these steps:

1. Open Microsoft Backup.

2. Choose the Schedule Jobs tab.

3. Click Add Job, and click Next to start the Backup Wizard. In the next page, choose a backup type. We prefer to choose folders manually, but you can choose to back up only the system state or back up the entire PC.

4. Manually select what you want to back up as detailed previously.

5. When prompted by the Backup Type, Destination, and Name page, click Browse. Choose a location and create a name for the backup. Click Next.

6. In the Type of Backup dialog box, for the type of backup, select Normal. If you want to experiment with other backup types, refer to the help files included with the application.

7. Choose Verify Data after Backup, and click Next.

8. Choose either to append the data to an existing backup or to replace the existing backups. We generally append the data; it's faster. Click Next.

9. In the When to Back Up page, select Later and create a job name. Click Set Schedule.

10. In the Schedule Job Options dialog box, select Properties. The Schedule Job dialog box appears in Figure 12-16.

11. Configure when you want to run the backup utility. You can create a schedule for the job to be run once, daily, weekly, monthly, at system startup, at logon, and when idle. Click OK.

12. Enter a job name in the Scheduled Job Options dialog box, and click OK.

13. Enter an administrator's password when prompted. Click OK. Click Finish.

14. Exit the backup utility.

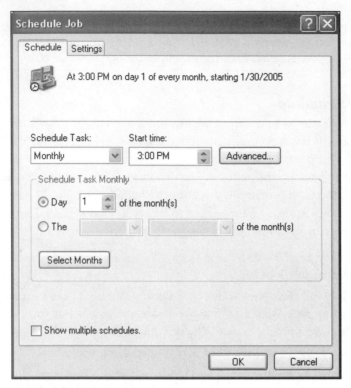

**Figure 12-16**
Create a schedule for the backup utility to run.

# Know How Often to Back Up and What to Back Up

In this section, we're going to spell out, in simple terms, just how often we think you should back up your data. One size certainly does not fit all, though. Your needs will differ depending on how often you use your computer and for what purpose. For example, we back up this book's data daily; we'd hate to lose a whole day's worth of work (or worse, a whole week) and have to rewrite lost pages. However, you may not need to back up your personal data each day as we do; if you don't use your computer much or don't make changes to files you've already backed up, you may only have to back up your personal data once a month. Ultimately, it's up to you to decide.

Because everyone's computing habits are different then, you'll have to look at the information in Table 12-1 objectively. We're going to state the *least* amount of times we think you should back up specific kinds of data. You'll eventually decide how often to back up, though—only you know how much data you can stand to lose.

So how do you decide what's right for you? Well, consider this: say your son just had his fifth birthday party and you took digital pictures. After uploading them to your PC and deleting them from your digital camera, you shut down the computer for the night. The next day, the PC doesn't boot. Perhaps you realize the cat's been sleeping and shedding on the tower, or maybe someone spilled red Kool-Aid on it. Although it's only been a day, you've lost all the pictures of that party. There's no way to get them back, short of a miracle. That would have been a moment when a daily backup would have been useful.

With that in mind, look at Table 12-1. This table should at least remind you of what should be backed up regularly, but the guidelines for how often are ultimately up to you. We've documented what we believe is the least you should do.

**Table 12-1   Know What to Back Up and How Often**

| What to Back Up | How Often |
|---|---|
| Photos, movies, documents, personal folders, music | Once weekly for the avid user, once a month for the occasional user (or as data changes). |
| Wills, insurance policies, power of attorney documents, personal letters | Once, and then each time they change. |
| System state, drivers, fonts, service packs, and other important folders with Microsoft Backup | Three to four times a year. |
| Downloaded applications and their registration codes | Anytime a new application is downloaded, installed, and is one you want to keep. |
| Client files and work files | Daily, weekly, or as they change. |
| Internet favorites and cookies and Outlook Express address book and mail messages | Monthly. |
| System information, including important system files such as the Registry, fonts, drivers, and downloaded updates and service packs | Two or three times a year. |
| System Restore | System Restore should be enabled. It will make a backup of your system each day. |

# Test and Organize Backed-Up Data

There's only one thing worse than having a hard drive crash with no backups, and that's having a hard drive crash and finding out your backups are corrupt, aren't up-to-date, are missing some important files you didn't think to back up, or are so unorganized that they aren't useful. It happens, and when it does, it's a nightmare.

In the following section, we'll concentrate on *not* letting that happen. You'll learn that testing the backups and organizing the backups you've recently created is just as important as remembering to back up in the first place. And we'll show you how. Let's start with your CD and DVD collections.

## Testing and Organizing CD and DVD Collections

It's easy to test a CD or DVD. Just pop the disk in the disk drive, open it in My Computer, and verify that you can view and use the information on it. If the data's there, using it is easy. Simply drag and drop the backed-up data (if it isn't from Microsoft Backup) from the CD or DVD to the new or repaired PC's hard drive. Because the data on a CD or DVD is so versatile, you can copy the data to another Windows operating system or even copy some of your personal data to a Mac if you want to.

It's not quite as easy to keep the data organized. There are a hundred ways to go wrong. You can burn CDs haphazardly and have data spread across several disks. You can have disks everywhere—in desk drawers, in a closet—or maybe you don't keep them stored in the proper cases. Perhaps the disks aren't dated, or you have a lot of duplicate data. You may have backups with no label on the CD or DVD and not have a clue what's on it. You may even have copies of files that have undergone revisions and not know which ones are new and which ones are old. These backups are going to drive you crazy if you ever have to use them.

---

**TIP:** *If you already have a mess like this on your hands, start fresh today with all new backups, and store the old ones in the garage or basement.*

---

In order to avoid these problems, you have to start at the source. You have to take the initiative to avoid gunk before, during, and after making your backups. The following list will help you start anew:

√  Each time you burn a CD or DVD, write the date on it. Organize backups by date on a shelf, in an organizer, or in a drawer.

√  Place burned CDs and DVDs in protective cases. Inside the case, include a note of what is on the CD or DVD—documents, pictures, music, movies, or other data.

√  Create subfolders when creating new data on your hard drive. Doing so will allow you to back up only the new data and avoid the duplication that exists when entire folders are repeatedly backed up.

√  Test all CDs and DVDs before storing them.

√ Always have one backup created by Microsoft Backup with the system state in case of emergencies. It's even better if you can burn a copy of your entire root drive to a DVD.

√ Don't forget to back up fonts, drivers, downloaded programs, registration codes, service packs, and other data a few times a year. Store these in a safe place, in dated order.

√ Applications you've purchased, operating system disks, driver disks, and office application disks must be kept safe too. Figure 12-17 shows one kind of organization.

In Figure 12-17, there are four CD organizer notebooks. One holds personal backups, organized from newest to oldest, one holds operating system disks, one holds general applications, and one holds driver disks and driver backups.

**Figure 12-17**
This is one way to organize disks.

*WARNING! If you decide to use a CD notebook like this, make sure you keep all registration codes with the software. Some of the codes are written on the box the software came in or on a separate paper. If you throw these out, you won't be able to reinstall your software should you need to.*

# Testing and Organizing an External Hard Drive

Testing the data on an external hard drive is just as easy as testing the data on a CD or DVD; you just need to browse to it and see if the data is there. If it's there, you only need to be able to open and use it. If anything ever happens to your PC, you can simply drag and drop the data to recover.

Unfortunately, external drives almost always end up looking like what's shown in Figure 12-18. In this figure, you can see that there are various folders in no particular order, there are zipped files next to Word documents, and there are screenshots randomly saved throughout. There are also a couple of files that don't seem to do anything, like the one with the tilde (~). This is *not* how your external drive should look.

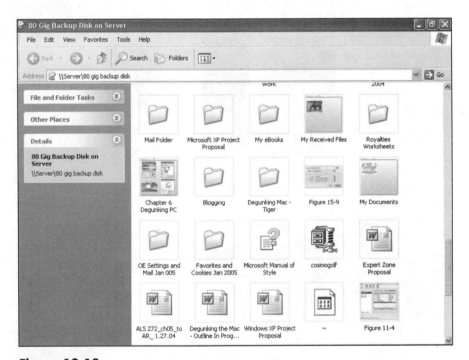

**Figure 12-18**
Don't let this happen to your external hard drive.

Again, avoiding the issue is the best option. Of course, for most of you, this probably comes too little and too late. If your backups look like these, it's time to take control.

To avoid a gunked-up hard drive or to degunk the one you have, perform the tasks here in the following order:

1. Regularly delete (or delete now) any files you no longer need.

2. Create folders for the items you've backed up—Pictures, Music, Movies, Documents, Work, Clients, Ongoing Projects, Finished Projects, and so on—and move stray files and related folders into them.

3. Create a folder called Mail, and move all of your Outlook Express backups into it.

4. Create a folder called Internet, and move all of your Internet-related backups into it, including downloaded files.

5. Create a folder called Microsoft Backup, and store backup files there you create with the backup utility.

6. From the View menu, point to Arrange Icons By, and select Name to organize alphabetically or Modified to arrange from newest to oldest.

7. When saving new backups, always browse to the correct folder or create a new folder that represents the data.

Finally, to be on the safe side, borrow or purchase an external DVD+RW drive. Make copies of the data stored on your external hard drive. Do this once a year.

## Testing and Organizing Windows Backups

The only way to really test the backups you've created with Microsoft Backup is by restoring the data through the Restore and Manage Media tab in the backup utility. As shown in Figure 12-19, it's easy. Simply select the specific backup in the left pane and click Start Restore. You can choose to restore the data to its original location, an alternate location, or a single folder. For testing, we'll suggest you choose to restore to a single folder. After the restore process, you can browse to that folder to see if the data was restored properly. (Of course, when restoring after a crash, you'll choose to restore to the original location.)

We'll talk more about restoring (which is, in essence, the same as testing) in the final sections of this chapter.

---

*TIP: Notice in Figure 12-19 that a note is present that says, "If Files Already Exist: Do Not Replace." You can change this behavior from the Tools, Options dialog box.*

---

If the backup fails or causes you any problems at all, don't worry; you can always create a new backup, and the utility creates a System Restore point before starting. If something goes wrong, you can always use System Restore to return to the PC's state prior to the backup.

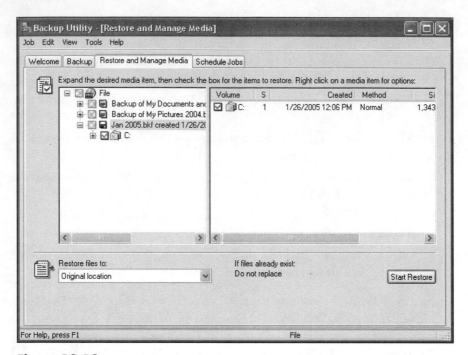

**Figure 12-19**
Use the Restore and Manage Media tab to test a backup.

---

**NOTE:** *Microsoft Backup offers a lot more than what we've shown here. If you're really interested in this backup utility, browse through the help files. You can create all kinds of backups, create alternating schedules for different backup types, and configure options for restoring and backing up files.*

---

# Restore Data from Backups

Having backups won't do you any good if you don't know how to use them. We can guarantee you'll need them if you have to reinstall everything on your PC or if your PC's hard drive conks out and you have to purchase a new PC. If you've tested your backups already, you're halfway there, though. Let's look now at performing a *real* backup.

## Restoring Personal Data from CDs, DVDs, and External Hard Drives

Restoring personal data stored in folders on a CD, DVD, or external hard drive is as simple as dragging the data from the media to the appropriate folder on the recovered or new PC. To drag and drop data from the My Documents folder on the external media to the My Documents folder on the new PC, for instance, just open the folder on the external media, choose Edit and Select All, and then drag and drop. You can perform the same tasks to copy and move the data from the My Movies or My Pictures folders to their appropriate counterparts too. Just repeat the steps with all of the folders of personal data you've backed up.

## Restoring Mail and Internet Data

If you've backed up the mail and Internet data to a CD, DVD, or external drive, you can't really drag and drop that data easily. (You can, but not easily!) To restore mail and Internet data, you'll need to import the data back into the original program, and this will generally require that you use the same utility that you previously used to export it.

For instance, to restore an address book in Outlook Express, you'll choose File, then Import, and then Other Address Book. You choose Other Address Book because you previously saved the address book in a CSV, or comma-separated values, file. That's now a "real" address book. You'll then browse to the file on the CD, DVD, or external drive and choose OK and the address book will be restored automatically.

Importing messages in Outlook Express requires a little more knowledge. Here's how to import messages you've backed up previously:

1. Open Outlook Express, and on the File menu, point to Import, and choose Messages.
2. In the Select Program page, select Microsoft Outlook Express 6 (or Microsoft Outlook Express 4 if that's what you use). Click Next.
3. In the Import From OE6 page, select Import Mail From an OE6 Store Directory. Click OK.
4. In the Location of Messages page, click Browse and locate the saved message files. Click OK and then Next.
5. In the Select Folders page, select All Folders as shown in Figure 12-20. Click Next.
6. Click Finish when the process is complete.

There are a few other things you've backed up you can import. In Outlook Express you can choose File, Import, and Mail Account Settings to import the settings for your e-mail account(s). In Internet Explorer, you can use File, Import and Export to import backed-up favorites or cookies. Figure 12-21 shows this interface. It's as easy as making the choices and clicking Next. No trick to it!

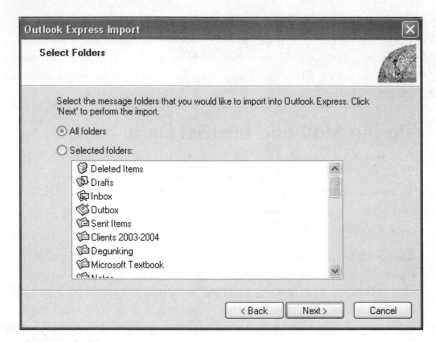

**Figure 12-20**

Choose All Folders when importing backed-up mail messages.

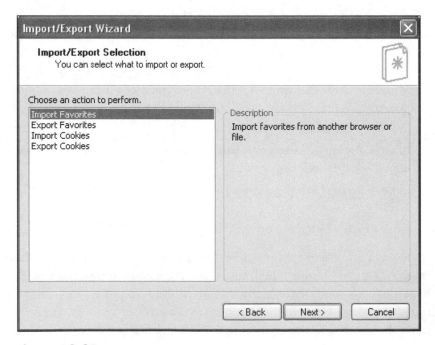

**Figure 12-21**

Internet Explorer's Import/Export Wizard helps you import cookies and favorites easily.

## Restoring Application-Specific Files

Application-specific files require a little sleuthing to restore. First, you'll have to remember the location from which you backed them up. If you can remember that, simply drag and drop from the media to the appropriate folder on the PC. If you can't remember where that is, you'll need to open the application, create a file, and choose Save As. Wherever the data saves by default is where you'll need to restore backed-up files.

In programs such as Microsoft Outlook that offer Import commands from the File menu, you'll want to import data using their specific utility. In Microsoft Outlook, you'll choose the File menu, then Import and Export, and finally, Outlook. Figure 12-22 shows a page of the wizard. You can use the wizard to import backed-up data.

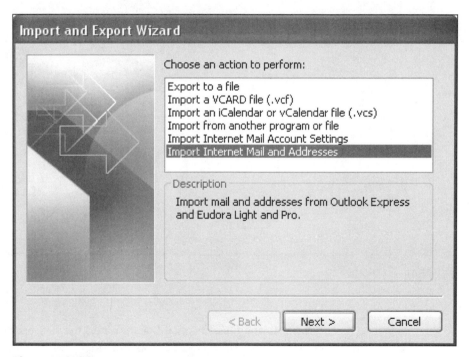

**Figure 12-22**
Some programs offer wizards to import data you've backed up.

## Restoring with Microsoft Backup

If you need to restore using a backup created with Windows Backup, you'll need to perform the restore on the same PC or on one with the same operating system as the one you had previously. You can't restore a backup created on a Windows 2000 PC to a Windows XP PC; it just doesn't work that way. As you work though the restore process, you'll select the backup you want to use, select where to restore the backed-up files (there are three options: Original Location, Alternate Location, and Single Folder), set the restore options, and then start the restore operation.

To restore using Windows Backup, follow these steps:

1. Open Windows Backup.

2. Expand File, and select the backup to use. Figure 12-23 shows this option.

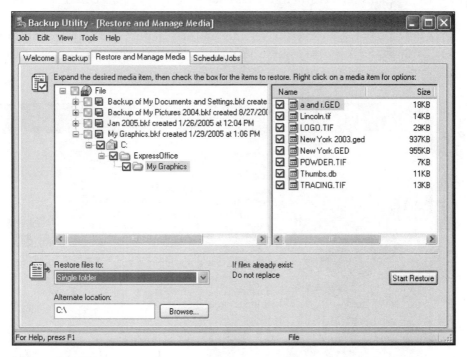

**Figure 12-23**
Selecting a backup.

3. Select an option for restoring files. Original Location puts the files back where they were initially, and Alternate Location and Single Folder allow you to browse for the location to save to. If you choose one of the latter two, click Browse and locate a place to save the data.

4. Click Start Restore.

5. In the Confirm Restore dialog box, click Advanced to view the advanced options, or click OK. We advise leaving the advanced options as they are.

6. When the restore process ends, click Close and exit the backup utility.

## GunkBuster's Notebook: Choosing and Installing a UPS Device

Although a UPS (uninterruptible power supply) device is technically not a device that is used for *backing up* data, it is a device that can save you from *losing data*. A UPS device protects PCs, printers, external hard drives, home theater equipment, and fax machines when a power outage occurs by offering electrical current to them when the electrical service is interrupted. For a PC user, this means the PC will not shut down when the power goes out; hence, the user will not lose any data. Many new UPS devices also protect against electrical surges and sags, as an expensive surge protector would. This offers additional protection.

There isn't much to setting it up either. Just plug it in for a day or so and let it charge, and then attach your devices. You can get a decent UPS device for around $100. These will usually offer a 10- to 15-minute battery backup, which will give you time to safely shut down your equipment. UPS devices can also contain the following:

√ Six to 12 electrical outlets for connecting peripherals and PCs

√ Protection from brownouts, blackouts, and surges

√ Network and phone line surge protection

√ Power management shutdown options that save and close all open files and applications and provide an unattended operating system shutdown.

√ USB connectivity

√ Audible alarm

# Summing Up

In this chapter you learned a lot of different ways to back up your data. You learned that CDs and DVDs are a good option for most people, that external drives make for easy daily backups, and that Microsoft Backup can be used to create full or system state backups and can perform those on a schedule.

You also learned that although backing up is one task, organizing backups is another. Backups should be organized by date; CDs, DVDs, and files and folders should be properly named and dated; and backups should be stored off-site or at least in another room to protect them from any disaster that might also befall the PC.

Finally, you learned how to restore using various types of backups. It's easy to restore personal folders from CDs, DVDs, and external drives, but it's a little more complicated to restore mail, Internet, and application data.

We'll continue with our quest to degunk your PC. In the next and final chapter, we'll look at how to get better performance. As you might guess, you can add RAM or upgrade internal parts, but you can also add hardware, such as a TV tuner.

# Enhancing PC and Media Performance

## Degunking Checklist:

√ Physically install more RAM to enhance the performance of your PC.

√ Learn if and when you should upgrade your CPU if your current CPU is not keeping up.

√ Add a TV tuner card and its remote control device.

√ Upgrade your video or sound card, or add a FireWire port.

√ Learn why you need hardware profiles and how to create them.

√ Tweak your system properties.

√ Explore ways to enhance media performance.

√ Enhance Windows Media Player's performance (and security).

There is always a way to enhance performance. To enhance the performance of a car, you add a faster engine; with a PC, you add a faster CPU. To enhance your health or lengthen your life, you may opt to add vitamins to your diet or start an exercise regimen; for a PC, that may mean upgrading your sound card or upgrading the CPU or motherboard. No matter what you want to enhance, there's usually some way to do it. (Just look at the spam in your Inbox!)

You can also enhance *media* performance. In a home theater system, you can add TiVo, a digital video recorder, or surround sound speakers; a PC's equivalent may mean a larger hard drive and an upgraded video card. On the PC, you might also tweak your media player's settings. You want the player you use for viewing and listening to media on your PC to run as efficiently as possible.

In this final chapter, we'll look at a myriad of different options for enhancing both PC and media performance. You'll learn how to upgrade hardware, tweak system settings, and improve media performance by tweaking Windows Media Player.

---

**WARNING!** *Some of the suggestions in this chapter require you to open the PC's tower and work inside it. Before doing anything inside the PC's tower, read the information about ESD (electrostatic discharge) in Chapter 3. ESD is static electricity, which produces the "shock" you feel when touching a door knob or metal object. Some shocks can't be felt though, and are harmless by our human standards. However, any amount of ESD is a computer-killer.*

---

# Add RAM to Enhance Performance

Adding memory is the easiest and fastest way to speed up and improve the response time of your PC. These days, purchasing an extra 128 or 256 MB of RAM won't break the bank. RAM stands for Random Access Memory and it's where XP stores data it needs or thinks it will need to perform a task like print a document, perform a calculation, or receive and open an e-mail. If your PC has 256 MB of RAM or less, you really need to upgrade to at least 512 MB. If you have 512 MB, you'll see a noticeable difference by upgrading as well. If you're into performance, if you play games, if you work with large files such as digital photos, or if you do a lot of multitasking between programs, you need to grab as much RAM as you can. My new Sony has three slots that can hold 512 MB each. You might discover you have the same options.

RAM is an important component because the PC uses it for the temporary storage of data and code that it needs to perform a task like cropping or recoloring an image, multitasking between programs, and using copy and paste. It's fast, and the PC can access it much more quickly than data from the hard drive. When RAM gets full though, and there's no free space left for storing data temporarily, the PC sends data over to the hard drive in an area called a paging file. Accessing data from the paging file takes much longer than accessing it from RAM, so if you are low on RAM, you're sure to experience slower response times than you need to.

# Physical Installation

So, just how hard is it to purchase and install extra RAM? It isn't difficult at all! These days, you simply figure out what kind of RAM you have, walk into a computer store, and purchase it right off the rack. It used to be much more complicated than this, and you'd have to order directly from the manufacturer, or worse, take your PC to a shop. (Depending on your computer, you might still have to order directly from the manufacturer, but this is fading out quickly.)

The first step involved in adding more RAM is to take a few minutes and determine how much RAM your PC already has. You can do this in a number of different ways, including viewing the My Computer's Properties page or by watching your PC boot up (if this information isn't hidden with a splash page). Figure 13-1 shows the information in My Computer.

You can also find out from System Information. Just click Start, click Run, and in the Run dialog box type msinfo32.exe. Click OK. Once you know how much RAM you have, you can decide if more would be better. In most cases, the answer is yes. There are many types of memory though, so you'll have to make sure you get the right kind.

## *Finding the Right Memory for Your Machine*

There are lots of kinds of computer memory: SIMMs, DIMMs, PC133, PC2100DDR, PC100, and more. You can't just go out and buy a memory stick; you have to know what kind you need. If you have the information booklet that came with your PC, you can find out what kind of memory you should get by glancing through the specs page. You can also take the booklet to the store with you and show it to the sales staff. If you purchased a computer from a major manufacturer like Gateway, Hewlett-Packard, Dell, IBM, or Compaq (just to name a few), and you can't find your information booklet, simply call tech support or visit the company's Web site. You'll find the information there.

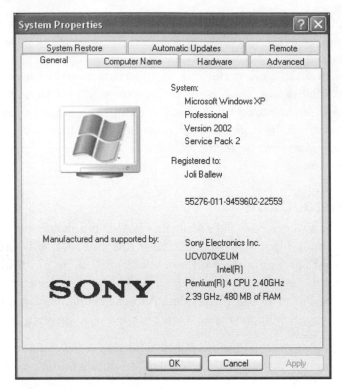

**Figure 13-1**

The System Properties General tab shows how much RAM is available.

---

*TIP: We can't promise this will always work, but in general, typing www.<the company name>.com brings up the company's Web site. For instance, www.gateway.com, www.dell.com, www.IBM.com, and www.hewlettpackard.com all link to their respective Web sites. If you can't find the Web sites using this technique, simply search for it on the Web using any Web browser.*

---

### GunkBuster's NoteBook: Using the Web to Decipher Your RAM

Many Web sites sell RAM (like **www.crucial.com**), and these sites enable you to order the RAM you need directly from the Internet. Just enter into the Web form what type of RAM you want, pony up a credit card number, and wait for it to be delivered. There's no need to even go to the store!

If you aren't sure what kind of memory you need because you own a used computer or simply just don't know, many sites offer

a look up option, where you can type in your computer type, model, motherboard model, and other data to find out. Many sites offer a downloadable tool that will scan your computer and search out the required information. Crucial has a downloadable tool called the Belarc Advisor. We ran it on our systems and were quite impressed. Even if you plan on purchasing your RAM in a store, you can use the automated tools that they make available to easily determine the RAM that you will need.

### Installation Instructions

Once you have the RAM in hand, you'll need to install it. Your RAM should come with installation instructions, but for the most part, installing RAM is as simple as turning off your computer, unplugging it, locating the slot on the motherboard, and popping in the RAM. Some pop straight in, and some slide in from an angle. Be careful when you install it though, you don't want to shock the board or the RAM. Make sure you touch the chassis and have unplugged the computer before performing any installations. Read the instructions carefully because different memory types install in different ways; however, installing RAM is generally quite simple.

### Watch the Boot Up Process

Once the RAM is installed, you can watch the boot up process (if your computer doesn't have a splash screen that hides it). Here you'll see the RAM being counted prior to the computer starting. You can also view the new RAM information from the My Computer's Properties page or from System Information. You want to make sure your new RAM has been detected properly. If it hasn't, try installing it again, or contact the manufacturer from where the memory was obtained for technical support.

# Upgrade the CPU

If you have an older PC that runs well and you have an attachment to it, or if you just aren't ready to purchase a newer PC, it is possible to upgrade the CPU (central processing unit) of your older PC to get better performance. The CPU is the PC's "brain" and manages what goes on inside the computer. A faster CPU will usually translate to better performance. However, upgrading a CPU is no piece of cake, and many people find that it only causes them problems. Before you delve into the process of finding an upgrade, purchasing that upgrade, and installing it, read the rest of this section.

On an older PC, upgrading a CPU, and only the CPU, will give you some performance boost, but most likely, you won't get all of the new CPU's available power. For that, you'd need to replace the motherboard and the RAM too. Just as you can't get glossy color photos from an inkjet printer with no color cartridge installed, you can't use a CPU's advanced technology if you don't have the required internal parts.

We figure if you really want a performance boost, and you're going to spend the money and time to get there anyway (including upgrading the CPU and motherboard, and adding new RAM), you might as well head out and purchase a new PC tower. You can use your old monitor, keyboard, mouse, and other hardware; there's no need to purchase a complete system. In the short run *and* the long run, we believe this is a better idea.

All this is a little technical. Let's take a break from the system stuff for a moment and look at something a little more fun. Want to watch TV at the office? Stay tuned!

# Install a TV Tuner Card

If you want to watch TV on your PC, you'll need to install a TV tuner card. TV tuner cards are the latest hardware option for the media-savvy. With most cards on most PCs, you can watch over 100 channels of high-quality television, watch DVDs, and even plug in S-video or composite input and audio input. Most cards come with remote controls too, and software that allows you to surf through TV channels just as if you were sitting in front of an actual television. Higher end models also allow you to schedule and record TV programs, and zoom in, pan, or freeze video action.

Installing is generally touted as something like this on the manufacturer's Web page: "Simply install the card and the user-friendly software, connect the TV cable, and sit back and enjoy high-quality video right from your PC." Now, installing the card *is* actually pretty easy, we have to give them that. However, there are thousands of Web pages devoted solely to FAQs, technical help, and troubleshooting tips for getting the TV cards working properly, as well as thousands of forum entries from those lost in the process.

In this section, we'll discuss just how to go about installing and configuring a TV tuner card, the software, and the remote control, and how to avoid the pitfalls that cause most problems along the way. If you're thinking of installing a TV tuner card, read the manufacturer's instructions first, and then read this. After that, you'll be ready for the installation.

## Meeting System Requirements and Installing the Card

There are specific system requirements for all hardware products, and TV tuners are no exception. For the most part though, if you have Windows XP on a new machine, you'll probably meet those requirements easily. However, you should make sure by reading the information on the box very carefully. If you need to upgrade something, say RAM or the video card, do so before continuing.

---

*TIP: The next section details how to upgrade video and sound cards.*

---

As with installing any card, make sure you are properly grounded, and then seat the card into the proper PCI slot. Press firmly and secure the card with a screw. Again, by reading the manufacturer's instructions, you can make sure you do this properly. Some may require the card be placed in the last slot, away from the other cards, and some may require just the opposite. Once installed, close the case, and start the PC.

## Installing the Software

Software differs from manufacturer to manufacturer, but for the most part, you'll pop a CD in the CD ROM drive and follow the prompts. It's important to install the software *and* the driver, if both exist. The most common problems with installing TV tuners are either the driver installation or the failure to install and configure the included software.

If you find you are having problems after installing both, open Device Manager and verify that the TV Capture and TV Tuner entries are there and functioning correctly. If you see a yellow exclamation point or a red x, visit the manufacturer's Web site for help, and most likely, an updated driver or software.

To open Device Manager:

1. Right-click My Computer and choose Properties.
2. Select the Hardware tab, and then click Device Manager.
3. Any hardware with a red x or yellow exclamation point is hardware that is not functioning properly.
4. Double-click any red x or yellow exclamation point to begin the trouble-shooting process. Click Troubleshoot This Device from the available options.

## Configuring and Troubleshooting the Remote

When configuring the remote, you'll need to plug in the remote control sensor to the TV card and verify it is a secure connection. You'll also need to put the batteries in the remote. These two issues are the most common problems found when remote controls fail. Some manufacturers also require you to install additional software for the remote, and some remote controls require you to press a "connect" button, as you would with a wireless keyboard or mouse, to initially make the wireless connection to the TV tuner card.

Beyond that, there should been a green IR (infrared) icon in the Notification area of the Taskbar, which often turns red when the remote is used. Problems can occur if the driver is not installed properly, or if other IR signals are nearby. Microwaves are notorious problem causers. Although there's a lot to it, you can install a TV tuner card, and it's well worth it.

# Upgrade Video and Sound Cards

Although upgrading a CPU isn't easy (or suggested), and adding a TV tuner card requires multiple steps and a bit of patience, upgrading video and sound cards is usually pretty simple stuff. We say "usually" because, for the most part, all PCs already have a video card and a sound card, and they are removable and replaceable. This statement is only true for PC towers, though. You'll have a harder time replacing video and sound cards on proprietary PCs that require proprietary hardware, laptops, or all-in-one PCs (where the monitor, hard drive, and stand are all one unit), or any PC where the sound or video card cannot be removed. If you have a PC with a tower though, it's really easy to upgrade. (If you don't, we suggest taking your PC to the dealer or to a computer repair shop for the upgrade.)

## Selecting a Card

Before you purchase a new video or sound card, you need to open the case and see what's already installed. If the video card or the sound card is in a "slot," it can be removed and replaced with an upgraded model. There are different kinds of slots though, and you'll be looking for a PCI (peripheral component interconnect) slot and AGP (advanced graphics port) slot. A PCI slot is thin and white, and can hold a video card or a sound video card, among other things. (PCI slots also hold USB cards and modems.) Most PCs have at least four PCI slots. Newer PCs may also have an AGP slot. An AGP slot is wider, and brown. In this case, the AGP slot will house the video (or graphics) card.

Once you know what type of slot your PC offers, and what type of slots house your cards, you can shop for a card to replace the one(s) you have. Make sure the card you purchase is better than the one you own, though; you don't want to replace one mediocre card with another. This is definitely a case of "getting what you pay for," so search for a good card, with onboard RAM (so it can hold its own data instead of swapping out to the RAM on the motherboard), and that your PC meets the card's minimum requirements.

## Installing the Card

With the hardware requirements met, you'll need to open the PC's tower and install the card. If you've never installed a card before, read the manufacturer's warnings regarding ESD (electrostatic discharge) first. There's also a section on ESD in Chapter 3. Once you are properly grounded and ready to move forward, remove the screw that holds the old card, remove the card, and seat the new card into its slot. Press firmly and secure the card with the screw. If you're careful enough, you may be able to sell or reuse the card you remove.

Again, reading the manufacturer's instructions will help you perform the installation properly. Once installed, close the case and start the computer. Note that you may also have to install a driver for the new card. If so, insert the CD and work through the installation process.

---

**TIP:** *Adding and installing a FireWire card is the same as adding a video or sound card. Your PC has to meet the minimum requirements, you have to have an available PCI slot, and you have to install it just as you would any other card. Many FireWire cards also come with available USB ports as well.*

---

# Configure Hardware Profiles

Wouldn't it be great if you could walk into your house and say, "Hello, house, it's me, <insert your name here>," and all of the home's *hardware* settings, such as the temperature of the heat and air, the dimness or brightness of the lights, and the slant of the window shades, would position themselves automatically to your set preferences? What if you could also tell your home to turn on the TV and put it on a specific channel? Well, that day is *almost* here for our homes, but it's *already* here for our PCs. It's easy to configure too; you just need to create a hardware profile.

In this section, you'll learn how to create and configure a hardware profile for your PC. Very simply put, a hardware profile is a set of instructions that tells Windows which hardware to start automatically when you start your PC. A hardware profile also tells Windows which settings to use for each hardware device. (You help configure these settings as you use your PC.) Windows XP uses the profile to decide what drivers and services to load on boot up too, among other things.

---

**TIP:** *You can have multiple hardware profiles.*

---

### About Default Hardware Profiles

When you installed or purchased your PC, it came with one profile, named creatively enough, Profile 1. This profile tells Windows to start all of your installed devices and their drivers when the PC boots. This includes printers, scanners, Web cams, microphones, monitors, external drives, external DVD or CD players, keyboards and mice, and anything else that you've physically connected.

You can easily create a hardware profile so that when you boot it up, Windows automatically uses what you've configured as personal hardware settings, and enables or disables the hardware you do and don't want to use. While creating these profiles makes the configuration of the PC as perfect as possible for your needs, it also allows the PC to perform better. Remember, the PC only needs to do what you need it to do; if it does more than necessary, you're losing performance you could otherwise have.

---

**NOTE:** *A laptop comes with two hardware profiles: Docked and Undocked. The default settings for these will depend on the hardware you configure for both states. There'll be a section on laptops later.*

---

Creating different hardware configurations can be quite useful too. You can have different hardware profiles for each user who accesses the PC, or for different jobs performed by a single person at the PC. For instance, a teenager could create a gaming profile, while you could create a working one. The gaming profile could have advanced hardware devices configured such as handheld gaming hardware, while the working profile could have these disabled. The gaming profile could also have RAM configured differently than the working profile, and you could disable printers, scanners, and other unnecessary hardware. Remember, the more resources your PC has available, the better it will perform, and this is especially true for gamers.

---

**TIP:** *Of course, you'll set your preferred screen resolution, hardware settings, mouse and keyboard settings, and other preferences too, all of which will either be part of the hardware profile or your user account preferences. Whatever the case, they'll be available (or not available) at boot up.*

---

## Normal and Working Profiles

Normal and working profiles are generally left as the original Profile 1. These are the settings you're using now if you haven't created any other profiles. Profile 1 enables all hardware, enables all necessary drivers, and uses your currently configured settings for sound and video, RAM (virtual memory), and services (among other things). If you're not familiar with services, they are what Windows uses to perform tasks and offer information, compatibility, and, well, services, to you and the PC. You may recognize these, which are all services:

√   Fast User Switching Compatibility

√   Help and Support

√   Messenger

√   Plug and Play

√   Themes

√   Windows Time

For a normal setup, all of these services—your personal sound and video settings, your hardware, your RAM configuration, and more are, for the most part, the way you should have it configured.

---

**TIP:** You can view services by opening Administrative Tools (you may have to choose Start and then Search to find them if you have Windows XP Home Edition), and by opening Services.

---

## Gaming Profiles

If you have a gamer in the house, he or she may want to configure a gaming profile. A gaming profile will need to be optimized for game playing, and thus will be a bare-bones working configuration, and a maxed-out gaming one. For a gaming profile, you can disable printers and scanners, and you might want to disable Web cams or network cards too. You can also tweak virtual memory settings (refer to the section "Tweak Virtual Memory Settings" later in this chapter). You can even enable specific functions of sound and video devices, or enable gaming hardware in Device Manager.

Beyond the obvious though, you can also disable quite a few services. A gamer won't need the Routing and Remote Access service, for instance, nor will he need the Help and Support service. Disabling services is easy; knowing which ones are safe to disable is a little more difficult. Let's look at the former first. To disable a service, follow these steps:

1.   Open Administrative Tools. Administrative Tools is available from Control Panel in Windows XP Professional, and by searching in Windows XP Home Edition. Older versions of Windows won't have these tools. To find out if your version has these tools, click Start, choose Search, and type Administrative Tools.

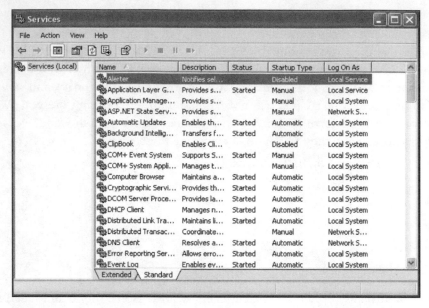

**Figure 13-2**
The Services window shows all services, which are started automatically,
manually, or disabled.

2. Open Services. See Figure 13-2.

3. Select a service and double-click it. For the purpose of instruction here,
select Alerter. The Alerter service notifies selected users and computers of
administrative alerts. By default it is disabled.

4. To change a services startup type, next to Startup Type choose Disabled,
Manual, or Automatic. This is shown in Figure 13-3.

5. Click OK when finished and close the Services window. (You may want to
click Cancel to make sure you do not make unwanted changes.)

So what services are not necessary? Well, that all depends on what you do and
don't want your PC to be able to do. Here are a few of the services a gaming
profile should have disabled:

√ Alerter

√ ClipBook

√ Computer Browser

√ Error Reporting Service

√ Help and Support

√ Indexing Service

√ Net Logon

**Figure 13-3**
Double-click any service to modify it.

√   Performance Logs and Alerts

√   Remote Desktop Help Session Manager

√   Remote Registry

√   Removable Storage

√   Routing and Remote Access

√   Server

√   Smart Card

√   Smart Card Helper

√   Themes

√   Windows Installer

√   Windows Time

√   Print Spooler

Without going beyond the scope of this book, we'll leave it up to you to look deeper on your own to find out what each of these services do and what they're used for. You probably have a good idea about some of them, though. For instance, you wouldn't need the print spooler service if you're planning on disabling your printers for this profile. The point we want to make is a simple one: reduce the load on your PC for better gaming performance.

### Laptop Profiles

Creating hardware profiles for a laptop is probably the best use of hardware profiles, and perhaps why profiles were created in the first place. That's because laptops are used in a variety of ways, as they can be docked and connected to additional hardware or a network, or undocked and connected wirelessly, or by modem to another network or the Internet. A docked laptop may also use a better monitor, a real mouse, a full-sized keyboard, a network printer, or a Web cam. When the computer is not docked, and you don't have that hardware available, there's no need to have it enabled and the drivers installed. There's also no need for the laptop to attempt to connect to a network that isn't there. The laptop might also be used to join a domain at work, but used to join a workgroup at home. All of these factors make creating or tweaking profiles on a laptop a necessary part of owning one.

When creating or tweaking a laptop's docked and undocked profiles, make sure you answer the following questions ahead of time, and configure the profile accordingly:

√   In its docked state, what hardware does the laptop connect to?

√   In its undocked state, what hardware does the laptop connect to?

√   In its docked state, what network hardware does the laptop connect to?

√   In its undocked state, what network hardware does the laptop connect to (perhaps a wireless connection is available)?

√   When docked, what is the name of the workgroup or domain?

√   When undocked, what is the name of the workgroup or domain?

√   When docked, is a modem used?

√   When undocked, is a modem used?

√   When docked or undocked, is a network card used? Bluetooth?

√   When docked, what screen resolution do you prefer? When undocked?

√   When docked, do you have external speakers?

√   When undocked, do you prefer to turn off the sound?

√   What power settings are configured while docked?

√   What power settings are configure when undocked?

We're sure you can think of other things as you sit down with each configuration and really think about what you use and what you don't. Once you know, create or enable the profiles as shown in the next section, log on to those profiles, and configure the settings that are right for you.

### Creating a Hardware Profile and Configuring a Default

Creating a hardware profile requires three steps. First, you create the profile in System Properties. After rebooting and selecting that profile, you configure it in Device Manager. Finally, you decide if you want a certain profile to start automatically, or after a specific amount of time, and you make that configuration change. The three procedures are detailed in this section.

First, create a hardware profile. Hardware profiles are created in the System Properties dialog box, from the Hardware tab:

1. Right-click My Computer and select Properties.

2. In the System Properties dialog box, choose the Hardware tab. The hardware tab is shown in Figure 13-4.

**Figure 13-4**

The Hardware tab offers the Hardware Profiles button.

3.   Click Hardware Profiles.

4.   Under Available Hardware Profiles, shown in Figure 13-5, click Profile 1 (or in the case of a laptop, Docked Profile or Undocked Profile). Click Copy.

**Figure 13-5**

Copy the existing profile to create a new one.

5.   In the Copy Profile dialog box, type a name for the new profile and click OK.

6.   Select the new profile, and click Properties.

7.   In the new profile's Properties dialog box, check Always Include This Profiles As An Option When Windows Starts. (If this is a laptop, check This Is A Portable Computer, and choose a state - unknown, docked, or un-docked.) See Figure 13-6. Click OK.

8.   In the Hardware Profiles dialog box, select Wait Until I Select A Hardware Profile. Click OK.

9.   Click OK to close the System Properties dialog box.

Next, you configure the new hardware profile. To configure the new hardware profile with hardware settings, hardware to start or disable, and any other preferences:

**Figure 13-6**

Configure the new profile to appear as an option at startup.

1.  Restart the computer and choose the new profile.

2.  Right-click My Computer and choose Properties.

3.  Select the Hardware tab.

4.  Select Device Manager.

5.  In Device Manager, choose devices to enable, configure, or disable. As an example, to disable any hardware device, double-click it, choose the General tab, and under Device Usage, select Do Not Use This Device In The Current Hardware Profile (Disable). This is shown in Figure 13-7. You can enable or configure devices in the same manner.

6.  When finished, close Device Manager and click OK to close the System Properties dialog box.

Finally, with the hardware profiles configured, you have three options for boot up. You can configure the PC so that a specific profile is automatically used each time you boot the PC, you can choose to show all of the profile choices for a specific amount of time and then have a specific one start automatically, or,

**Figure 13-7**
Disable any devices you won't need.

you can choose to show all choices and not boot until one is selected. To set any
of these configurations, follow these steps:

1. Right-click My Computer and select Properties.

2. In the System Properties dialog box, choose the Hardware tab.

3. Click Hardware Profiles.

4. In the Hardware Profiles dialog box, under Hardware Profiles Selection,
   make the appropriate choice. They are:

5. Wait Until I Select A Hardware Profile. Check this is you don't want the PC
   to boot until after you make a selection.)

6. Select The First Profile Listed If I Don't Select a Profile In _____ Seconds.
   (Select this if you want a profile to automatically start after a certain amount
   of time has passed. If you want the first profile listed to start automatically,
   select 0 seconds.)

7. Click OK twice to exit.

# Tweaking the System

There are a million ways to tweak a PC and make it perform better; you know that from what you've learned in this book, and hopefully what you learned in *Degunking Windows*. In this section, we'll take it a step further, and focus solely on tweaking the System settings. You've seen the dialog box we'll use here more than a few times while working though this chapter? It's the System Properties dialog box. This time though, we'll focus on a different tab, the Advanced tab.

The Advanced tab of the System Properties dialog box, shown in Figure 13-8, has three sections: Performance, User Profiles, and Startup And Recovery. We'll focus on the first of those, enhancing performance.

## Tweak Effects, Processor Scheduling, and Memory Usage

How you configure your PC to use colors, themes, and visual styles affects how well your PC performs. So does how you configure your CPU to function. Do

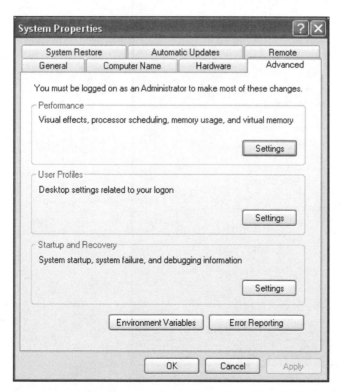

**Figure 13-8**

The System Properties dialog box offers the Advanced tab for configuring advanced system setting.

you want the processor to adjust performance for your applications or background services? You probably want it for your applications. Finally, how you configure the memory in your PC to be used also plays a role in performance. Let's look at all three, and configure them for the best performance possible.

To tweak system performance settings:

1. Right-click My Computer and choose Properties.

2. From the System Properties dialog box, select the Advanced tab.

3. Under Performance, select Settings.

4. From the Visual Effects tab, shown in Figure 13-9, select Adjust For Best Performance. (Note that if you have custom setting configured, they will be lost if you click Apply or OK.)

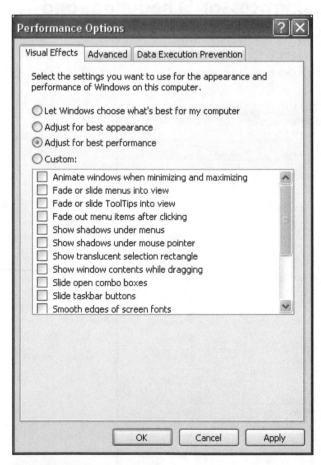

**Figure 13-9**
Configure for best performance.

5. From the Advanced tab, under Processor Scheduling, select Programs. This is the default, and will give programs a greater share of processor time than it will to background services.

6. From the Advanced tab, under Memory Usage, select Programs. Only select System Cache if you are using the PC as a server.

7. Click OK to apply the changes. Click OK to close the System Properties dialog box.

## Tweak Virtual Memory Settings

We talked earlier about adding RAM. We decided that the more RAM you have, the better performance you'll get. That's because when RAM is full, Windows sends the data and code it needs to hold temporarily to an area of the hard drive reserved for such events, and data and code are swapped back and forth as needed. Because it takes longer to access data from the hard drive (in an area called the paging file), you'll obviously want to have as much RAM as you can afford (assuming you are into increasing the performance of your computer)! However, no matter how much RAM you have, the data stored there will eventually be swapped, so you want to make sure that the settings configured for virtual memory are the best they can be.

Virtual memory is the imaginary memory area that makes the computer act like it has more memory (RAM) than it actually does. Virtual memory is implemented using a paging file or swap file, which is generally located on the C: drive. You can set the size of this file manually if you'd like, or you can accept the defaults. There are two options to change: the initial file size and the maximum file size. Changing these setting may increase the performance of your PC.

The initial file size box is the area where you provide the number of megabytes for the virtual-memory paging file on the selected drive, and it is where you set the initial (or beginning) size of the file. The maximum size box is the area where you provide the maximum number of megabytes that can be used for the file. The numbers configured here define the size of the paging file. If you want, you can leave your initial virtual memory settings to whatever Windows suggests, which is about 1.5 times the amount of RAM on the system, and the maximum paging file size about three times the amount of RAM. However, there are a few tweaks you can make if you desire:

√ If you have less than 512 MB of RAM, leave the page file as is, using the default settings.

√ If you have lots of RAM, say a gig or more, set the initial page file to about half of the physical RAM and set the maximum size at three times the RAM.

√   If you don't have much free hard disk space and upgrading is not feasible, set the initial page file to 2 MB.

√   Keep in mind that an extremely large maximum page file does not necessarily increase performance, and may actually hinder it. You don't want to allow too much of the hard drive area to this file.

√   Even if you have a gig or so of RAM, don't turn off the page file. Some programs can crash if no virtual memory is available.

If you'd like to tweak the virtual memory settings, here's how you set a custom page file in Windows XP:

1.   Right click My Computer and click Properties.

2.   Click the Advanced tab, and under Performance, click Settings.

3.   In the Performance Options dialog box, click the Advanced tab.

4.   Under Virtual Memory, click Change.

5.   Configure the settings as you desire, and click Set. OK your way out of the dialog boxes. See Figure 13-10. If prompted, reboot your computer.

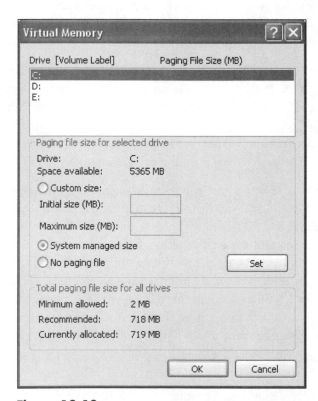

**Figure 13-10**

Virtual memory settings can be tweaked to enhance performance.

A number of third-party programs are available to help you boost the performance of your machine, including some that will automatically tweak the paging file. Walk into any computer store or search the Internet for "Windows XP performance enhancement software" and you'll find plenty!

---

*TIP: On the Internet, check out www.acceleratedsoftware.net for some great acceleration tools.*

---

# Enhance Media Performance

You can only do so much to enhance the performance of your PC with hardware; eventually you'll run out of places to add RAM, ports to add hardware, or slots to add cards. You'll need to start working on the inside of the PC, specifically the Windows operating system. While we discussed degunking the operating system in depth in our first book together, *Degunking Windows*, we'll touch on a few of the degunking tasks here too. It is certainly appropriate when talking about improving your PC's media performance to include some tweaks regarding the operating system itself.

In this section we'll first talk about improving overall operating system performance, because the better your PC runs, the better your media will play. We'll then teach you where to find the latest and best free media tools from the Internet, including PowerToys, media bonus packs, and plug-ins. You can use this software to enhance PC and media performance as well. Finally, we'll show you how to secure the application you likely use for viewing and listening to media, Windows Media Player.

## Tweak Computer Performance

You can't render a movie in Movie Maker 2 in short order without having the appropriate system resources. Windows Media Player will drag along, hang up, and even close unexpectedly if your PC is bogged down with other tasks. CD and DVD burning software might create a coaster out of your recordable CD and DVD if you listen to streaming video or edit a picture while burning it. The only way around these problems is to make sure your PC is in good shape, has enough RAM and processing power, and that you aren't slowing it down with unnecessary tasks while it's trying to perform tasks of its own.

### Common Sense Tricks for Better Performance

One of the major reasons PCs have problems and perform poorly is that they simply have too much to do. Themes and screen savers that use system resources, and programs and files that take up valuable hard drive space, can cause performance problems. When cleaning up your PC to enhance its performance, make sure you've dealt with these things appropriately. Turn off themes and system-intensive screen savers that require computations or lots of video memory, uninstall programs you don't need and no longer use, and rid your hard drive of unnecessary files.

Another reason PCs and media hang up, freeze, or perform poorly is that the application, perhaps Windows Media Player or QuickTime, needs all of the resources it can get its hands on. If the application needs RAM, and you're using what RAM you have to print a large document or perform a complicated edit in Photoshop, performance will certainly suffer. Use a little common sense; don't try to render a movie while at the same time burning a DVD, and make sure your applications are getting the attention they need from both RAM and the processor.

## GunkBuster's Notebook: Disable Programs that Run in the Background

You can also enhance computer, and thus media performance by making sure you don't have unnecessary programs running in the background that you don't know about or need. If you've downloaded a lot of programs, shareware, freeware, or third-party applications from the Internet, chances are you're going to be more than a little surprised at what you find running behind the scenes.

The System Configuration Utility can be used to see what is running in the background, and to disable what you have running. To open and use this utility:

1. Click Start, click Run, and in the Run dialog box type msconfig.exe. Click OK.

2. Click the Startup tab, shown in Figure 13-11, and scroll down to the bottom of the list.

3. Look at the items in the list and uncheck anything that you don't use, yet know what it is.

   Click OK to close and reboot.

If you're ever unsure about what an item does, a quick search on Google for the entry will generally produce results. If you find out a particular entry is a sound card driver, it would make sense to leave that component selected.

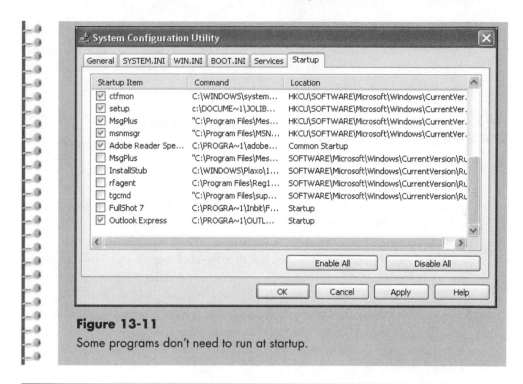

**Figure 13-11**

Some programs don't need to run at startup.

**TIP:** *Don't disable anything you aren't familiar with. Windows XP needs RUNDLL32, for instance. Only disable what you recognize and know you don't need.*

# Use Free Media Player PowerToys and Plug-Ins

PowerToys are (generally) free applications that you can use to enhance the usefulness of an existing Windows XP media component and other XP components. Some PowerToys enhance functionality too, such as allowing you to add a scientific calculator or change how Alt-Tab works. PowerToys generally allow access to previously inaccessible areas of a component. Plug-ins are modules that add functionality to an existing component and are integrated into the application itself. Plug-ins "plug into" existing applications and become part of them.

We have a few favorite PowerToys we'd like to introduce here. First is the TweakMP PowerToy. Using TweakMP, you can take control of Windows Media Player by performing actions previously unachievable, such as automatically leveling the volume of songs as they are burned to a CD.

The Windows Media Bonus Pack for Windows XP is another of our favorites. It offers PowerToys too, along with sound effects, the Media Player Tray Control, the Personal License Update Wizard, and more. With these PowerToys and plug-ins, you can take complete control over Windows Media Player.

After introducing these two items, we'll show you where to find even more PowerToys and plug-ins for Windows Media Player, and the most useful features of each. Following that, we'll show you how to find other PowerToys, and how to distinguish the useful from the not-so-useful.

---

**TIP: All of the software in the next few sections can be obtained from www.wmplugins.com, and they are all free.**

---

### TweakMP

TweakMP is an easy-to-use PowerToy and plug-in that offers several features for taking control of Windows Media Player. It only works with Windows XP, though, and you'll have to download it from **www.wmplugins.com**. It lets you set general options such as what double-clicking an item in the Media Library achieves (playing or queuing an item), and what happens when songs are played (such as adding the item to the Now Playing playlist). With TweakMP, you can also configure how and when full-screen controls are shown when you're in full-screen mode. For instance, you may configure Media Player to show full-screen controls every time you move the mouse, or only when the mouse is moved to a specific area of the screen.

What we find really useful in this PowerToy, though, is the ability to automatically level the volume of songs when copying them to an audio CD. You know the drill: you copy songs to your hard drive from various sources, perhaps you obtain some tracks from your iPod, some from a CD from your music library, a few from MusicNow, one from an Internet radio station, and another from a digital recording of an analog LP. When you burn these mismatched tracks to a CD, some are inevitably too soft, and an equal number are too loud. You find yourself constantly changing the volume while listening to the CD.

To get around this, you can use automatic leveling from TweakMP's CD Options page:

1. Open Windows Media Player. Click Start, point to All Programs, point to Accessories, point to Entertainment and select Windows Media Player.

2. To open TweakMP, click Tools, point to Plug-ins, and choose TweakMP.

3. From the General tab, you can configure general options such as what double-clicking an item in the queue achieves. To enable automatic leveling when you burn CDs, click the CD tab. Select Automatically Level The Volume Of Files When Copying To An Audio CD. See Figure 13-12.

4. Close the dialog box when finished.

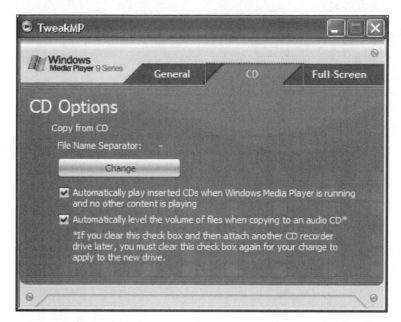

**Figure 13-12**

With TweakMP, you can bend Windows Media Player to your will.

### *Windows Media Bonus Pack for Windows XP*

The Windows Media Bonus Pack is jam-packed with useful features too. We'll detail a couple of them here. One of our favorites is the Windows Media Player Tray Control. With this feature, you can relegate Media Player to the Notification Area, thus keeping it off of your Desktop. By right-clicking the Windows Media Player Tray Control icon in the Notification area, you can then control the player without accessing the player's interface. This is a perfect addition to your computer at work, and might keep you out of hot water with the boss. (In fact, simply clicking once on the icon starts or stops the currently playing track.)

To use the program you'll first need to download and install it. As with the other plugins and PowerToys mentioned in this section, you can get it from **www.wmplugins.com**. Here's how to use it once you have it installed:

1. Click Start, point to All Programs, point to Windows Media Bonus Pack, and select Windows Media Player Tray Control.

2. Right-click the tray control icon in the Notification Area as shown in Figure 13-13. The icon you're looking for is the one shown on the far left in this image.

From the choices you'll see from right-clicking, you can play, pause, or stop current media, move to the previous or next track in the queue, mute, turn the

**Figure 13-13**
The Windows Media Player Tray Control lets you
control the player from a small icon in the
Notification area of the Taskbar.

volume up or down, or, hide the media player. You can close the tray control,
close Media Player, or both, and set options for the Tray Control, such as running it at startup. The Windows Media Player Tray Control is the perfect solution at work, when you don't want your boss to know you're also listening to
music or watching videos! All you'll need is a set of tiny earphones.

The other applications and utilities in the Windows Media bonus pack for
Windows XP include:

√ Movie Maker Creativity Kit

√ Plus! MP3 Audio Converter LE

√ Media Library Management Wizard

√ Personal License Update Wizard

√ Windows Media Player Playlist Import to Excel Wizard

Our other favorite bonus pack application is the Windows Plus! MP3 Audio
Converter LE. If you've been collecting music since the beginning of the age of
collecting digital music, you probably have a library full of MP3s. MP3s are an
older technology though, and Windows Media Audio (WMA) files are a much
better option. Converting your existing MP3s to WMA files will save space on
your hard drive because WMA files produce much smaller files than MP3s do;
you'll also be able to carry more tunes on your portable media player, as long as
it supports this format. Most of the newer portable players do, but you should
check yours just in case before conversion. Additionally, WMA files, with their
default bit rate of 128 Kbps, are considered CD quality, and one of the reasons
why this file type is quite popular and widely used. You open the converter
application from the Windows Media Bonus Pack folder the same way you
opened the tray control program, from Start, and All Programs. And, unlike
other conversion applications, it's free!

When you first use the Plus! MP3 Audio Converter LE, you'll be asked whether
you want to convert an entire folder of files or only a single file. If you have
hundreds of MP3s, the former is the obvious way to go. You can then specify
search options, including the folder to browse to, whether or not to include
files in subfolders, and what types of audio files to search for. You can also

choose the bit rate to use, if you're in the know about these things, as well as other options. Figure 13-14 shows these options. When you're ready, click Next and Start Conversion, and leave the rest in the hands of the application.

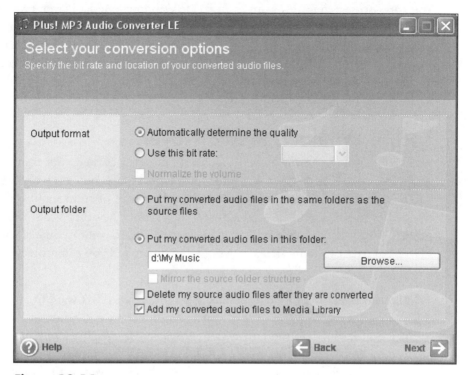

**Figure 13-14**
Convert older MP3 files to WMA files to save space on your hard drive.

---

**TIP:** *If you don't want people to see what you've recently been listening to or watching after using Windows Media Player, you'll want to clear its history files. The MRU (Most Recently Used) list in Windows Media Player can be cleared by right-clicking the Windows Media Player Tray Control and pointing to Options. Just choose Clear MRU.*

---

## Other Popular PowerToys and Plug-Ins

The PowerToys and plug-ins introduced here are only a small fraction of what's available. You can see hundreds of additional PowerToys and plug-ins by browsing to www.wmplugins.com. The PowerToys and plug-ins that are available are categorized by featured items, most popular, and highest rated, so that you can decide which ones you can trust and which ones are suspect. Although many of the available items are simply visualizations and skins (interface images, colors, and themes), which don't really *do* anything, others are quite useful, such as

PlayerPal. With the PlayerPal PowerToy, you can control Windows Media Player from anywhere on your network, using your own Web browser. You can search for music, add tracks, or even add albums, just to name a few things.

You can also search for plug-ins from inside Windows Media Player. From the Tools menu, point to Plug-ins, and choose Download Plug-ins. You'll be taken to Microsoft's Windows Media Web site. There you'll find plug-ins for creating audio effects, for DVD decoders, MP3 encoders, and more. Anything you find on these Web sites can be trusted, but if you aren't sure you believe us, check the user ratings before downloading.

# Secure Windows Media Player

Securing Windows Media Player might not have ever crossed your mind, that is, until your kids made their way into your media library, and you wondered if you could set parental controls on your DVDs! You can of course, and you can take other steps to protect yourself and your family in other ways. You can protect your identity while online and using the player, you can disable Media Player Update if you find that annoying or intrusive, and you can protect yourself in ways you never before thought possible.

Windows Media Player is pretty secure as is though; we don't want to give you the wrong idea here. When the player goes online to get lyrics and media information, it doesn't send anyone any *personally identifiable information* about you to any Web sites it visits. Microsoft doesn't know what music you listen to either, or what videos you download and watch. However, in the interest of those who want to feel even more secure, or to set parental controls for the kids, this is the section for you.

## *Set Parental Controls*

If you have Windows user accounts and passwords set up for everyone who accesses your computer, you can use the DVD ratings included on DVD disks to control which users can access and watch what DVDs. The Motion Picture Association of America rates DVDs as G, PG, PG-13, R, NC-17, and Not Rated. If you set parental controls, anything that is rated higher than what you specify won't be played unless the viewer has a valid administrator account and password.

To enable Parental Control in Windows Media Player:

1. Select Tools, and choose Options. Select the DVD tab.
2. Check the Parental Control box, and then select a rating, as shown in Figure 13-15.
3. Click OK when finished.

**Figure 13-15**

Configure parental controls so your kids can't see DVDs
you don't want them to.


## Protect Your Identity

When playing CDs and DVDs while online, Windows Media Player will connect to the Internet and return information about the media you're playing,
such as the songs included on the CD, album cover art, artist information, DVD
information, and more. Windows Media Player allows you to change the behavior though, by changing your privacy settings.

To see your privacy options and change them:

1. Open Windows Media Player.

2. From the Tools menu, choose Options.

3. Select the Privacy tab. The options are shown in Figure 13-16.

4. One of the options is Send Unique Player ID To Content Providers.
   Information it sends isn't personally identifiable, but it may send information
   about connection time, IP address, OS version, player version, player identifi-
   cation number, date, protocol, and so forth. The purpose of this, of course, is
   to provide your content provider with information that will help them serve

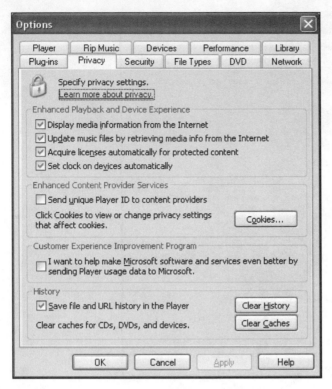

**Figure 13-16**

Configure privacy options to further secure Windows
Media Player.

you better and give you a better experience and higher quality output.
However, if sending this information seems intrusive, you deselect it.

5.  You can also disable Retrieve Media Information For CDs And DVDs from
    The Internet. When this is checked, and it is by default, the player will
    attempt to obtain information about your CDs and DVDs from
    www.windowsmedia.com, including artist name, track name, and similar
    data. Information about your music will be gathered and sent to a database,
    for the purpose of enhancing your musical experience. If you do not want
    to share information about your CDs and DVDs, and you do not want to
    obtain information from Windows Media, deselect this box.

6.  Read the other options, and deselect as warranted. Click OK when finished.

# Summing Up

In this last chapter, you learned how to improve the performance of both your PC and its media performance. You learned that adding RAM is a great way to increase performance, and why upgrading a CPU or motherboard might not be the best solution for an aging computer. You also learned how to add or upgrade hardware, including adding a TV tuner card and a remote control, and upgrading sound and video cards.

You learned how to "virtually" tweak your PC by creating hardware profiles, modifying system properties, and configuring the virtual paging file on the hard drive. And finally, you learned how to get better media performance through PC performance, and by tweaking Windows Media Player.

# Appendix A

# Get Rid of Unwanted Hardware and Degunk Your New PC

Hopefully, while degunking your existing PC, you found quite a few things you could get rid of, namely unnecessary printers, Web cams, digital cameras, and other hardware. You may have upgraded hardware too, thus creating *more* items to dispose of, including used video and sound cards. What are you going to do with all of that unnecessary and outdated hardware?

The answer to that question is a bit more complex than simply throwing the items in the trash. The consequences of that solution are filling up our landfills and oceans with waste that does not degrade easily. The waste we're creating has a name too; it's recently been termed *e-waste*. E-waste is becoming quite a hazard to our landfills, rivers, and oceans and is posing a serious threat to our water and air. With that in mind, we've added this appendix. We want to show you ways to *recycle* your old hardware instead of tossing it in the trash.

Tossing out old hardware goes hand in hand with the inevitable collection of new stuff. You purchase new video or sound cards, new DVD burners, and new network equipment. You may even get a new PC, or an additional one. Some of the new stuff, especially a new PC, has to be degunked before you can even use it. New PCs come with 30- and 60-day trial software, ads and desktop icons to join AOL or other Internet service providers, and tons of other gunk. It's difficult to know everything that you can and can't get rid of, or even how to get rid of it safely.

We'll look at that in this chapter too, and fill you in on the steps involved in degunking a new PC.

# Get Rid of Unnecessary or Outdated Hardware

E-waste. E-garbage. These are the names given to waste from disposed-of electronic equipment: PCs, digital cameras, Web cams, old PC cards, printers, and other hardware. This waste does not degrade in your local landfill. Because of that, it creates an environmental hazard, and not just for people, but also for birds, animals, and sea life. So, everyone should make a point to recycle equipment instead of throwing it away. Of course, it will *eventually* get thrown out, but perhaps by that time, there will be better measures in place for dealing with it.

---

**TIP: Before getting rid of any working PC, make sure there's no personal information on it. The best thing to do is use the PC's restore disk(s) or reinstall the operating system with a "clean" install.**

---

## Choosing a Family Member

We're going to bet that your grandmother doesn't know the difference between a parallel printer connection and a USB printer connection. In fact, we'll go out on a limb and say even if she *did* know the difference, she wouldn't really care that USB is faster than parallel, as long as you're giving her a printer with working cartridges. You do have an option for that printer you need to get rid of.

You may have kids or grandkids too, who are just itching to get their hands on a digital camera. You wouldn't give an 8-year-old a *new* camera, but giving them your old one is certainly a way to recycle it while at the same time teach them about responsibility and taking care of expensive equipment.

Finally, you may have friends or other relatives who would appreciate older equipment. For instance, the teenager next door who is experimenting and building their first PC could use your old video or sound cards, or even an old PC. Builders are known for recycling parts from other's PCs, including reusing old hard drives, CD drives, and floppy drives. They may even be able to use the motherboard.

## Selecting a Charity, School, or Organization

There are lots of other ways to get rid of old hardware, including giving to charities, schools, and organizations. Giving used and working equipment to a charity or organization is one of the best ways to recycle it. You can choose any charity you like, give them a call, and tell them what you have. If you choose a local charity, you can deliver it yourself, saving shipping charges.

You can also give older equipment to schools, although some schools can't accept it. There is a lot of red tape involved in giving to schools and colleges, but if you have a favorite alma mater, you can certainly give it a whirl.

Of course, churches also are a good way to go. Churches have many uses for older equipment, including giving to charities they sponsor, using the equipment in their own church and classrooms, and giving the equipment to members who need it. They may even set up a computer lab with your donated equipment!

---

**TIP:** To find a local charity, search the Internet for "*<your city and state here> donate used computers.*" You can also call your city's public information line for suggestions.

---

## Sell the Hardware

You can sell used equipment too. There are hundreds of sites on the Internet devoted to such, including eBay. You'll need to take a picture of the hardware, write down the specifications, and make sure the equipment is working properly. You can also sell equipment through your local newspaper, a fundraiser, or a garage sale.

## As a Last Resort, Contact City Services

If you can't give away or sell your old hardware, you'll have no other option than to throw it away. There are good and bad ways to throw it away though; you don't want to put that old monitor on the front lawn and wait for city services to come and pick it up. They'll only take it to the landfill, where it will not be disposed of properly. Instead, you'll want to look for other options. Other options include contacting city sanitation and/or recycling services or looking for third-party recycling centers.

---

**TIP:** You **can** put an old **working** monitor by the curb for a day or so and hope that someone drives by and picks it up. That often works as a quick way to recycle unwanted working equipment.

---

To test how recycling works in your area, make a phone call to the city's Public Information Office. Tell them you have computer equipment you need to get rid of and you'd like to either give the working equipment to a charity or throw it away. If you have non-working equipment, state that as well.

If you go this route in Dallas, Texas, for example, you'll be referred to the city's sanitation department. From there, you'll be referred to a local company named Computer Reset (**www.computerreset.com**). This company, like many others that do this type of work, recycles parts, repairs computer equipment, and sells PCs and salvaged parts. It doesn't charge for taking in your old equipment.

While third-party companies like Computer Reset use what they can and resell what they can, they also go to great pains to recycle the rest. They break down scrap metal and haul it off for recycling, they remove circuit boards and sell them to companies who grind them up for their precious metals, and they ship used monitors overseas to people who use the parts inside them for components in their own. These companies even take printers, VCRs, and other equipment. It's a good way to get rid of equipment and feel good about it. At least the entire thing isn't going to end up in a landfill somewhere.

## GunkBuster's Notebook: Don't Create Environmental Gunk

In larger cities, monitors and other electronic equipment left by the curb are picked up by bulk trash pickup services, generally a city service. The trucks then carry the equipment to the landfill, where they *may* put the hardware in a portion of the landfill designated for such refuse. (Many don't separate the bulk at all though, and just dump all of the trash together when they drop it off at the landfill.) They'll then plow over and crush the equipment. This is not a solution for disposing of e-waste, though, because it does not help recycle the equipment in any way and the resulting crushed elements still make their way into the local water and environment.

The only solution, at this time, for most people to safely and responsibly get rid of unwanted equipment and hardware is to contact their city sanitation service, specifically the recycling part of this service, and ask for specific instructions on getting rid of it. They can lead you in the right direction.

# Degunk Your New PC

If you've purchased a new PC, you need to read this section. New PCs these days come with all sorts of gunk preinstalled, including free trials from Internet service providers, free trials of software, and installed software you don't want and don't need. You could have a couple of gigabytes of gunk on there you'll never use!

Here are some examples of what you can expect to find on a new PC from a major retailer or PC manufacturer. While reading through this list, try to decide if you'd use or appreciate this software or if you wouldn't:

√   A free trial of Microsoft Office.

√   A free trial for America Online and similar companies.

√   Unexpected Desktop pop-ups from the manufacturer, prompting you to upgrade your warranty, register, or visit its Web site.

√   Proprietary software from the manufacturer that you won't use, such as media music services, media installers, and "experience" software. Figure A-1 shows a search for "vaio" on a fairly new Sony Vaio PC.

√   Third-party software you may not be interested in, including mapping software, encyclopedias, CD burning software, greeting card creation software, and image-editing software.

√   Bundled office software including Microsoft Works, which you won't need if you already use Microsoft Office.

√   On PCs that are media centers, multiple DVD burning software applications.

√   Third-party software such as Quicken, Microsoft Money, Quick Time, MusicMatch, and Microsoft Picture It! (This type of third-party software will often time-out 30 to 60 days after you first use it.)

You need to get rid of what you won't need or won't be using right away. Don't let your brand-new PC become bogged down before you ever get the chance to gunk it up yourself! But, how do you know what to keep, what you need, and what you can safely delete? It isn't that complicated, really. Let's start with the free trials.

## Free Trials

On almost any new PC, you can expect to find a free trial of something. It may be a free trial for AOL or another Internet service provider, which you can access from the Desktop, or it may be free trial software for an application, which you can access from the All Programs menu. Figure A-2 shows an example of an AOL shortcut icon on the Desktop. (You can tell it's a shortcut

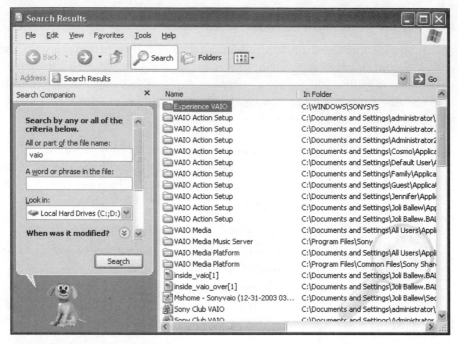

**Figure A-1**

Gunk, gunk, gunk, and more gunk. What *is* all of this stuff?

**Figure A-2**

New PCs often come with gunk on the Desktop.

because of the arrow.) Of course, this is gunk, but how do you get rid of it? Can you? Should you? Will you mess up your new PC if you do? Those are all tough questions, and not too many people know the answers.

### Free Trials on the Desktop

You may know that right-clicking any Desktop icon and choosing Delete will remove the icon from your Desktop, and you can do that to get rid of the gunk there, but what you may not know is that it will not remove the actual gunk from your PC. Right-clicking the AOL & Internet Free Trial! icon in Figure A–2 and choosing Delete will delete the icon *only*. It *won't* delete the actual files from your PC. It's the files that take up hard drive space, not the icon. To delete the actual files, you need to look a little deeper.

The best way to delete files from a PC is from the Add or Remove Programs window, shown in Figure A-3. As you can see though, there's no AOL entry in there. Tricky, tricky. In this case, you'll have to delete the files manually.

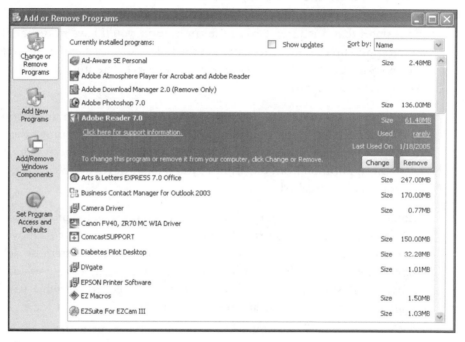

#### Figure A-3
Sometimes there is no way to uninstall files using traditional methods.

---

**TIP:** *Before manually deleting any files, you should create a restore point in System Restore. System Restore is available from Start, All Programs, Accessories, and System Tools.*

---

Here's how to manually delete the files:

1. Right-click any shortcuts on the Desktop that represent free trials of software you know you will not need.

2. From the resulting menu choices, select Properties.

3. From the Properties dialog box, choose Find Target.

4. Notice what is in the folder. In almost all cases, you can delete everything in there. If you're deleting Internet access choices, you may have several as we do, including ATT, AOL, and EarthLink.

5. To delete any item, right-click it and choose Delete.

6. Close all windows and dialog boxes, and then right-click the unwanted Desktop icon and choose Delete to get rid of it.

7. Restart your PC and verify there are no errors on bootup. If there are, use System Restore to revert the PC to its prior state.

## Free Trials in the All Programs Menu

If you see free trials in the All Programs menu, or if you open an application and it states that it is a free trial of the application, you'll have to decide if you want to pony up the extra money to get the full version or if you want to delete it from your PC altogether. Of course, we're here to delete stuff, so we'll assume that's what you want to do.

As with the Desktop, right-clicking any item in the All Programs menu and choosing Delete will only remove it from the list; it won't remove the gunk from your PC. The actual files will still be on there somewhere. And if you delete the application from the list now, you'll likely never notice it again and it will never get uninstalled.

Unlike deleting files by finding the target folder as we did in the previous section, you're going to want to get rid of applications using the Add or Remove Programs applet in the Control Panel. You can really mess up a system by deleting program files haphazardly, especially by finding a folder and deleting its contents, and we won't suggest it again. First, let's use this applet to see what you have installed that you don't want, and then let's delete what you don't want:

1. Open Control Panel and the Add or Remove Programs applet.

2. Scroll through the list and see if you can locate the trial software. It should be there. Also look for software you know you'll never use, such as Quicken, Microsoft Picture It!, or Microsoft Money.

3. Each time you find an application you never intend to use, select it and choose Change/Remove. When prompted, select Remove or Uninstall.

4. In most instances, the process will occur automatically, although you may be asked to assist by responding that yes, you're sure you want to uninstall the program, and by clicking Next a few times to complete the process.

**WARNING!** *If you're ever prompted, while uninstalling **anything**, to delete files that may be shared with other applications, always choose No to All. You do **not** want to delete shared files. Doing so could cause bootup error messages or problems with other applications.*

We suggest, as noted before, that you create a System Restore point prior to uninstalling programs or deleting files. That way, if something goes wrong, you can always revert back. We'll also suggest here that you reboot immediately after deleting programs and that, when you're finished, you use Disk Cleanup and Disk Defragmenter to clean up the computer.

## Software from the Manufacturer, Third-Party Software, Duplicate Software

The process for getting rid of software from the PC's manufacturer or from a third party is the same as getting rid of free trial applications. It's best done through the Add or Remove Program applet in Control Panel. This is especially true of software installed by the PC manufacturer.

To see what's installed on your PC, browse through the All Programs menu and look for your PC manufacturer's name. Figure A-1 showed the search results for a Sony Vaio, and the same entries are also in the Add or Remove Programs applet in Control Panel.

When it comes to uninstalling this kind of software, it's hard to know what you can and can't uninstall. It seems quite logical you'd need to leave anything the manufacturer installed intact. That's simply not true. The operating system contains the files needed to run the PC, and additional files added by the manufacturer are almost always unnecessary.

Here's a quick "for instance": Our Sony Vaio has lots of media applications (as you saw in Figure A-1). A quick search on Google informs us that one of those applications is for turning our PC into a server so that networked computers can access media files. Whew! We're not going to do that, and thus, this software isn't necessary. Again, this is true for almost all manufactured PCs. You can safely delete these additional files once you know you do not want to use their respective applications. (Again, though, create a restore point, just to be on the safe side, and Google anything you're not sure about.)

Finally, some third-party software (and even free trial software) offers an Uninstall option right in the All Programs menu. Figure A-4 shows an example. If this is offered, use it.

**Figure A-4**
Some programs have an uninstall option in the All Programs menu.

> ## GunkBuster's Notebook: Duplicate Applications
>
> Just because something came preinstalled on your new PC is no reason to keep or use it. Likewise, there's no reason not to uninstall applications you don't want to use or programs you have equivalents for. Don't keep it just because you think you "paid" for it; that's not a good enough reason.
>
> Here's an example of duplication. We prefer Microsoft Office for writing, Microsoft Excel for creating spreadsheets, and Microsoft Access for our databases. Just because our new PCs come with Microsoft Works doesn't mean we need to change, and it doesn't mean we shouldn't uninstall the program. If we're not going to use it, it's just gunk.
>
> You'll have to take inventory too. If you use Photoshop CS and your new PC came with Microsoft Picture It!, you may want to uninstall the latter. If your new PC came with Quicken but you use Quick Books, uninstall the former. Don't let someone else gunk up your brand-new PC.

# Summing Up

In this appendix, you learned different ways to safely dispose of unwanted hardware, including entire PCs. You learned why it's important to dispose of hardware responsibly and how disposing of it improperly can harm the environment and add to the amount of e-waste we create each year.

Recycling is the best way to get rid of hardware. You can pass it on to family members or friends or give it to a charity, school, or organization. You can sell it too, at a garage sale, through the newspaper, or at one of hundreds of Web sites devoted to recycling hardware, including eBay.

Finally, you learned about degunking a new PC. Throwing out *old* hardware almost always instigates the purchase of *new* hardware. These days, PCs come with all sorts of gunk, including software, trial programs, and proprietary applications. You learned why, how, and when to get rid of things you don't need.

# Index

# H

# N